D1116282

# THE STRUCTURED CROWD
## Essays in English Social History

# THE STRUCTURED CROWD

## Essays in English Social History

**HAROLD PERKIN**
*Professor of Social History*
*University of Lancaster*

**THE HARVESTER PRESS · SUSSEX**
**BARNES & NOBLE BOOKS · NEW JERSEY**

First published in Great Britain in 1981 by
THE HARVESTER PRESS LIMITED
*Publisher: John Spiers*
16 Ship Street, Brighton, Sussex

and in the USA by
BARNES & NOBLE BOOKS
81 Adams Drive, Totowa, New Jersey 07512

© Harold Perkin, 1981

*British Library Cataloguing in Publication Data*

Perkin, Harold
  The structured crowd.
  1. England – Social conditions – 19th century
  2. England – Social conditions – 20th century
  I. Title
  309.1′42′07      HN385

  ISBN 0-85527-413-1


Barnes & Noble Books
ISBN 0-389-20116-2

Typeset by Inforum Ltd, Portsmouth
Printed in Great Britain by
Redwood Burn Limited, Trowbridge and Esher

To the President, Asa Briggs, and the members
of the Social History Society of the United Kingdom,
without whom the subject would scarcely exist.

# Contents

# INTRODUCTION

A crowd flowed over London Bridge, so many,
I had not thought death had undone so many.
T.S. Eliot, *The Wasteland*

Social history, I argue in the first essay in this book, is or ideally
should be the history of society in all its aspects. Society as seen by
the casual outsider, a visitor from another society or another planet,
is a crowd, in the dictionary definition 'a press, mob or throng of
people collected confusedly together'. It is only on closer inspection
that the outsider realizes that the crowd is not undifferentiated but is
divided into many kinds of people, male and female, old and young,
healthy and fragile, above all well and ill dressed, rich and poor, the
self-confident and the diffident, and only after close questioning can
he know that the differences are systematic and based on historically
deep-seated and complex interrelationships. In other words, the
immense crowd which makes up any society, and certainly English
society since the onset of industrialism, is a highly structured one. If
history, in the familiar phrase, is a seamless web, social history is a
rich brocade with ramifying threads which weave an ever-changing
pattern of social differences, most notably inequalities of wealth,
status, and power which express themselves in those shifting
hierarchies of classes, orders and ranks which we call the structure of
society.

Yet 'the structure of society' is too static a phrase to describe this
dynamic complexity, and the skill of the social historian lies, like that
of Leonardo da Vinci in his drawings of water flowing around the
piers of bridges, in revealing both the movement and the
permanence of the design. The metaphor is apt. The crowd which
flowed over London bridge in Eliot's poem was a structured crowd:
every one somebody's son or daughter, wife or husband, father or
mother, landlord or tenant, master or servant, boss or worker, buyer
or seller, professional man or client, politician or voter, holiday
maker or purveyor of treats. And they were all, consciously or
unconsciously, related in a more general way, by the bonds of
language, inherited ideas and beliefs, and all the common
experiences of a shared community. It is the social historian's task to
trace out and explain these relationships, not merely to describe the
structure of the crowd and how its various types and groupings
interconnect and fit together but also how it flows in changing yet

seemingly permanent waves and eddies over time. And this four-dimensional, spatial and chronological, structured flow he must somehow reduce to the two-dimensional pattern of his rich brocade, or more strictly to the one-dimensional flow of the narrative line.

One way to set about it, like Leonardo, is to make working sketches as the opportunity arises, artificially detached bits of the seamless web, essays in the original meaning of the word – tries, attempts, experiments. In three decades of a working career a social historian's note books accumulate a large folio of such sketches. Many will be failures, some may get published and succeed to that degree, a few may grow into books and supersede themselves. The following essays are a small selection, mostly of the second kind, which have been written for different purposes, almost all as lectures or papers for a wide variety of audiences and published in very diverse and scattered places. In each essay I have tried to isolate a small aspect of the flowing crowd and to show how it is structurally connected to the main river, the rest of society and its structural experience. Some of the attempts are central to the main theme and are concerned with the flowing structure itself: the role of aristocratic landowners, bourgeois entrepreneurs and a precocious wage-earning proletariat, as well as of consumer demand and social emulation, in 'The Social Causes of the Industrial Revolution' (Essay 2), the engagement of the 'productive' classes against the 'unproductive' in a neglected movement of 'pure' class antagonism in 'Land Reform and Class Conflict in Victorian Britain' (Essay 7); the emergence of a truer, more self-generated history of the working class from the 'false consciousness' of some middle-class intellectuals' versions in 'The Condescension of Posterity' (Essay 10); the changing recruitment of 'top people' in 'Who runs Britain? Elites in British Society since 1880'(Essay 11); and the subtle changes in the consciousness of the class society itself as expressed in its literature during its century of greatest dominance in 'Social Change and the Novel, 1840–1940' (Essay 6). Others are ostensibly more peripheral and yet throw a surprising light from the sidelines on the central theme: the purveyors and consumers of street literature in 'The Origins of the Popular Press' (Essay 3); the hidden springs, going back to the original land settlements and the structure of the new communities which they created, of the striking differences in "The 'Social Tone" of Victorian Seaside Resorts' (Essay 5); the increasing importance to modern society of higher education by and for the professions in 'The Professionalization of University Teaching'

(Essay 8); and the surprisingly long history that lies behind public inquiries and protest meetings in 'Public Participation in Government Decision making: the historical experience' (Essay 11). Yet others reflect a concern with social thought – the common coin of accepted ideas rather than the high-flown conceptions of great thinkers – and its two-way relation with society: the still over-simplified and misunderstood transition from *laissez-faire* to state intervention in 'Individualism versus Collectivism in Nineteenth-century Britain: a False Antithesis' (Essay 4), and the ancient and modern habit of seeing future society in terms of the present in 'The History of Social Forecasting' (Essay 12).

The whole baker's dozen, culled from a much larger corpus of work, is topped and tailed by two essays on the state of social history in the early 1950s and the late 1970s: 'What is Social History?' (Essay 1) in which, as the first assistant lecturer in the subject, I set out my credo on the need for a new, vertebrate, integrated social history with a central, unifying theme; and 'Social History in Britain' (Essay 13) in which I review the gratifyingly enormous advances made in and by the subject over the twenty-five years in between. That is a long time to devote to one central, unifying theme, even one so compelling and various as the development of modern English society since the Industrial Revolution. As I look back over a quarter of a century of Sisyphean labour, I find myself still rolling the same stone up the same hill; but around me I see a much larger and, to my eyes, more confident and successful band of fellow workers, most of them members of the Society for Social History of the United Kingdom, founded as recently as 1976. One of them, my friend and mentor the President, Asa Briggs, pushed the stone further and broke more of the ground before me. To him and all of them, with gratitude from a fellow labourer on the same sunlit, vintage slopes, I dedicate this book.

*Borwicks,*                                             HAROLD PERKIN
*Caton,*
*Lancaster*

# 1
# WHAT IS SOCIAL HISTORY?*

SOCIAL history as a separate discipline is the Cinderella of English
historical studies. Judged by the usual criteria of academic disciplines, it can scarcely be said to exist: there are no chairs and, if we
omit local history, no university departments, no learned journals,
and few if any textbooks. There seems to be something approaching
agreement about its second eldest sister. Some years ago J.F. Rees
wrote:

There is now a virtual consensus of opinion on the scope of economic history. It
includes a study of the state of agriculuture, industry, commerce, and transport,
together with an elucidation of the more technical problems of currency, credit, and
taxation.

He goes on to say,

These subjects necessarily involve an examination and description of social conditions. In fact the line between the economic and the social cannot be strictly drawn.[1]

Sir Maurice Powicke wrote in a similar vein: 'Political and social
history are in my view two aspects of the same process. Social life
loses half its interest and political movements lose most of their
meaning if they are considered separately.'[2]

On social history, then, there seems to be only confusion. Is it, in
the words of G.M. Trevelyan, 'the history of a people with the
politics left out',[3] or, in those of A.L. Rowse, how society consumes
what it has produced?[4] Is it economic history without the more
technical problems of currency, credit, and taxation, or even without
the economics? Is it, stripped to the skeleton, simply how men spent
their leisure hours.[5] All these definitions seem to me inadequate.
Should we, and if so how can we, distinguish it from political or
economic history, or even from general history? For, as the late Sir
Lewis Namier remarked, 'human affairs being the subject-matter of
history, all human pursuits and disciplines in their social aspects
enter into it'.[5] What is the field of the social historian? How can we
find a place for him?

*First published in the Bulletin of the John Rylands Library, Manchester, XXXVI, 1953;
this revised version was published in Approaches to History, H.P.R. Finberg, (ed.),
London: Routledge & Kegan Paul, 1962.

I suspect that the social historian, like many others, is here the victim of a metaphor which bedevils even the most casual methodological remark. I mean the agrarian metaphor of 'fields of study'. According to this the busy cultivators of the academic soil divide it up into allotments on each of which, by a natural division of labour, each cultivator raises the kind of crops (of facts, hypotheses, and generalizations) the ground and green fingers will yield. The ploughland, plotted and pieced, of human knowledge is parcelled out like a great open field after enclosure – and woe to the tenant who cannot show a title-deed! The social historian finds his crops still stubbornly growing athwart his neighbours' hedges, and he must trespass, or become a hired labourer serving several masters. Finding a place for him seems an ungrateful task.

But 'studies', 'subjects', 'disciplines' are not fields, and facts are not crops to be privately harvested and garnered. Facts belong to that category of goods which can be shared without being diminished. All facts are grist to the student's mill, provided his mill will grind them. The outcome of his labours depends on his choice of facts, and this depends on his interests, on the questions he wishes to ask.

Historians know this better than most students, for does not 'history' come from a Greek word for an equiry? All historians start with a question, however frequently they have to change it as they work. What happened? How did it happen? Why? Or at the very least: what will these documents tell me about the past? The social historian differs from other historians only in the questions he asks and the answers he seeks. Finding a place for him does not entail a reallocation of holdings. It merely involves allowing him access to the evidence.

Social history might be thought to be the historical counterpart of sociology, which 'ideally. . . has for its field the whole life of man in society.'[6] But all historians ask questions about the life of man in society. What characterizes the questions of the social historian? The word 'social' is, *prima facie*, not a help. The Oxford English Dictionary gives thirteen major usages (some of them obsolete). Not one of them covers all that is implied in 'social history', or, if it does, covers too much. By virtue of its derivation the word seems at one time or another to have attached itself (in the human sphere alone) to any and every idea or relationship in any way connected with the grouping of men for whatever purpose. For 'social' is an omnibus word covering in the first instance all those human activities which display awareness of others. Semantics fails us: we must fall back on common sense.

W.W. Rostow, attempting to 'relate economic forces to social and political events,' has written: 'It is a useful convention to regard society as made up of three levels, each with a life and continuity of its own, but related variously to the others. These three levels are normally designated as economic, social, and political.'[7] However useful, it is still, of course, a convention. All three 'levels' inhere, if anywhere, in each and every member of society. Society, like the universe, is one and indivisible. It is impossible to isolate, except metaphorically, any one of the 'levels,' however lively and continuous its existence within the whole. To claim primacy for the impulses from one level is no more than to assert that in each man one kind of interest, appetite, desire, or motivation, predominates. The economic interpretation of history asserts the primacy of the economic motive in each man over all others. (Oddly enough, the Marxist view is more a sociological than a purely economic interpretation. 'All history is the history of class struggle' is a socio-political rather than an economic maxim. It is true that Marx believed that a man's class and therefore his position in the struggle is determined by his relation to the system of production, but Engels the capitalist goes to prove that men are not invariably motivated by their economic interest alone, while Marx himself goes to prove that men can elect to espouse the cause of a class to which they do not themselves belong). Put in this way the determinist case becomes an interpretation of the nature of man. It may still hold, but the proofs are metaphysical, and the determinist must meet Gilbert Ryle's thesis that a man is a single entity, not a bundle of discrete parts and qualities.[8] Men in the past, as we today, lived simultaneously on all three levels, without any division of themselves into abstract 'men', either political, economical, or social.

But, like the universe, society cannot be viewed from all sides at once. The spectacular success of the natural sciences since the seventeenth century springs from the device of abstraction, by which the scientist is able to concentrate on a limited number of eminently answerable questions. Abstraction does not change the world, it merely focuses the attention of the observer. In the study of history, of men in past society, it is the difference in focus which justifies the three-fold division of labour. Each specialist has his own focus of attention, his own point of view, his own techniques and tools, his own informing link with an appropriate analytical science (political science, economics, or sociology). It is the labour, we note, not the final product, and in many cases not the raw material, which is divided. Social history is not a part of history. It is, in Arthur

Redford's phrase, all history from the social point of view.
   But what is the social point of view?

The social level (as viewed by Rostow) is very broad indeed. It includes the way
people live, the culture and religion which they generate and regard as acceptable,
their scientific pursuits, and above all the general political concepts which serve to
rationalize their relationship to the community.[9]

This last point is surprising, though less so in a later form: 'the
manner in which general ideas are formed which serve as the basis
for a considerable array of political positions on particular issues'.
G.M. Trevelyan, who took a similar view of the intermediate rôle of
social life between what are usually called the economic basis and the
political superstructure, defines the scope of social history as

the daily life of the inhabitants of the land in past ages: this includes the human as well
as the economic relation of different classes to one another, the character of family and
household life, the conditions of labour and of leisure, the attitude of man to nature,
the culture of each age as it arose out of these general conditions of life, and took ever
changing forms in religion, literature and music, architecture, learning and thought.[10]

So far, so good: but one feels it is not far enough. Social history, on
this pattern, is still auxiliary, peripheral, invertebrate, not, in Arnold
Toynbee's terminology, an intelligible field of study, or even an
articulation of one. There are some for whom even this is too much,
who would confine social history to the kitchen, the wardrobe, the
sports field, the ballroom, the garden-party, the taproom, and the
green circle round the maypole. All these are fascinating places,
provided they are seen in significant relation to the wider world of
which they form part. What is to be avoided is antiquarianism, the
compilation of undigested facts in unpalatable lists without significance or inspiration. Social history of this kind is prone to suffer
from the defect remarked by H.P.R. Finberg in the local historians of
the old school: it lacks a central unifying theme.[11]
   Local history of the new school, as it has developed in the twentieth century under Sir Frank Stenton, W.G. Hoskins, and others,
give us the clue. Its central unifying theme seems to be none other
than the social history of local communities. I am far from sugges-
ting that social history, like the Department of English Local History
at Leicester, should take 'the local history of all England for its
province', though this would certainly have many advantages: Sir
Maurice Powicke long ago acclaimed 'the study of local history as
the basis of the intimate understanding of social change'.[12] What I
have in mind is that the social historian should take his society, and

try to see it whole. That is, in addition to studying the daily life of its members – in the wide sense intended by Trevelyan – he should concern himself with society *qua* society, with social activities and institutions as such, irrespective of their end or purpose. This is the plan adopted by A.L. Rowse in his excellent study of the structure of society in *The England of Elizabeth*. There he essays to 'expose and portray' the whole society, to 'extract the juices of the social' from government and economic matters, parliament and the church, law, education, and the cultivation of the land; wherever in short they can be found. 'Only so is it possible to write the book and give it a coherent form.'[13]

The political and the economic historian are aware of the social framework underpinning the economy and the political system at every point. The shape and structure of society, its growth and decline, the physical distribution of its members by region and district, town, village, and homestead, and their social distribution in the bands of prestige we call classes or the pyramids of connection the eighteenth century called 'interests'[14] – all these affect and are affected by events on the levels of politics and economics. The political or economic historian is often driven to ask questions about them, but they are not his primary concern. He is not interested in them for their own sake, but only as they affect the economy or political affairs. Except indirectly, they are not his questions: but they are the social historian's starting-point.

The best example of what I mean is the study of population, now a discipline in itself, with its own name, techniques, and journals. Its protagonists point out that demography requires the aid of many different specialisms – statistics, medicine, biology, dietetics, economics, sociology – and its findings must be taken into account by all who study society, from whatever point of view. In the words of one of them, 'the significance of population phenomena lies in the meaning for human activity. Population numbers mean markets, military forces, land values. Deaths mean ill-health and disabilities.'[15] The political or economic historian can no more ignore population than parliament or prices. An explanation of 'bastard feudalism' or the break-up of manorialism without reference to the decline of population in the fourteenth and fifteenth centuries would be *Hamlet* without the prince indeed. Nor is mere reference to an otherwise independant variable enough. If we knew the precise relationship between population growth and the agricultural, industrial, medical, and sanitary improvements during the British Industrial Revolution we should have gone far towards explaining the process of industrialization as a whole. A generation ago we could point to the medical advances of the eighteenth century as evidence that population was more cause than effect in the onset of industrialism.[16] Now the whole question has been reopened on a subtler basis by a series of analyses designed to show how complex was the interaction between population and economic growth.[17] Cause and effect were so intertwined as to require the most patient demographic research and refined statistical techniques to extricate them.[18] Meanwhile, the most that can be said is that, whatever caused the initial population surge of the mid-eighteenth century, its failure to be met by the usual Malthusian check was not unconnected with the larger supplies of food and opportunities for jobs provided by economic growth – a surprising return after a century and a half to the general, if not the particular, position of Malthus. A necessary adjunct to political and economic history, the study of population is central to the social 'historian's purpose. Demography as a practical science is a branch of social history.

As for the study of institutions, the House of Lords or the City is just as legitimate a topic for the social historian as the kitchen or the wardrobe. Indeed, the social origins of the peerage and the social connections of City-men both cry out for systematic investigation.[19] Every institution, from trial by ordeal to the modern factory, from partible inheritance to political patronage, has its social aspect. Its interest for the social historian is intensified if it throws light on the way in which the society maintains and renews itself, distributes prestige or status, and solves or frets at the recurring problems of adjustment to its environment and its neighbours.

Light may be found in the most improbable place. Sir Maurice Powicke says of the thirteenth-century tournament:

The inducements to violence were too great to allow room for restraint. In the early days, if not later, prisoners might be held to ransom; the booty in valuable horses and equipment might always be large; victory could lead to fortune as well as to fame. The Earl Marshal's prowess in the tournament had laid the foundation of a career which had led to a rich marriage and an earldom; and, although he was certainly an exceptional man, it would be easy to underrate the influence of these martial gatherings on the social fortunes of young men in succeeding generations.[20]

There is a clear example of social mobility, all the more important in an age when the opportunities for social advancement were relatively few.

Pilgrimage to the relics of saints might be thought a social activity of some interest, but not much far-reaching significance. In a book remarkable for its consistently social approach to European history, R.W. Southern writes of the tenth and eleventh centuries:

The deficiencies in human resources were supplied by the power of the saints. They were the great power-houses in the fight against evil; they filled the gaps left in the structure of human justice. The most revealing map of Europe in these centuries would be a map, not of political or commercial capitals, but of the constellation of sanctuaries, the points of material contact with the unseen world.[21]

So succinctly is characterized the religious orientation and springs of action of an entire, if small, international society. When he recalls that Rome was the sanctuary of many saints, above all of the two great apostles, a flood of light is thrown on the origins of Papal supremacy.

Social history, then, is nothing more and nothing less than the history of society. If this is an Odyssey indeed, it has its wayside hazards. On the one side there is, since nothing human happens outside society, the whirlpool of exhaustiveness, of totality, the desperate, plunging end of those 'still climbing after knowledge infinite'. On the other side prowls the devouring monster of social science.

First, the history of society is not the history of everything that happens in society. That is total history, ideal history, that complete understanding of mankind's past which every true historian dreams of, works towards, and (since he cannot travel simultaneously by land, sea, and air) forsakes only as a means, not as an end. The social historian must avoid the attempt to be everywhere at once. He must keep firmly in view his immediate goal, the understanding of the life of men in the past, in its setting of society and institutions.

Secondly, social history is not a branch of sociology. It does not seek practical knowledge, descriptive laws, governing principles, predictive generalizations, or what G.C. Homans, emulating Clerk-Maxwell, calls the nine field-equations of the science of human relations. It is, first and last, a kind of history. Like all history, it is concerned with 'concrete events fixed in time and space',[22] that is, with particular societies at particular times in particular places. These the social historian studies for their own sake, as an end in themselves, without reference to the practical utility of what he discovers. If an ulterior end is required, it is the hope that 'Histories make men wise.' Economic history in its early days had to resist the economists' demand that it be 'governed by the desire to illustrate economic laws.'[23] The social historian differs from the sociologist precisely as the economic historian from the economist. Like the latter, the former pair are colleagues, partners, members of the same team. They cannot afford to neglect each other's insights and *expertise*. If they do, sociology, deprived of the temporal breadth and multiple sensibilities of the historian, becomes historically parochial, restricting itself to such societies and institutions as happen to have survived, without the means of knowing how they came to survive; while social history, deprived of the heuristic depth and theoretical penetration of the sociologist, becomes academically superficial, an antiquarian pursuit of facts-in-themselves, without the means of relating their significance. Yet neither is the master, neither the servant of the other. Both are equals in the study of society, approaching it from different directions and for different purposes. The social historian confronts the same material, may even borrow the sociologist's techniques, but he asks different questions, seeks a different end.

Social history, to justify itself, must ultimately issue in actual social histories. At present it seems to be in, or just emerging from, the situation Cunningham remarked of economic history over forty years ago:

> There have been numerous histories of one or another department of economic activity, as for example, merchant shipping, or agriculture, or of particular localities; but comparatively little progress has been made in surveying the growth of economic activities in their interconnection, and the development of the body economic as a whole.[24]

Now there is nothing at all to be said against histories of departments of any kind of history, least of all social history. The more there are, the nearer draws the possibility of a comprehensive social history, and the better it will be when it comes. Moreover, there is no need for the specialist historian to consider too closely into what category his interest falls. Let him follow his question, his problem, or his material where it will lead. If he cuts across categories, if like Newton he can unite two hitherto unrelated levels of experience, so much the better. He may be a genius, a man who sets the world thinking in a way which was not possible before. His work in any event will have value for general history, and for some historians in particular. But, to paraphrase Cunningham, there will still be a need to survey the growth of social activities in their interconnection, and the development of the body social as a whole.

Of what ought a comprehensive social history to consist? It should concern one society, fixed in space and time: ancient Babylon, Periclean Athens, imperial Rome, Latin Christendom in the eleventh and twelfth centuries, China under the Great Khan, Elizabethan England, Glossop since the Industrial Revolution. How should the historian approach his society, unfold its themes, write its history, so far as the evidence permits? He should try to see his society as a structured, functioning, evolving, self-regenerating, self-reacting whole, set in its geographical and cosmic environment. He should present the natural history of the body politic, exposing and explaining its ecology, anatomy, physiology, pathology, and, since the body politic may be presumed to exist on more than the physical plane, its psychology too: its awareness of itself, its conscious aims, criteria, and ideals.

This, of course, is a tendentious metaphor which must not be pushed too far. Society is no more a body than it is a machine; it is a *social* entity, an integrated collectivity of human beings, and therefore in important ways both something more and something less than an individual man or woman. Above all, though it has no soul and no putative expectation of eternal life, it has the remarkable property of self-regeneration, that is, of reproducing not some other creature in the same form but *itself* in a great variety of forms. It is a dynamic system which, unlike the body, does not need to organize its members according to a pre-ordained pattern, but can interchange them and evolve new organs according to its requirements. The body metaphor had the tendency in those societies which invented or utilized it of suppressing this potentiality and defending the *status quo ante* – a tendency easily circumvented by those assailants wise enough to appeal to their own version of the *status quo*. Yet the metaphor has the merit of insisting on the essential unity of the thing studied, and, avoiding its obvious traps, we may with its aid usefully explore the implications of the five interrelated aspects of social history.

By the society's ecology is meant its relation to the physical environment, first of all to the geographical background with which it is intimately intermingled, the hard facts of topography, soil, climate, fauna, and vegetation, and the ways in which they have been modified by human action. Adaptation is a two-way process. As society adapts itself to the environment, so it learns to adapt the environment to itself. The well-known English contrast between 'woodland' and 'champion', between the hamlet-and-homestead settlement of the highland zone and the nucleated-village settlement of the lowlands, is the product of such mutual adaptation – mutual, since open-field villages were by no means unknown in the north and west, and British settlement in the south and east before the

English came seems to have been mainly of the highland type. Moreover, East Anglia after the Danes came – if not earlier, after a possibly Jutish immigration – enjoyed down to modern times a highland type of settlement on a lowland topography. This paradox is traceable to the inheritance customs of East Anglian peasants, partible inheritance in an area with abundant land to be reclaimed from waste and fen.[25] The younger son used his inheritance as a base from which to drive back the marsh and reclaim a home, necessarily segregated, for himself. Partible inheritance characterizes socage tenure, and down to this day adjacent fenland parishes bear witness in their differing population densities to their diverse proportions of medieval sokemen and different rates of reclamation.[26] Thus intimately did community and landscape adjust to one another.

At the other extreme from the local is the larger environment of the cosmos. Nothing, it may be thought, changes less from one society or one generation to another than the unchanged and unchanging universe. On the contrary, nothing in human experience can change more and with profounder implications for society than man's view of the universe and his place in it. Quaint, arbitrary, and artifical to the modern scientist, the Aristotelian–Ptolemaic cosmology (responsible for the body-metaphor besides much else in our social thinking) was as hard and ineluctable a fact to the medieval European as the stubborn soil or the capricious weather. It had the special virtue of linking human society to everything that existed from the archangel to the lowest worm that crawled, and so endowed it with the same ontological certainty. The prince among his subjects was the natural equivalent of God among the angels, man among the creatures, the lion (or the elephant) among beasts, the eagle (or the phoenix) among birds, the whale (or the dolphin) among fishes. Harmony in the body politic echoed the cosmic harmony of the circumambient spheres; treason and civil strife made discords which heaven rejected and cast out with disgust.[27] When the New Philosophy put all in doubt, shattered the music of the spheres, and overturned the ladder and scale of creatures, European man gained power over nature and, collectively, over his own social organization, at the cost of this old assurance of the continuity of the social, natural, and supernatural worlds. A society's cosmology is from one point of view an aspect of its psychology: from its own it is an integral part of its objective environment.

By way of adaptation a society's ecology leads straight to its anatomy. The structure of society is a great deal more than its class-system. In the first place, it embraces the whole of the social 'given element' into which the individual is born: the size and shape of society, that is, the population and its distribution by geography and age as well as by occupation and social position; the pattern of institutions, from marriage or inheritance customs to feudal homage, patronage, or contract of employment; and the complex of associations – family, church, guild, chivalrous order, school, hospital, workhouse, club, trade union, professional body, and even factory, political party, or organ of government, in, and only in, their social aspects – in and around which the individual must move and have his being.

Secondly, class is not the only or inevitable division of a hierarchical society. The very concept of class, in the modern sense of broad, mutually hostile, horizontal bands based on conflicting economic interest, is a product of the British Industrial Revolution. Until then the word was used in its neutral, 'classifying' sense, and its place supplied by the 'ranks', 'orders', and 'degrees' of a more finely graded hierarchy of great subtlety and discrimination.[28] In that older society the horizontal solidarities and vertical antagonisms of class were usually latent, overlain by the vertical bonds of patronage and dependency and the horizontal antagonisms between different interests, such as the landed, East and West Indian, cloth-manufacturing, and wool-exporting interests. In the small communities – village or tiny town – which made up most of the old society, a man was highly conscious of his exact position in the social hierarchy, not by comparison with his anonymous fellows on his own level elsewhere, but by his face-to-face relationship with his immediate neighbours above and below him. In regard to such a society the concept of class is a bludgeon rather than a scalpel, and crushes what it tries to dissect.

Nor is it much improved by turning it round and calling it status group, at least in the Germanic sense of *Stand*. *Stände* are but classes ancient enough to have acquired a customary title, and to exchange a crudely economic for a quasi-legal criterion. They are appropriate to a schematized feudalism, just as classes are to a schematized capitalism, and in real life schematically correct classes are rare. Modern distinctions, based often enough on a narrow historical experience, fail us, and we must fall back, as in social anthropology, on the terminology used in the society itself. In this case, as explained by a somewhat old-fashioned Irish judge in 1798, 'Society consists of noblemen, baronets, esquires, gentlemen, yeomen, tradesmen, and artificers',[29] though he might have added husbandmen and the 'labouring poor'.

The structure of society may be a dynamic rather than a static system, even when maintaining itself in substantial equilibrium. The 'storm over the gentry' in the century between the English Reformation and the Great Civil War,[30] whatever the outcome of the controversy, has illuminated, if rather fitfully, one of the most important features of English society, not only in that period, but from the fourteenth to the nineteenth century: the continuous recruitment to the landed aristocracy and gentry of 'new men' from trade, industry, the professions, and occasionally from agriculture. In the Tudor and early Stuart era of profit-inflation, a buyers' land market, and swollen opportunities at Court, the upward flow may have been brisker than at any time before the Industrial Revolution. But it was in principle the same social process which begins with families like the Howards, de la Poles, and Pastons in the fourteenth and fifteenth centuries and is still going strong with the Peels, Strutts, Addingtons, and Scotts (Lords Eldon and Stowell) in the early nineteenth. It is, indeed, a part of the larger mobility of English society, that two-way flow of blood and wealth – an upward flow of rising men from all the lower to all the higher levels, balanced by a downward flow of younger sons from higher to lower, to which must be added an upward flow of heiresses and a downward as well as a sideways flow of dowried daughters – which made England a more open, expansive, and yet a more stable society than any Continental nation. Its dynamic stability created a resourceful landed aristocracy continually replenished from below and in close contact through its own sons with the society it dominated; an active middle layer of business and professional men with powerful incentives to enterprise but none to remain in the towns and form a permanent, frustrated, revolutionary *bourgeoisie*; and 'lower orders' stimulated by social emulation to the twin prerequisites of industrial expansion, proletarian wage-earning, and consumption via the market. In France, by contrast, the segregation from trade and the professions of the privileged old *noblesse,* completed and confirmed by Louis XIV, not only severely impeded French economic development[31] but was perhaps the greatest single cause of political discontent. France had a political, England an industrial revolution: the difference arises from their contrasting social structures.

The third step is to see how the structure works, how the body politic functions. Its physiology includes how the society gets its living, how it exploits its natural and human resources, how it distributes and consumes what it has produced, what activities other than the means of life it pursues by way of ends in themselves, by what social controls it maintains itself in being and defends itself from unacceptable structural change, and how it regenerates itself and passes on its knowledge and skills, its attitudes and ideals, from one generation to the next. In other words, the historian must 'extract the juices of the social' from agriculture, industry, and trade, the distribution of income and capital, government and public order, legislation and public morality, education in all its many forms, religion, intellectual and scientific thought, literature, music, the arts, sports and games, pastimes and amusements. Here we seem very near the whirlpool of totality, if not to have plunged right in.

Yet the problem of keeping a steady course is not so difficult as it at first appears, nor is the pull of the whirlpool peculiar to the social historian. Let us look at what J.J. McCulloch considered the pre-requisites of the good economist.

The economist will not arrive at anything like a true knowledge of the laws regulating the production, accumulation, distribution, and the consumption of wealth if he do not draw his materials from a very wide surface. He should study man in every situation; he should have recourse to the history of society, arts, commerce, and civilization, to the works of legislators, philosophers, and travellers, to everything in short that can throw light on the causes which accelerate or retard the progress of nations.[32]

In this breadth of view, McCulloch was joined by John Stuart Mill and, more recently, by Arthur Lewis.[33] Neither he nor they intended the economist to be also a professional social historian, art critic, archaeologist, political scientist, philosopher, or explorer. They simply meant that he should seek his answers wherever they might be found.

Relevance is a matter of questions asked and answers obtained. The political historian cannot refuse to deal with the Black Death, enclosures and engrossing of farms, the Reformation, population growth, inflation, the invention of gunpowder, the General Strike, or the hydrogen bomb, on the grounds that disease, agriculture, religion, demography, currency, technology, industrial relations, and science are not his subjects. They are all his subjects in so far as they affect his central theme, the public issues upon which turned the politics of the age.

The social historian has his own central theme by which to test the relevance of his questions. He will welcome answers to them from any source. He is not concerned with agriculture, industry, and commerce for their intrinsic interest, but he can scarcely give any account of the functioning of society without reference to them.

Social structure is by no means the same thing as the distribution of income. 'The essence of social class,' says T.H. Marshall, 'is the way a man is treated by his fellows (and, reciprocally, the way he treats them), not the qualities or the possessions which cause that treatment.'[34] But a study of a class-system without the economic qualities and possessions of its members would be divorced from reality. Moreover, many of the statistics used by the economic historian, of income and wealth, occupations and unemployment, immigration and emigration, for example, are immediately relevant to the social historian, answering some of his most important questions. The political historian, taking into account the wealth of nations and the sinews of military power, will readily concede the point.

In the same manner, the social historian cannot ignore the social implications of politics, legislation, and administration. Social policy in the days of Burleigh or of Beveridge, the social causes and effects of war, the social foundations of a ruling aristocracy, the social consequences of taxation and welfare measures, the class connections of political parties, all affect the functioning of society, and are his concern. This point the economic historian, who has since the time of Adam Smith had to take into account the policies and actions of government, will readily concede.

Many of the answers the social historian seeks, or the evidence for them, are already to be found, then, between the covers of books labelled political or economic history. This he can only welcome, as teacher and researcher. If it were not so the teaching of social history would be next to impossible, since so few satisfactory textbooks yet exist, and under-graduates cannot work entirely from the sources. As for research, history is a co-operative not a competitive endeavour, and we owe a duty to our colleagues and predecessors to use whatever they have discovered of relevance to our interests. Economic and political activities are not the social historian's first interest. He is concerned with them only as they affect social activities and institutions. It is a matter of focus, of priorities, of emphasis. He will follow in the wake of the political or economic historian just long enough to get his questions answered. Though he may for a time fish the same waters, he will use a different net and steer a different course.

There is another approach to the whirlpool of totality, that of the dilettante. Faced with a great multitude of topics, any one of which might become a lifetime's study, the social historian may lose himself in the intellectual dispersion of the jack-of-all-trades. Religion, science, philosophy, literature, music, painting, architecture, gas-

tronomy, costume, furniture, courtship, sport, and entertainment –
the list of sirens, each no less seductive than the rest, is endless. Yet
the same sense of direction, the same steady navigation, will save
him from drowning. He should follow them so far, and only so far,
as they lead him in the direction of his central theme.

Let us take, for example, one of the humblest and most antiquarian
of these topics, the study of costume. What could be less relevant or
more frivolous than how the members of a society were dressed? On
the contrary, no single source of evidence can, at a glance almost, tell
the historian so much about this society: its comparative prosperity,
the distance between rich and poor, the grading of the social hierarchy, its occupational, religious, military, or ceremonial inclinations,
its frivolous or serious cast of mind, its attitudes towards women,
children, servants, or the poor, something even of its moral standards and its ideal type of man or woman. Sir Walter Raleigh's £600
*ensemble* compared with the puritan suit of drab testifies as elo-
quently to courtly society as his 'Say to the Court it glows, and
shines like rotten wood.' Pepys's £20 beaver hat compared with the
cottager's fustian is as specific a comment as Gregory King's political
arithmetic. Madame Récamier's republican Greek tunic compared
with Marie Antoinette's aristocratic panniered gown makes its point
as radically as Rousseau's *Contrat Social*.

Probing more deeply, we can see in the familiar fashion cycle,
unique to Western civilization from the later Middle Ages till only
yesterday, a clue to the expansion of European and still more of
English society. The fashion cycle requires a special kind of society
with a peculiar structure, aristocratic but not exclusive, hierarchical
but open to infiltration from below, so that emulation by their social
inferiors will force the leaders of society to change their style of dress
periodically in order to maintain their visible supremacy. The social
emulation and mobility to which the fashion cycle testifies were a
source of energy which helped to drive the engine of expansion.
England, where the fashion cycle reached furthest down the social
scale, affecting according to eighteenth-century observers like Pehr
Kalm the very labourers,[35] enjoyed the highest rate of mobility and
the most far-reaching industrial and colonial expansion. Used thus
to illuminate the structure and functioning of society the most
peripheral of topics is reduced to perspective and becomes of
relevance and value to the central theme.

The fourth aspect, the society's pathology, is concerned with
social problems and the attempts at remedying them. These are what
Cunningham had in mind when he wrote; 'We cannot understand

the past unless we attempt to realize the precise problems of each age and the success or failure which attended human efforts to grapple with them.'[36] The social historian might begin with the five giants of our modern domestic epic, want, disease, ignorance, squalor, and idleness; but there are many others to be found in most societies in most ages – vice and crime, intolerance, civil strife, and the ravages of war. Their remedies take him, without apology, into the sphere of government policy, social administration, police and punishment, as well as individual and organized charity, mutual aid, and simple good-neighbourliness.

One of the most ubiquitous of problems is that of social conflict between different groups, orders, classes, or interests within the society's structure. Whether all history is the history of class struggle, whether exploitation and resentment at it, the diminishing size of the exploiting class and the increasing immiseration of the exploited, the final bloody revolution and its classless sequel, are all inevitable concomitants of class society, are questions which can only be answered empirically, and cannot be determined here. One sceptical gloss may be permitted, however. The age which evolved the modern concept of class to describe the massive discontents released by the Industrial Revolution, on the legend of which Marx erected his theory, seems to have been an era not of *class* but of *pre*-class conflict. In a viable class society, such as the mid-Victorian which immediately succeeded it, conflict is institutionalized and rendered acceptable by channelling it through such institutions as industrial negotiation and parliamentary elections. The violence of the age of the Luddites and of the Chartists seem rather to have been the birthpangs of an older society unable to accept or deliver itself painlessly of the new society struggling in its womb. In that older society conflict was not the bargaining of reluctant but inevitable partners forced to adjust their differences by non-violent strike action and negotiation, but the violent disloyalty of insubordinate servants, to be suppressed by legal and military violence.

Paradoxically, even as Marx wrote, the new class society itself was undermining his theory of class struggle: in exact measure as it emerged into the light, and mature class attitudes replaced the outraged paternalism and Oedipean adolescent rebellion of the old society, so the violence subsided and was overtaken by the remarkable and, in Marxist terms, inexplicable pacification of mid-Victorian England. May it not be that non-violent class conflict is the normal relationship between marital partners who cannot live together without bickering, but who apart cannot live at all? And violent revolution the pathological variant, the rending divorce, to which most marriages do not lead?

Social problems are solved or evaded in the light of the fifth and last aspect, the society's psychology, the way it reacts upon itself. It includes the aims which it consciously pursues, the moral criteria by which it judges its success, the public opinion which it applies to its own behaviour and concerns, and the ideals which satisfy its aspirations. It has some affinity with social psychology, the study of group behaviour, but we must not be misled by the metaphor into thinking it is the same thing or its historical counterpart. It has more affinity with the sociology of knowledge, which sets out to discover the social provenance of ideas and ideologies, and provides the historian with hypotheses which can be tested against the experience of his society.[37] He can, for example, ask whether nineteenth-century Britain, the society in which Marx lived for most of his life, bears out the Marxist view that men's ideas are determined by their relation to the means of production, and if so, what was Marx's own relation to the economic system. He can ask whether Dicey's division of the century into three distinct periods of social-legislative opinion, labelled 'Blackstonian optimism', 'Benthamism or Individualism', and 'Collectivism', can be squared with the empirical facts. Or he can ask why so many reforming minds of the century, including Marx and most of the Benthamites, classical economists, Christian Socialists, Fabians, and Oxford Idealists, belonged to none of the three great classes of landlords, capitalists, and proletarians, but to the 'forgotten middle class' of salaried, feed, or dependent brain-workers. The answers to these questions will bring about – are already bringing about – a revolution in nineteenth-century historiography.[38]

Central to this aspect is perhaps the most significant feature of modern developing societies, their increasing self-awareness and control. In our own society self-awareness began even before the great antiquaries of Rowse's 'Elizabethan discovery of England'[39] with the violent xenophobia of the later medieval period. It sought precision through Graunt, Petty, King, and the political arithmetic of the seventeenth century; gained intellectual depth and a sense of growth in the eighteenth with Adam Ferguson, Adam Smith, John Millar, James Steuart of Coltness, and the Scottish historical school of philosophy; made the crucial transition from self-knowledge to social engineering with Edwin Chadwick, Kay-Shuttleworth, Leonard Horner, and the great civil servants of the nineteenth century; and in the twentieth on the social science of Booth, Rowntree,

Bowley, and Beveridge founded that great machine tool of social engineering – still underemployed and its potentialities unrealized – the Welfare State. How far this evolution is peculiar to Britain and how far it is a necessary concomitant of industrialization, 'development', or 'modernization', is a further question for empirical enquiry.

But whether it knows or not, every society has its ideals: of what constitutes the good life and how society should help which individuals to pursue it, of what society should be and what its relations with its *alter ego*, the state. All such ideals inevitably come back to the ideal of what the individual is, or should in the best circumstances become. The ideal social type in feudal society was the chivalrous knight, serving God and his lord according to his oath. In the succeeding post-feudal, pre-capitalist society, it was the landed gentleman, the leisured amateur, freed by his unearned income to pursue the ends of life, which by definition were his own pleasures. In Victorian society it was the resourceful entrepreneur, who eschewed idleness and laboured in his vocation, providing work for the deserving and the workhouse for the undeserving poor. What does the twentieth century take for its ideal type? Is it not, East and West, in developed and developing societies alike, the professional expert, who alone amongst the non-proletarian classes enjoys ungrudged, unchallenged prestige and security?

Beneath the ideal of what a man should be there lies the deeper ideal of what human life is for. This is the fountainhead of the society's psychology. From it flows the quality and texture of its social thought, and ultimately of society itself. According as it finds the meaning and purpose of life in serving God or the five-year plan, in harrowing the heretic or consoling the brief pilgrimage of fallen man, in bringing light to the Gentile or death to the non-Aryan, in the *recherche du temps perdu* of a supposed golden age or in the *ignis fatuus* of a hypostasized posterity, in negotiating the narrow isthmus between two eternities or in furthering the ever-widening march of progress, in pursuing truth in the interstices of an authoritarian dogma or to the libertarian abyss of existential doubt or universal holocaust, so, consciously or unconsciously, it will create itself in the image of its ideal. Nor does its true belief necessarily cry out in the market place, orate in the forum, or speak in the flat tones of the administrator. It often speaks with the quiet voice of conversation in a private room. It is in the daily talk of ordinary men and women that the real values of a society are felt and heard. And it is at this most intimate of levels that the social historian must seek, if he can, the psychological generating power of his society.

We have now come full circle, from cosmology to the meaning and purpose of life *sub specie aeternitatis*. In the topology of a unitary object every surface is interconnected and every path leads back to where it started. The body politic's ecology, anatomy, physiology, pathology, and psychology overlap and interconnect because a society is an organic whole in which the functioning of every part affects that of every other. Moreover, just as no man is an island, so no society can live for long in isolation from the great society of mankind. Hence to all the foregoing we must add a further dimension: the mutual relations and influence of diverse societies, the comparative study of their structure and institutions, and ultimately perhaps their involvement in the tortuous evolution which, willy-nilly and for better or worse, has made the modern world one, and all its societies members one of another in the same fateful progress to survival or perdition.

If so capacious a study as social history, thus delimited, sounds a superhuman task, that is because, in relation to any one human being, it is so. No one historian can or should hope to say all there is to say about a society: life is too manifold and too short for that. But a man's reach should exceed his grasp, or what's a subject for? Fortunately for historians, of the making of history there is no end, and much study is a joy to the profession. In practice the teaching of an articulate social history is no more impossible than the teaching of an articulate political or economic history. One of the amenities of history as an educational discipline is that it tailors itself to the capacities of teacher and taught. What can be done at their level in the available time they may do, with pleasure and profit from the very beginning without having to wait for distant returns.

Two formidable problems still remain, of presentation and of sources. The first is the 'rank-and-file dilemma' which Hexter has compared to Heisenberg's indeterminacy principle in quantum physics.[40] The historian cannot simultaneously pursue all the aspects of a complex society and show the whole society in motion. He cannot write both narrative and topical history at the same time. But somehow he must try. A great deal may be learnt from local studies, in the handling of small societies over short periods. To larger studies periodization is the key: since the social historian must move forward by periods, he will choose them with an eye to their essential unity as temporal articulations of the whole society. In English social history he will find the old periodization a hindrance, as indeed it is increasingly felt to be by political and economic historians. He will find useful articulations in viable periods by taking the ages between or dominated by great geological shifts in the structure of society: true feudalism, succeeded via the decline of military service, serfdom, and population by 'bastard feudalism'; Tawney's century between the Reformation and the Great Civil War; the Augustan age from the Restoration to the onset of the Industrial Revolution; the Industrial Revolution, so much more than an economic phenomenon; G.M. Young's early Victorian England, succeeded by the different age between it and the First World War; the as yet twilit passage between the world wars; and the amorphous, unorganized history of post-war England. Any periodization has its difficulties. There is no ideal solution and only one touchstone, that the history, like poetry, should seem to come unforced, like the leaves to a tree.

As for sources, the social historian, like McCulloch's economist, must 'draw his materials from a very wide surface'. They may be found in whatever has come down to us from the past, in whatever form: in print or manuscript, from love letters to Census returns; the myriad artefacts, from clothes to cooking-pots, which are the instruments of daily life; the products of past culture, from temples to miniature painting; or the marks of old habitation, from lost villages to landscape architecture, on the face of the country. He must know only how to use them. With documents he should be a skilled researcher; with objects, an amateur archaeologist; with Census returns or political arithmetic, a critical statistician; with *objets d'art*, not a connoisseur but at least a dilettante; with works of literature, a literary historian if not a critic. With them all he should have a keen eye for what the mediocre as well as the good of its kind can tell him about the social life of the past. He cannot hope and should not try to do other men's work for them; but what he can do he should do better. He cannot afford, for example, the intolerance of some literary critics towards all but the most perfect products of the creative imagination. F.R. Leavis believed that to use literary evidence intelligently the student of society needs to be a trained critic.

Without the sensitizing familiarity with the subtleties of language, and the insight into the relations between abstract or generalizing thought and the concrete of human experience, that the trained frequentation of literature alone can bring, the thinking that attends social or political studies will not have the edge and force it should.[41]

All this is true – but what does it profit a historian of early Victorian England if it teaches him that the *only* work of Dickens worth his serious attention is *Hard Times?*[42]

Moreover, Leavis was less acutely aware of the need of the student of literature to have studied from non-fictional sources the society of which the literature is the outgrowth. Failure to do this well enough has led some literary critics into a kind of legendary history, geared to what Frank Kermode has called 'a myth of catastrophe',[43] the fall from a primordial state of innocence and grace before the 'dissociation of sensibility' and the debasement of popular culture. The mere historian will not question the values upon which the theory of the golden age is erected, but he will question its periodization and its sources. T.E. Hulme found it in the age before the Renaissance and rationalism did their deadly work; W.B. Yeats, before Shakespeare; Leavis himself, before Milton, since rather unkindly rehabilitated by T.S. Eliot; Mrs Leavis, before W.H. Smith and the cheap editions on the railway bookstalls; and now Richard Hoggart, in his childhood, before the working class was corrupted by the popular press. One wonders if they had ever read a broadsheet ballad, a 'penny dreadful', or a gallows sheet – the literary sources most relevant to any pronouncement on popular culture.[44]

On his part, the self-respecting social historian will not rely on evidence from one source alone. He will not, for example, expect Moll Flanders to typify the women of Defoe's England – but he may legitimately expect her story to make concrete the human experience behind the 'great debate of the poor',[45] the statistics of London poor relief, the settlement Acts, the harshness of the penal code, and the chronic fear betrayed in the parish records of the birth of fatherless children.

The multiple sensibility of the historian will connect the most diverse sources. The Cambridge University registers show that the heirs of eighteenth-century landowners did not distinguish themselves academically to the same extent as their fellow students and younger brothers.[46] How this conclusion comes alive when we find a manuscript letter from the anxious widow to her eldest boy at Magdalene;

Your promises aided by my strong affections prove powerful enough to make me give in to what you desire, even to forget past miscarriages if you'll be serious and make the best use of your time you possibly can for the future and study as much as in you lies to retrieve the precious time you have unhappily lost. In order to that you must drop all the Idle part of your acquaintance and they'll not care to trouble you if they find you intent upon a Book. Don't make much of your Self in a bad way. No philosopher in Cambridge will find occasion for more than four-score pound a Year.

Perhaps he had justified her earlier fears when Sturbridge Fair was drawing near, 'that all the silly Students will lose their time and innocence there', and ignored her advice 'to get your Tutor to go along with you'. We are not surprised to learn that there is no record of Jack Egerton's graduation, or that his brothers Samuel and Thomas, who did not go to a university, became successful merchants in Venice and Holland.[47]

Again, the first modern occupational Census of 1851 comes to life in Ford Madox Brown's *Work,* painted in the following year.[48] An invaluable document precisely because it is not great art and leaves nothing to the imagination, it offers a microcosm of mid-Victorian society: the equestrian, leisured gentry; the earnest middle-class ladies with crinoline, sunshade, and evangelical tract – *The Hodman's Haven, or Drink for Thirsty Souls;* the thirsty hodman downing a pint; the clean-drawn navvy in all the dignity of labour; the uppish craftsman with buttonhole, watch-chain, and *The Times;* the sleeping tramps; the shame-faced, yet pre-Raphaelite, ragged messenger-boy; the sandwich-board men and women; the orange-girl being moved along by the peeler; the intellectuals leaning on the fence – said to be Carlyle and F.D. Maurice; the merry urchins, the underfed baby with its sad, old-man's face, and, of course, the mongrels. On the frame there is the homily, 'In the sweat of thy face shalt thou eat bread'. Even the work has a mid-Victorian flavour: they appear to be mending a sewer.

The social historian need not be a specialist in every discipline connected with his sources. Herbert Butterfield has shown how, without being a scientist, one can offer a more rounded and satisfying history of science than the teleological version which usually passes for it. One does not have to be a scientist to trace the significance of a theory of impetus, which the scientist, impatient to follow only the main line leading to the present, is likely to ignore.[49] Nor does one have to be a musician, a town-planner, a theologian, or a bookmaker to trace the significance of music, urban growth, religion, or gambling in the social life of the past. An educated man, it has been said, is one who can read every page of *The Times* or the *Guardian* with intelligence; but that does not mean that he needs to be an expert in politics, diplomacy, law, finance, technology, court etiquette, fashion design, literary criticism, advertising, midwifery, marriage guidance, and life insurance, as well as the construction of crossword puzzles. The ideal social historian is the ideally educated man.

In spite of its difficulties and demands, the neglect of social history is only apparent. Cinderella has already moved to the centre of the stage and is giving cues to the other protagonists. Charles Wilson recently contrasted with the political and individualist preoccupations of the historians of Acton's generation 'the sociologized history of our own day which is less concerned with individuals and more with men as members of social groups'.[50] His words are borne out in whatever direction we look: in the biographical approach of Namier, Sir John Neale, and their followers to the history of Parliament, 'a demographic study of the most significant group-formation in the life of this country';[51] in the attempts on both sides of the gentry controversy to explain the Great Civil War in terms of the social upheavals of the preceding hundred years; in the interest in the social origins and interconnections of entrepreneurs;[52] in the recognition of the social factors necessary to economic growth;[53] or in the realization that modern international history turns on the competition of rival theories of the organization of society. In all of these the social approach offers insights and understanding not available to Acton's generation. It is a far cry from Seeley's 'History is past politics: politics is present history' to Trevor-Roper's 'Political history is often a commentary, a corrective and clarifying commentary, on social history, and as such cannot be divorced from it.'[54]

Can social history go further than this? Will Cinderella cease to be a handmaiden and become a princess in her own right? There are some signs of a coming transformation. Comprehensive social histories are in progress, or completed: A.L. Rowse's *The Elizabethan Age,* Edward Hughes's *North Country Life in the Eighteenth Century,* the multi-volume *International Social History* under the editorship of J.H. Plumb. Two front-rank academic publishers are devoting open series to the subject, while a third has widened its economic history textbook series to admit social history.[55] The *International Review of Social History,* published by the *International Instituut voor Sociale Geschiedenis* in Amsterdam, has been revived and by its publication of articles in English partly makes up for the lack of a native journal. Asa Briggs's appointment in social studies at the University of Sussex may perhaps by those who know him be regarded as the first chair in social history; at least there is no danger that the subject will be neglected in Brighton.

Perhaps the way forward may be through a new approach to general history, already heralded by the new approaches to political and economic history: the comparative study of what Pareto, Toynbee, and G.D.H. Cole have taught us to call élites.[56] In the interaction of their political power, economic strength, and social roots and connections all three kinds of historian may learn to work together as equal partners in a common enterprise. Sir John Habakkuk has already shown the kind of contribution which social history can make to such an approach by his studies of the nobility in eighteenth-century England and of the rôle of family settlements in the maintenance of their wealth and power.[57]

Such an approach to general history may well reveal the special primacy of the impulses from the social level. I am not putting forward a new species of determinism. Men, we may still believe, choose their ends, although in the light of what seems best for them in the short or the long run. But the ends men have sought – prestige, admiration, culture, fame, knowledge and understanding, family life, philanthropic endeavour, spiritual rebirth, unreflecting enjoyment, or a vicarious eternal life in the seed of their loins – have been as often social as political or economic, while wealth and power under scrutiny often turn out to be means to social ends. Determinism, as we have seen, is at bottom an interpretation of the nature of man. Determinists impute to the majority of men, or at least to a majority of those in key positions, the pathological ends of a few: power or acquisition as ends in themselves. Social ends are so various and manifold that they offer no temptation to oversimplify the multi-centred complexity of human nature. And, since it is only in society that men become human, let alone civilized, there is no better definition of human nature than Aristotle's, translated as he understood it: 'Man is a social animal'.

Every age has its own interest in the past, its own version of the perennial question of Milton's Adam, 'How came I thus, how here?' The interest of our own age can only be described as social. We want to know not only what laws were made and battles fought or even how men got their living, but what it felt like to be alive, how men in history – not merely kings and popes, statesmen and tycoons – lived and worked and thought and behaved towards each other. 'Social questions', Beatrice Webb confided to her diary in 1884, 'are the vital questions of today: they take the place of religion.'[58] In the 1960s they take the place of everything, at least in politics, especially in international politics. And what is politics but the questions we most want to debate in public? At this point Cinderella becomes a princess if not, as the respect and the reluctance of political and economic history to let her go her independant way would seem to suggest, the queen of historical studies.

# Notes

1 In A. Redford, *Economic History of England, 1760–1860*, London: Longmans, 1931, p.v.
2 F.M. Powicke, *King Henry III and the Lord Edward*, Oxford: Clarendon Press, 1947
3 G.M. Trevelyan, *English Social History*, London: Longmans, 1944, p.vii.
4 A.L. Rowse, *The Use of History*, London: Hodder & Stoughton, 1946, p.69.
5 L. Namier, 'History, its Subject Matter and Tasks', *History Today*, 11, 1952, p.161.
6 M. Ginsberg, *Sociology*, London: Butterworth, 1949, p.7.
7 W.W. Rostow, *British Economy of the Nineteenth Century*, Oxford, Clarendon Press, 1948, p. 134.
8 G. Ryle, *The Concept of Mind*, London: Hutchinson, 1949, *passim*.
9 Rostow, *op. cit.*
10 Trevelyan, *op. cit.*
11 H.P.R. Finberg, *The Local Historian and his Theme*, Leicester University Press, 1952, p. 17.
12 F.M. Powicke, *Historical Study in Oxford*, Oxford: Clarendon Press, 1929, p. 10.
13 A.L. Rowse, *The Elizabethan Age: I, The England of Elizabeth: The Structure of Society*, London: MacMillan, 1950, p. viii.
14 W.J.H. Sprott, *Sociology*, London: Hutchinson, 1949, p.98; S.H. Beer, 'The Representation of Interests in British Government: Historical Background', *American Political Science Review*, LI, 1957, pp. 613–50.
15 W.F. Ogburn, 'On the Social Aspects of Population Change', *British Journal of Sociology*, IV, 1953, p.26.
16 M.C. Buer, *Health, Wealth and Population in the Early Days of the Industrial Revolution*, London: Routledge, 1926; G.T. Griffith, *Population Problems in the Age of Malthus*, Cambridge, University Press, 1926; T.H. Marshall, 'The Population of England and Wales from the Industrial Revolution to the World War', *Economic History Review*, V, 1934–5, pp. 65–78.
17 K.H.Connell, 'Some Unsettled Problems in English and Irish Population History, 1750–1845', *Irish Historical Studies*, VII, 1950–I, pp.225–234; H.J. Habakkuk, 'English Population in the Eighteenth Century', *Economic History Review*, 2nd Series, VI, 1953, pp. 117–33, and 'The Economic History of Modern Britain', *Journal of Economic History*, XVIII, 1958, pp.486–501; J.T. Krause, 'Changes in English Fertility and Mortality, 1781–1850', *Economic History Review*, 2nd series, XI, 1958, pp. 52–70, and 'Some Implications of Recent Research in Demographic History, *Comparative Studies in Society and History*, I, 1959, pp. 164–88; T. McKeown and R.G. Brown, 'Medical Evidence related to English Population Changes in the Eighteenth Century', *Population Studies*, IX, 1955, pp.119–41.
18 Cf.D.E.C. Eversley, 'Population and Economic Growth in England before the 'Take-off' – Some notes on methodology and the objects of future research', a paper read at the Economic History Conference, Stockholm, August 1960, and kindly lent to me by the author.
19 G.E.C. *et al.*, *The Complete Peerage of England, Scotland, Ireland . . .*, London: St. Catherine's Press 1910–59, gives no systematic information about the origins of newly-created peers; on the social connections of City-men a beginning has been made by T. Lupton and C. Shirley Wilson, 'The Bank-Rate Tribunal: the Social Background and Connections of 'Top Decision Makers', *Manchester School of Economic and Social Studies*, XXVII, 1959, pp. 30–51.
20 *King Henry III and the Lord Edward*, p. 21.
21 R.W. Southern, *The Making of the Middle Ages*, London: Hutchinson, 1953, p. 137.

22  Namier, *op.cit.*, p. 157
23  W. Cunningham, *The Progress of Capitalism in England*, Cambridge University Press, 1916, p.6. n.2.
24  *Ibid.*, p.17.
25  Cf. G.C. Homans, *English Villagers of the Thirteenth Century*, Cambridge, Mass. Harvard University Press, 1941.
26  Cf. H.E. Hallam, *The New Lands of Elloe*, Leicester University, 1954; and *Settlement and Society: A Study of the early agrarian history of South Lincolnshire*, Cambridge University Press, 1965
27  Cf. E.M.W. Tillyard, *The Elizabethan World-Picture*, London: Chatto & Windus, 1950.
28  cf. R. Williams, *Culture and Society, 1780–1950*, London: Chatto & Windus, 1958 pp. xiii, xv; A. Briggs, 'The Language of Class in Early Nineteenth Century England', in A. Briggs and J. Saville, (eds), *Essays in Labour History*, London: Macmillan, 1960.
29  G.M. Young, *Victorian England: Portrait of an Age*, London: Oxford University Press, 1960 ed., p.6, n. I.
30  For full bibliographies of the controversy between Tawney and Trevor-Roper and their followers, see J.H. Hexter, 'Storm over the Gentry', *Encounter*, X, 1958, no. 5, pp.22–34; and P. Zagorin, 'The Social Interpretation of the English Revolution', *Journal of Economic History*, XIX, 1959, pp. 376–401.
31  Cf. R.B. Grassby, 'Social Status and Commercial Enterprise under Louis XIV', *Economic History Review*, 2nd series, XIII, 1960, pp. 19–38.
32  J.R. McCulloch, *Principles of Political Economy*, 4th ed., Edinburgh, 1849, p. 21
33  J.S. Mill, *Principles of Political Economy*, London, 1848; W.A. Lewis, *Theory of Economic Growth*, London: Allen & Unwin, 1955 esp. pp.5–6.
34  T.H. Marshall, *Citizenship and Social Class*, Cambridge, University Press 1950, p. 92.
35  Pehr Kalm, *Account of his Visit to England on his Way to America in 1748*, trans. J. Lucas, London, 1892, p.52; quoted by D. Marshall, *English People in the Eighteenth Century*, London: Macmillan, 1956, p. 178.
36  Cunningham, *op. cit.*, p.24.
37  Cf. W. Stark, *The Sociology of Knowledge*, London: Routledge & Kegan Paul,1958
38  On the side of social policy and administration, see J.B. Brebner, 'Laissez Faire and State Intervension in Nineteenth-Century Britain', *Journal of Economic History*, Supplement VIII, 1948, pp. 59–73; O. MacDonagh, 'The Nineteenth-Century Revolution in Government: a Reappraisal', *Historical Journal*, I, 1958, pp. 52–67; Henry Parris, 'The Nineteenth-Century Revolution in Government: a Reappraisal Reappraised' *ibid.*, III, 1960, pp. 17–37 For my own views see Essay 4, below, 'Individualism versus Collectivism in Nineteenth-Century Britain: A false Antithesis'.
39  Rowse, *op.cit.*, chap. ii.
40  J.H. Hexter, 'A New Framework for Social History', *Journal of Economic History*, XV, 1955, p. 423.
42  F.R. Leavis, *The Common Pursuit*, London: Chatto & Windus, 1952, p. 194.
43  F.R. Leavis, *The Great Tradition*, London: Chatto & Windus, 1948, pp. 227, 19.
44  F. Kermode, 'A Myth of Catastrophe', *The Listener*, 8 and 15 November 1956; cf. his 'The Dissociation of Sensibility', *Kenyon Review*, XIX, 1957, pp. 169–94.
45  See 'The Origins of the Popular Press', Essay 3 below.
46  Cf. C. Wilson, 'The Other Face of Mercantilism', *Transactions of the Royal Historical Society*, 5th series, IX, 1959, pp. 81–101.

47 H. Jenkins and D. Caradog Jones, 'Social Class of Cambridge University Alumni of the Eighteenth and Nineteenth Centuries', *British Journal of Sociology*, I, 1950, pp. 93–116.

48 *Egerton MSS.*, kindly placed at the disposal of the History school of the University of Manchester by the late Lord Egerton of Tatton: letter, E. Egerton to John Egerton, postmarked 25 March (1729), and *ibid.*, August 1728; W.H. Chaloner, 'The Egertons in Italy and the Netherlands, 1729–44', *John Rylands Library Bulletin*, XXXII, 1949–50, pp. 157–70.

49 In the Manchester City Art Gallery; reproduced in G.M. Young, ed., *Early Victorian England*, London: Oxford University Press 1934, I, opp. p.4.

50 H. Butterfield, *The Origins of Modern Science*, London: Bell, 1949, chap.i. Wilson, *op. cit.*, pp. 100–1.

51 Namier, *loc. cit.*, p. 162; Cf. J.E. Neale, 'The Biographical Approach to History', *History*, XXXVI, 1951, pp. 193–203.

52 Cf. e.g., *The Entrepreneur: Papers presented at the Annual Conference of the Economic History Society at Cambridge, England, April 1957*, Cambridge, Mass. Harvard University Press, 1957.

53 Cf. Lewis, *op. cit.*; W.W. Rostow, *The Stages of Economic Growth*, Cambridge University Press, 1960.

54 H.R. Trevor-Roper, *The Gentry, 1540–1640*, Cambridge University Press, 1953, p. 44.

55 Heinemann Kingswood Social History Series, edited by H.L. Beales and O.R. McGregor, Routledge & Kegan Paul, Studies in Social History, edited by myself; and Longmans, Economic and Social History of England edited by A. Briggs.

56 A similar suggestion, for the comparative study of the 'overmighty subject' at different periods, is made by J.H. Hexter, 'A New Framework for Social History', *op. cit.*

57 H.J. Habakkuk, 'England', in A. Goodwin, ed., *The European Nobility in the Eighteenth Century*, London: A & C. Black, 1953, and 'Marriage Settlements in the Eighteenth Century', *Transactions of the Royal Historical Society*, 4th series, XXXII, 1950, pp. 15–30.

58 B. Webb, *My Apprenticeship*, London: Longmans, 1926, p. 149.

## 2

# THE SOCIAL CAUSES OF THE INDUSTRIAL REVOLUTION*

In 1844 'A member of the Manchester Athenaeum' wrote:

It is not more than seventy or eighty years since that a few humble mechanics in Lanarkshire, distinguished by scarcely anything more than mechanical ingenuity and perseverance of character, succeeded in forming a few, but important mechanical combinations, the effect of which has been to revolutionize the whole of British society, and to influence, in a marked degree, the progress of civilization in every quarter of the globe.[1]

No one today would deny that the Industrial Revolution, that 'vast increase of natural resources, labour, capital and enterprise'[2] which began in Britain in the late eighteenth century and is still in process of transforming the whole world, was a social revolution, at least in its effects. It was a revolution in human productivity, in the capacity of men to wring a living from nature, which increased, by a multiple rather than a fraction, both the number of people who could be carried on a given area of land and their living standard or *per capita* consumption of goods and services. Whatever happened in the short run to the living standards of some or all of the wage-earners in the critical second quarter of the nineteenth century, in the long run there can be no doubt of the result: during the nineteenth century real income per head for a population which itself more than trebled is estimated to have quadrupled.[3]

Meanwhile, it transformed not merely the abundance of life, in both senses, but the scale, structure and context of the institutions in which it was lived. For better or worse it changed the size and shape of the workplace and working group in which most people worked, the size and shape of the community in which they lived, the kind of houses they inhabited, the sort of clothes they wore, the furniture and utensils they used, and the very food they ate. More than that, it changed their relations with one another, and therefore the institutions which were the outward expression of those relations. The family itself became a different institution when father, children and sometimes mother went out to work instead of working at

*Read before the Royal Historical Society, 13 October 1967, and published in *Transactions*, 5th series XVIII, 1968.

home – and the emancipation of women and teenagers is not unconnected with that change. The community became a different
institution when it changed from the village or market town
dominated by the squire or parson to the vast industrial town or city
where class conflict became the norm – 'The cities,' said Engels, 'first
saw the rise of the workers and the middle classes into opposing
social groups. It was in the towns that the trade union movement,
Chartism and Socialism all had their origin' – and so there arose a
completely new structure of society, based on a few broad conflicting classes rather than the many ranks and orders of pre-industrial
society. Even the state became a different institution when it was
forced to grapple with the manifold problems of a complex industrial society, and its servants grew from the 15,884 'persons in public
offices' of 1800 to the 108,000 bureaucrats of 1869.[5] Indeed, it can be
argued that the Industrial Revolution changed the national character
itself. By the moral revolution which accompanied it and which was
not unconnected with the imposition upon the rest of society of the
traditional puritanism of the industrial middle ranks now thrust into
dominance, the English were transformed from one of the noisiest,
most aggressive, brutal and bloodthirsty of nations into one of the
most inhibited, polite, prudish, orderly and (some would say)
hypocritical in the world.

But what caused this social revolution? Why did it happen at all?
And why did it begin first in Britain, and not some other country? In
recent years this has become a very practical question, to which
many under-developed countries would like an answer, though the
answer when it comes may be no more helpful than the country
yokel's, 'If I were going to Development I would not start from
here.' For the causes of the first and only spontaneous industrial
revolution, in which by definition no one knew or planned the end or
purpose of the process, are likely to be unique, and therefore unhelp-
ful to those who seek to imitate it. Indeed, they constitute in
aggregate nothing less than the whole antecedent history of the
country, at least since it began to diverge decisively from that of its
continental neighbours at some time between the Black Death and
the Reformation. Which causes are given primacy depends on the
interests of the particular historian, and the level of explanation
which he finds satisfying.

At the first level, the immediate causes were obviously technological and economic. The Member of the Manchester
Athenaeum attributed it to the steam engine and, more remotely, to
he diffusion of knowledge by the printing press. Others have stres-

sed the favourable economic and geographical factors which brought the great inventions to bear: abundant and conveniently situated supplies of coal, iron ore and other minerals, and water; an island position connected by excellent waterways to the expansion of world trade; land owned in conveniently large blocks by owners willing to develop it; a plentiful and comparatively well-paid labour force susceptible to the lure of rising wages; abundant supplies of capital at extraordinary low rates of interest; and, above all, a large number of active and willing entrepreneurs ready to unite all these factors into decisive and profitable innovation.[6]

At a somewhat deeper level than these necessary but manifestly insufficient economic causes we can point to Britain's political good fortune, to the centuries of freedom from invasion, to the internal unity which made her, after 1707, the largest free trade area in Europe, to the almost complete absence after 1660 of effective governmental interference with industrial innovation while commercial policy still protected infant industries, to the seventeenth-century victory of the Parliament of landowners over the Crown which not only produced internal *laissez-faire* a hundred years before Adam Smith but provided legislative encouragement for enclosures, turnpike roads, and navigable waterways.

At a still deeper level of causation there are the philosophical or intellectual causes, the profound change in human expectations of the improvement of life in this world which stems from the Renaissance and the scientific revolution, and the network of natural philosophers, schools and academies, and philosophical societies which, in this country more than most, harnessed this spirit to the actual improvement of agricultural and industrial processes.[7]

At the deepest level of all lie the religious causes which, more recently, have been transmuted into the psychological causes of industrialism. Weber's and Tawney's familiar explanation of capitalist acquisitiveness in terms of the Protestant personality has now been reinforced by Hagen's and McClelland's explanations of Methodist and Dissenting entrepreneurs in terms of their upbringing, the first in terms of a reaction in the child, through the influence of the mother, against the 'withdrawal of status respect' from the father's generation of religious dissidents, the second in terms of the 'need for achievement' instilled in the children of minority groups.[8] At this level of religious reaction and psychological need we come nearest to a purely social cause, albeit a rather particular one, of the Industrial Revolution.

Surely, you may think, there are enough causes here to satisfy the

most fastidious historian – and far be it from me to deny the validity
of any of them, at their own appropriate level. To a social historian,
however, trained to look at societies as a whole and consider the
significant differences in structure and outlook between them, it
would be a dereliction of duty not to ask whether there is not a
further level of explanation which has been missed, or at least somewhat neglected, a level in which all the other causes can be said to
converge in harmonious operation in a way which made them
collectively sufficient. I refer to what W.H.B. Court has called 'the
elementary but easily forgotten fact that the first requisite of
increased wealth is a society of the kind required to produce it'.[9] If
there was a central, integrating cause, which brought the others to
bear in mutually fructifying co-operation, it was the unique nature
and structure of English society as it had evolved by the eighteenth
century. The only spontaneous industrial revolution in history
occurred in Britain because Britain alone amongst the nations with
the full complement of economic resources and political and
psychological attitudes had the right kind of society to generate a
spontaneous industrial revolution. (Holland, the only other country
with the right kind of society, lacked the natural resources).

What kind of society was the right kind? Britain on the eve of the
Industrial Revolution may be called an open aristocracy based on
property and patronage. First, like most pre-industrial societies it
was an aristocracy, a tall pyramid with a tiny apex of rich landlords
and a broad base of the poor living near the margin of subsistence.
But, unlike most other European countries, the aristocrats were not
feudal lords living on feudal dues or labour services, unable to raise
their incomes save by cheating or oppressing the peasants, and
prevented by the law or custom of *dérogeance* from entering or even
sending their younger sons into commerce and industry. They were
real owners of the land, able to exploit it in whatever way they
pleased, to let it to large, commercial tenants on long or short leases,
to develop it for building purposes, or to mine the minerals which
elsewhere were reserved to the Crown. But more of that in its proper
place. At the base the lower orders were not in the main peasants
working tiny plots of land for which they paid feudal dues or labour
services, but landless labourers earning wages for work on other
men's land or materials, and at least half of them in 1760 worked for
part of their time outside agriculture.[10] These two groups alone were
enough to make Britain – or rather England, for Wales and the
Highlands of Scotland were more continental in structure – unique.
But what distinguished Britain most of all from the continent was

the size and ubiquity of the groups in between, the long, unbroken chains of the 'middle ranks'. To quote a nostalgic Tory of the early nineteenth century, looking back on the world he saw disappearing:

> In most other countries, society presents hardly anything but a void between an ignorant labouring population, and a needy and profligate nobility;. . .but with us the space between the ploughman and the peer, is crammed with circle after circle, fitted in the most admirable manner for sitting upon each other, for connecting the former with the latter, and for rendering the whole perfect in cohesion, strength and beauty.[11]

At the top the middle ranks overlapped the landed gentry in wealth, for the great merchants, bishops and judges were not distinguished from the landed aristocracy by the size of their income but by the fact that they had to earn it. At the bottom they included many skilled craftsmen who would now be considered working-class, and small farmers and traders with incomes no larger than the labouring poor, since the division was not based on manual work but on the possession of some property, however small, including the property of an apprenticed skill and its appurtenant tools or equipment. It was in fact this wide dispersion of small capitals which made Britain peculiarly ripe for economic growth. As Patrick Colquhoun saw in 1814,

> It is not . . . an excess of property to the few but the extension of it among the mass of the community which appears most likely to prove beneficial with respect to national wealth and national happiness. Perhaps no other country in the world possesses greater advantages in this respect than Great Britain, and hence that spirit of enterprise and that profitable employment of diffused capitals which has created so many resources for productive labour beyond any other country in Europe.[12]

This long and carefully graduated hierarchy, made up of layer upon layer of status groups – Blackstone is said to have counted no less than forty different statuses, from duke down through gentleman and yeoman to pauper and vagrant[13] – was not a class society, in the modern sense of a few, nation-wide, mutually antagonistic classes. The very word 'class' in its social context, as Asa Briggs has shown, only came into use during and as a result of the Industrial Revolution.[14] Before then there was little elbow room in the small towns and tiny villages of the old society for the broad antagonisms of class, and what there was in the form of incipient trade unionism or political opposition to the established order was labelled insubordination, and ruthlessly suppressed by the social discipline which was the other, unbenevolent face of paternalism. Class conflict was of course latent, and burst out from time to time in riots against high bread prices, machinery, or unpopular employers, but rarely issued in the permanent institutions, trade unions, political societies, and the like, which are the vehicles of class. What permanent antagonism there was, amongst those of the middle ranks, the provincial merchants and industrialists without government contracts, the independant yeomen farmers and craftsmen, who could afford it, took the sublimated form of dissent from the ruling aristocracy's church. Not that men were unaware of inequalities of wealth and status. On the contrary, they were acutely aware of their exact position in the extended hierarchy, and of their precise relation to those immediately above and below them. For, as we shall see, the important links in that society were not the horizontal bonds of class but the vertical connections of dependency or patronage.

The twin pillars on which this society rested were property and patronage. One's place in the hierarchy was wholly determined by the amount and kind of one's property – 'the great source' as John Millar observed, 'of distinction among individuals'[5] – or that of one's friends and relations. Whereas in feudal society, property, in theory at least, followed status – the knight invested with his fee in return for military service which only he was qualified to perform, the serf with his holding in return for servile labour which only he was lowly enough to render – in postfeudal England status followed property. Nobility itself came to follow property. Great estates, however acquired, drew to themselves a title, and patents were revived over and over again for the non-noble heirs of such dukedoms as Newcastle or Northumberland.[16] The English gentry, unlike their continental counterparts, were not a *petite noblesse*, and possessed no legal privilege: land alone granted them their status. Their younger sons did not inherit their status, and had to complete with those below them for positions in the professions and in trade and industry. There the cost of acquiring the necessary education or training, and of purchasing a foothold in the business or profession, effectively limited the *entrée* to men of property. The education of a lawyer or clergyman cost hundreds of pounds, and was of no avail without the further price of a partnership or advowson. Army commissions in 1765 cost from £400 for an ensign to £3,500 for a lieutenant-colonel.[17] Apprenticeship varied in cost with the trade, the place and the standing of the master; in London in 1747 from £5–£10 for a hatter, breeches-maker, millwright or potter to £50–£300 for a merchant or banker, while the 'Sums necessary to set up as Masters' ranged from £50–£200 for the first group to '£20,000 *ad. lib.*' for the second, and 'Unlimited' for an overseas merchant or insurance underwriter.[18] So finely adjusted to each status was the cost of acquiring it.

More important, the possession of property determined the distribution of power. Government at the centre and in the localities reflected the distribution of property. The king was the greatest property-owner, the first of the borough-mongering country gentlemen of England. The House of Lords consisted almost entirely of great landowners. Threequarters of the House of Commons consisted of landowners and their relations, and the rest were chiefly their friends and nominees or business and professional men with one foot on the land.[19] 'The chief qualification required of a Cabinet Minister' wrote Professor Aspinall, 'was not so much ability as aristocratic connections and a large landed property'; in 1726 a quarter of the active peerage held Court or Government office.[20] Office itself was defined by Blackstone in proprietorial terms, as 'a right to exercise a public or private employment and to take the fees and emoluments thereunto belonging', while in Sir Lewis Namier's words 'For the elector the vote, for the borough its representation, for the Member his seat in Parliament, were valuable assets from which advantages were expected.'[21] Local government most perfectly reflected the graduations of property, from the noble lords-lieutenant and the genteel J.P.s through the borough oligarchies of substantial traders and lawyers to the farmers and independent craftsmen who policed the parishes and overseered the poor. Indeed, it was the social power of property, the informal social control of the rich over their poorer neighbours, which underlay and gave life to the formally constituted institutions of government. As Defoe approvingly remarked,

'Tis in the power of the Gentry of England to reform the whole kingdom without either Laws, Proclamations or Informers; and without their concurrence all the Laws, Proclamations and Declarations in the World will have no Effect; the Rigour of the Law consists in their Executive Power.[22]

After property, and emanating from it, the twin factor in determining status and power was patronage. When a man of rank and wealth had an appointment to make or influence, from a bishop or a Clerk of the Pells to a workhouse master or kitchen maid, he looked first amongst his 'friends'. Sir Robert Walpole 'frankly owned that while he was in employment, he had endeavoured to serve his friends and relations; than which, in his opinion, nothing was more reasonable, or more just'.[23] Addison, the only man to rise by literary patronage to be a Secretary of State, was persuaded that there are few men of generous principles who would seek after great places, were it not rather to have an opportunity of obliging their particular friends, or those they look upon as men of worth, than to procure wealth and honour for themselves.[24]

Edward Gibbon assumed the common motive for standing for Parliament to be 'to acquire a title the most glorious in a free country, and to employ the weight and consideration it gives in the service of one's friends'.[25]

Who were one's friends? In eighteenth-century usage they were, first of all, one's relations. Richardson's *Pamela* escaped from the clutches of Squire B. not merely to her parents, but 'to her friends'. Mrs Malaprop in *The Rivals* exhorted her niece to take 'a husband of your friends' choosing', meaning her aunt's. John Millar, the Glasgow professor of law, was intended for the Kirk, but his father 'was not inflexible in his determination, so that with little opposition from his friends, Mr Millar was allowed to transfer his attention from the Pulpit to the Bar'.[26] William Wright in *The Complete Tradesman* argued the apprentice's right to the advantages 'for which he served his time, and, perhaps, for which his friends gave a considerable sum of money with him'.[27] Defoe, proposing a university as 'the way to make London the most flourishing city in the Universe', suggested that the 'pupils' could lie and diet 'at home, under the eye of their friends'.[28] Amongst a plethora of examples we may cite the Exchequer posts worth £13,400 a year which Walpole procured for his three sons.[29] They were, secondly, the members of one's household, such as the chaplain and children's tutor, son of his attorney, whom Lord Moira presented to no less than four livings in the Church.[30] They were, thirdly, one's tenants and villagers: the same Lord Moira educated a local farmer's son, John Shakespear, who became professor of oriental languages at the East India colleges at Marlow and Addiscombe.[31] They were, fourthly, one's political helpers and associates, such as John Calcraft, son of the Duke of Rutland's election agent at Grantham, who was by way of the Paymaster-General's office and the further patronage of Henry Fox to become agent for half the regiments in the army and founder of a landed and parliamentary family in Dorset.[32] They were, only finally, those amongst one's acquaintances whom one looked upon as men of worth: Lord Moira procured the Registrarship of Bermuda for his friend Tommy Moore, the poet, who sailed there in 1803 before he discovered it to be a non-residential sinecure.[33]

Patronage was, of course, ubiquitous in eighteenth-century politics, and Sir Lewis Namier and his followers have made us familiar with its political function of maintaining, in the absence of modern party discipline, a government majority in Parliament. Patronage was much more than a political device, however, which was only the visible topgrowth of a plant whose roots and branches ramified throughout the length and breadth of society. It was more even than a device for filling jobs, fostering talent and rewarding friends at every social level. In the mesh of continuing loyalties of which appointments were the outward sign, patronage or 'vertical friendship' was the master-link of the old society, a durable, two-way relationship between an infinite series of patrons and clients which permeated the whole of society. It was a social nexus less formal and inescapable than feudal homage, more personal and comprehensive than the contractual relationships of capitalist 'Cash Payment'. One foreign visitor described it as 'a species of slavery, to which absolute monarchies are entire strangers,' which in England 'consists in a connexion of dependency which unites all orders of the state, and every citizen dispersed throughout these different orders'.[34] For those who lived within its embrace it was so much an integral part of the texture of life that they had no word for it save 'friendship'. It was the module of which the social structure was built. Its vertical links united the interest pyramids – the landed, commercial, industrial and professional interests which embraced every level of society from the great landowner, merchant or judge down to the merest labourer – which, rather than the as yet unborn classes, were the warring factions of politics.[35] At the lowest level even the poor were drawn into the nexus: the 'respectable' poor, known and accepted by powerful friends, had first access to local charities, the village paupers recognized as their own by the gentlemen of the parish were automatically relieved, but the poor stranger, the vagrant, the 'masterless man' without a friend to speak for him, was turned away. Even criminal justice was modified by it: the word of a powerful friend could reduce a felony to a misdemeanour, or transmute a death sentence to transportation.[36]

Patronage, then, was the other face of property, and brings us back to the major principle on which the old society was based. For Locke, the philosopher *par excellence* of the old society, property was the *raison d'être* of government and of civil society itself: 'The great and chief end . . . of men uniting into commonwealths, and putting themselves under government, is the preservation of their property'.[37] And the key to Locke is the peculiarly English concept of absolute property bequeathed to his generation by the landed aristocracy which had fought for three centuries and more to establish it.[38] In feudal societies property, especially in land, was both something more and something less than ownership. While it gave rights over the persons of the peasants, it was also contingent, conditional, and circumscribed by the claims of God, the Church, the king, the inferior tenants and occupiers, and the poor. By a process lasting three centuries, from the commutation of labour services through the enclosures and engrossing of Tawney's century to the abolition of feudal tenures at the Civil War, the landed aristocracy and gentry defeated the claims of the peasants, the Church and the Crown, and turned lordship into absolute ownership.

This was the decisive change in English history which made it different from that of the continent. From it every other difference in English society stemmed. The defeat of the peasants and their transformation into large commercial rent-paying farmers on the one hand and a larger body of landless labourers on the other laid the foundations for two of the most important prerequisites of industrialism: an agricultural system capable of responding to market forces by extensive improvement in methods and techniques, and a labour force innured to wage labour which had perforce to turn to such non-agricultural work as offered, notably in that capitalist outwork system which became the half-way house to the factory system.[39] It also accounts for the unique English system of poor relief, exactly contemporary with these developments, and not needed in peasant societies where the holding supports everybody, or when famine comes they all starve together. At the other end of the scale absolute ownership gave the landowners a stake, via increased earnings or rents, in every kind of economic growth: enclosures and other agricultural improvements, the exploitation of minerals (reserved to the Crown over most of Europe), the building of towns, and the development of transport. Once the landed Parliament had defeated the king and abolished the prerogative courts through which he had controlled their activities, they quickly reversed the restrictionist policies of the Crown and enclosed, engrossed and generally expoited their estates to their hearts' and purses' content.

Yet the most important effect of absolute ownership was its indirect effect upon the middle ranks of society. The price of absolute ownership, of doing what one would with one's own, was two-fold. On the one hand, it meant allowing anyone, from whatever level of society, who could acquire the means of purchasing an estate, to join the ranks of absolute owners, and enjoy the same rights and status. On the other, by an ironical and brilliant adaptation of the feudal device for ensuring a supply of adequately armed and mounted knights, primogeniture, it meant that in order to keep the estates together, and maintain the full power of their property and patronage, the younger sons were sent out into the world to earn their living in trade and the professions. The result was that two-way flow of men and wealth so characteristic of English as distinct from continental society: a continuous upflow of new men from trade and the professions into the landed class, a continuous downflow of younger sons, with education, small capitals and great energy and determination to succeed, into the middle ranks. To this we should add, since the English landowners were anything but snobbish where marriage with money was concerned, an upflow of heiresses and a downflow of dowried daughters. The consequent social mobility had repercussions throughout the length and breadth of society. The funnelling-off into the landed gentry of the most successful merchants and professional men in each generation made room for newcomers on the ladder all the way down. As a Manchester cobbler put it in 1756,

See, as the Owners of old Family Estates in your Neighbourhood are selling off their patrimonies, how your Townsmen are constantly purchasing; and thereby laying the Foundation of a new Race of Gentry. . .and who, knowing both how, and when to be content, retire, decently to enjoy their wellgot wealth, leaving the Coast open, for new Adventurers, to follow their worthy Example.[40]

It was the openness of the hierarchy, the freedom of movement up and down the scale, and above all the absence of legal or customary barriers between the landed aristocracy and the rest, which gave English society its unique quality of dynamic stability. The two-way flow of men and capital acted like the circulation of the blood, producing growth without change of structure. At the same time, it syphoned off in every generation the newly rich and talented of the middle ranks, who might otherwise have been socially frustrated and politically discontented. France, where social climbing was frustrated, had a political revolution. Britain, where it was not, had an industrial one.

But why was an open aristocracy based on property and patronage the right kind of society to generate a spontaneous industrial revolution? We can best see this by considering, all too briefly, the traditional causes of the Industrial Revolution, and how it operated through them. Britain's political good fortune, obviously, was due to the policies, or lack of them, which stemmed from the domination of society and government by a landed aristocracy jealous of the

Crown and in close rapprochement through the patronage system and its own younger sons with the economic drives and aspirations of the middle ranks. The philosophical and intellectual causes benefited from the same aristocracy's self-interested search for profitable improvements in agriculture, mining, transport and, occasionally, industry itself, and their patronage of such innovators as Bakewell, Newcomen, Brindley, Telford, and George Stephenson. The religious causes owed a perverse debt to the partial toleration or inefficient intolerance, of the English aristocracy towards the Dissenters, though it is a moot point whether a disproportionate number of inventors and entrepreneurs were Dissenters because they were prevented by their nonconformity from entering other occupations or because men of their level of society were more likely to be Dissenters.[41]

The test of any interpretation of the Industrial Revolution, however, is whether it explains the direct, immediate, and necessary economic causes, the essential factors of land, capital, labour and, most easily forgotten, of demand. The provision of land for agricultural improvement, mining, transport, factories, and towns was so little of a problem in the British Industrial Revolution that it is often forgotten what an obstacle feudal, tribal or fragmented peasant land tenure can be in under-developed countries. Without the active co-operation of the self-interested, absolute owners of the land, in Parliament and in the land market, the vital preconditions of industrialism, in agriculture, mining, transport, and town development, would not have been forthcoming.

Capital was cheap and plentiful in Britain not because of an advanced banking system, which came into being only as a result of industrialism, but because of the readiness of savers to lend, privately and informally, to entrepreneurs, and, more often than not, this was due to the pressing into service of kinship and patronage connexions, of which the Quaker cousinships in banking, brewing, and ironfounding were only a special example. Most of the early industrial enterprises, however, were built up from very small beginnings by ploughing back the profits, and here that wide diffusion of small capitals which Colquhoun remarked came into play. Yet capitalists, as many under-developed countries have found, are more important than capital. Why did British industrialists scorn delights and live laborious days beyond the point at which most continental ones sat back and took things easy? Because British society offered motivations beyond the mere accumulation of riches. As Malthus put it in his defence of the 'strikingly beneficial' effects of social inequality,

If no man could hope to rise or fear to fall in society; if industry did not bring its own reward, and indolence its punishment; we could not hope to see that animated activity in bettering our own condition which now forms the masterspring of public prosperity.[42]

## And again,

It is not the most pleasant employment to spend eight hours a day in a counting-house. Nor will it be submitted to after the common necessaries and conveniences of life are attained, unless adequate motives are presented to the man of business. Among these motives is undoubtedly the desire of advancing his rank, and contending with the landlords in the enjoyment of leisure, as well as of foreign and domestic luxuries. But the desire to realize a fortune as a permanent provision for a family is perhaps the most general motive for the continued exertions of those whose incomes depend upon their own personal skill and efforts.[43]

## Coleridge observed in 1830:

To found a family, and to convert his wealth into land, are twin thoughts, births of the same moment, in the mind of the opulent merchant, when he thinks of retiring from his labours.[44]

Their words are borne out by the country houses and estates of all the great industrialists from Arkwright, the Peels, and the Strutts in cotton to the Guests, Wortleys, and Hardys of Low Moor in iron.[45]

Social emulation also played a significant part in the mobilization of a labour force for the new industries. A wage-earning proletariat, inured to the regular hours and discipline of the factory, is one of the most hazardous requirements of industrialism, and its assembly even in Britain was no easy matter.[46] But here at least the landless labourers and piece-rate outworkers of the domestic system were used to earning money wages, and spending them as soon as earned. Whereas the continental peasant, when he had a windfall, hoarded it against a rainy day, to buy a cow or half an acre, to dower a daughter or buy out the younger son, the English wage-earner spent his wages on bread, beer, clothes and household utensils. Getting and spending gave the factory masters a magnet for drawing the workers into the mills. It was a shrewd stroke of Arkwright's to offer prizes for the traders who brought the best foodstuffs and household goods to Cromford market.[47] What brought the new workers into the mills was not so much the whips and scorpions of unemployment and starvation – which in the case of the handloom wavers manifestly did not work – as the chance to purchase the whiter bread, the darker beer, the flesh meat, the pottery, utensils, furniture, clocks and watches, and the new cottons themselves, which the new industrialism was turning out in such quantities.

This brings us to the most important economic factor of all, consumer demand. Industrial innovation is of no consequence without the massively expansive consumer demand to call it forth and sustain its growth. Foreign trade has been credited with causing the British Industrial Revolution, but at no time did exports account for more than a fraction of aggregate production, and in any case exports were merely the reverberation of British demand for foreign goods.[48] At bottom the key to the Industrial Revolution was the infinitely elastic home demand for mass consumer goods. And the key to that demand was social emulation, 'keeping up with the Joneses', the compulsive urge for imitating the spending habits of one's betters, which sprang from an open aristocracy in which every member from top to bottom of society trod closely on the heels of the next above. The *British Magazine* declared in 1763:

The present rage of imitating the manners of high-life hath spread itself so far among the gentlefolks of lower-life, that in a few years we shall probably have no common people at all.[49]

Henry Fielding blamed 'the late increase of robbers' on social emulation:

while the Nobleman will emulate the Grandeur of a Prince: and the Gentleman will aspire to the proper state of a Nobleman; the Tradesman steps from behind his Counter into the vacant place of the Gentleman. Nor doth the Confusion end here: It reaches the very Dregs of the People. . .[50]

This was the most significant difference between British and continental demand: in Europe emulative spending stopped short at the *bourgeoisie,* and never reached the mass of the peasants; in Britain knee breeches and peruques, bonnets and panniered dresses, according to foreign visitors like Per Kalm and P.J. Grosley, could be seen on the very labourers in the fields.[51] In the 1790s a Swiss journalist on a visit from Paris remarked:

There is as great an inequality of ranks and fortune in England as in France; but in the former the consequence and importance of a man as a member of society is far more respectable. Individuals of the lower classes are better cloathed, better fed, and better lodged than elsewhere; and often, as far as I could learn, with no better means than the same classes enjoy with us. Pride and a desire to preserve the public esteem seem to force upon them that attention to their conduct and outward appearance.[52]

If there was one cause, then, that must bear more than any other the weight of responsibility for the British Industrial Revolution, it is social emulation, English snobbery, 'keeping up with the Joneses' – a fitting verdict on the greatest single achievement of the greatest nation of snobs.

There remains, of course, the problem of timing. If the old society was ripe for an industrial revolution at least since the Civil War and Revolution of the seventeenth century, why did it take a hundred years or more to reach the harvest? The short answer is that every kind of growth takes time, and the growth of so dynamically stable a society as Britain's could go on for generations without breaking out of its pre-industrial husk. As Colquhoun shrewdly observed, in 1814,

It is with nations as it is with individuals who are in train of acquiring property. At first progress is slow until a certain amount is obtained, after which, as wealth has a creative power under skilful and judicious management, the accumulation becomes more and more rapid, increasing often beyond a geometrical ratio, expanding in all directions, diffusing its influence wherever talents and industry prevail, and thereby extending the resources by which riches are obtained by communicating the power of acquiring it to thousands, who must have remained without wealth in countries less opulent.[53]

Thus after about a century of accelerating growth, with significant surges in the 1680s and the 1740s, the British economy in the last two decades of the eighteenth century suddenly, like a steam engine coming to the boil, an atomic reactor becoming critical, or an aeroplane taking off, reached the point at which self-intensifying forces came into operation, and achieved a completely new and higher level of activity.

There is, however, a longer and more satisfying answer, connected with the most intimate and psychologically inaccessible of human activities, procreation. However rightly shaped for economic growth was British society by the early eighteenth century, however poised for take-off the manifold economic forces, the machine could not begin to move while the chocks of stagnating population remained firmly in place. Whatever caused the check to population in the first half of the century, whether smallpox, gin, bad weather, or lack of employment opportunities and marriage,[54] it was enough to cancel out all the forces making for rapid economic growth. For industrialism requires a very delicate adjustment of demographic growth: not too fast, because that will lower wages and thus both consumer demand and the incentive to labour-saving investment; nor too slow, for that will raise wages so high as to entrench on profits and the capacity for investment. In the last quarter of the eighteenth century British population hit the critical rate of growth squarely in the middle: slow enough to maintain, or even slightly improve, real wages and yet to encourage labour-saving innovation, fast enough to keep down labour costs and yet to expand aggregate demand for food and mass consumer goods. Thus for once it was possible to divert flows of income towards capital investment without a self-defeating effect on the purchasing power of the lower orders and therefore on aggregate demand.[55] The effect was to remove the built-in brake from the economic system and allow full play to the built-in dynamism of the open aristocracy. In other words, after a long period of laboured acceleration, the lift at last overcame the drag, and the machine was airborne.

Only a machine of the right shape and power, however, could have succeeded in taking off. The economic boom and population surge of the late eighteenth century were European wide, and presented an opportunity for any continental country to seize. In the event only Britain was equipped to seize it. That she was so was due to the unique nature and structure of British society.

## Notes

1　L. Faucher, *Manchester in 1844,* Manchester, 1844, translator's preface by 'A Member of the Manchester Athenaeum', p.VI.

2　T.S. Ashton, 'Some Statistics of the Industrial Revolution in Britain', *Manchester School*, XVI, 1948, 215.

3　According to contemporary estimates, reduced to the average of 1865 and 1885 prices on the Rousseaux index, from £12.01 in 1800 to £48.57 in 1902 – Phyllis Deane, 'Contemporary Estimates of National Income in the Second Half of the Nineteenth Century', *Economic History Review*, 2nd series, IX, 1957, 459.

4　F. Engels, *The Condition of the Working Class in England* (trans. and ed. W.H. Chaloner and W.O. Henderson, Oxford, Blackwell, 1958), pp. 137–8.

5　Emmeline W. Cohen, *Growth of the British Civil Service, 1983–1939,* London: Cass, 1965, p. 23n.; H. Mann, 'On the Cost and Organization of the Civil Service', *Statistical Journal*, XXXII, 1869, 49.

6　For two recent conspectuses by economic historians of writings on the causes of the Industrial Revolution, see R.M. Hartwell, 'The Causes of the Industrial Revolution: an Essay in Methodology', *Economic History Review* series, XVIII 1965, 164 ff., and M.W. Flinn, *Origins of the Industrial Revolution*, London: Longmans, 1966.

7　*Cf.,* inter alia, C.L. Becker, *The Heavenly City of the Eighteenth-Century Philosophers,* New Haven, Conn: Yale University Press, 1932, and N. Hans, *New Trends in Eighteenth-Century Education,* London: Routledge & Kegan Paul, 1951.

8　M. Weber, *The Protestant Ethic and the Spirit of Capitalism,* New York: Scribner, 1930; R.H. Tawney, *Religion and the Rise of Capitalism* (1926); E.E. Hagen, *On the Theory of Social Change,* Homewood Illinois: Dorsey, 1964, esp. pp.290–303; D.C. McClelland, *The Achieving Society,* Princeton, N.J.: Princeton University Press, 1961, esp. pp.145–9.

9 W.H.B. Court, *A Concise Economic History of Britain from 1750 to Recent Times*, Cambridge University Press, 1954, p.16.

10 P. Mathias, 'The Social Structure in the Eighteenth Century: a Calculation by Joseph Massie', *Economic History Review*, 2nd series, X (1957), 45.

11 'Y.Y.Y.' [David Robinson], 'The Church of England and the Dissenters', *Blackwood's Edinburgh Magazine*, XVI, 1824, 397.

12 P. Colquhoun, *A Treatise on the Wealth, Power and Resources of the British Empire*, London, 1814, p.6.

13 R.R. Palmer, *The Age of Democratic Revolution*, 1760–1800, Princeton, N.J.: Princeton University Press, 1959, I, p.63.

14 A. Briggs, 'The Language of "Class" in early Nineteenth-Century England', in A. Briggs and J. Saville, (eds), *Essays in Labour History*.

15 J. Millar, *The Origin of the Distinction of Ranks* (1793), p.4.

16 The dukedom of Newcastle was revived three times between 1694 and 1756 for heirs female, and that of Northumberland recreated in 1766 for Sir Hugh Smithson on his marriage to the heiress of the estates – 'G.E.C.', *et al, The Complete Peerage of England, Scotland, Ireland. . .*, London: St. Catherine's Press, 1910–59, IX, pp.529–31, 743.

17 E. Robson, 'Purchase and Promotion in the British Army in the Eighteenth Century', *History*, XXXVI (1951), 59.

18 R. Campbell, *The London Tradesman*, London, 1747, pp.331 ff.

19 G.P. Judd, *Members of Parliament, 1734–1832* New Haven, Conn: Yale University Press; 1955, p.71.

20 A. Aspinall, *The Cabinet Council, 1783–1835,* Reading University 1952, p.199; J.H. Plumb, *Life of Sir Robert Walpole*, London: Cresset Press, 1956, I, p.8.

21 Cohen, *op cit.*, p.21n.; L.B. Namier, *The Structure of Politics at the Accession of George III*, London: Macmillan, 1929, I, p.199.

22 D. Defoe, *The Poor Man's Plea in relation to . . . a Reformation of Manners*, London, 1700, p.129.

23 Plumb, *op. cit.*, I, pp. 247–8.

24 P.H.B.O. Smithers, *Life of Joseph Addison*, Oxford: Clarendon Press, 1954, p. 122.

25 R.E. Prothero, ed., *Private Letters of Edward Gibbon*, London, 1896 I, p.24.

26 J. Craig, 'An Account of the Life and Writings of the Author', prefixed to Millar, *op. cit.*, p.VI.

27 W. Wright, *The Complete Tradesman; or a Guide in the Several Parts and Progressions of Trade*, Dublin, 1787, p.3.

28 D. Defoe, *Augusta Triumphans, or the Way to make London the most flourishing City in the Universe*, London, 1841 ed., p.5.

29 H.J. Habakkuk, 'England', in A. Goodwin, ed., *The European Nobility in the Eighteenth Century*, London: A & C Black, 1953, p.7.

30 J.M. Lee, 'The Rise and Fall of a Market Town: Castle Donington in the Nineteenth Century', *Transactions Leicestershire Archaelogical and Historical Society*, XXXII, 1956, 65–9.

31 *D.N.B.*, LI, pp.345 ff.

32 E. Hughes, 'The Professions in the Eighteenth Century', *Durham University Journal*, XIII, 1952, 51; *D.N.B.*, VIII, pp.235 ff.

33 Lee, *loc. cit.*, *D.N.B.*, XXXVIII, pp.340 ff.

34 P.-J. Grosley, *A Tour to London* (trans. T. Nugent, 1772), II. p.272.

35 *Cf.* R. Pares, *King George III and the Politicians*, Oxford: Clarendon Press, 1953, p.3: 'The distribution of power between the classes was hardly an issue in politics before 1815.'

36 *Cf.* the small proportion of those convicted of capital offences who were actually executed: of 2,783 felons thus convicted in England and Wales in 1805 only 350 were sentenced to death, and of these only 68 were executed – P. Colquhoun, *A Treatise on Indigence* (1806), p.47.

37 J. Locke, *Two Treatises of Civil Government,* Everyman ed., London: Dent, 1955, p.180.

38 *Cf.* W.P. Larkin, *Property in the Eighteenth Century, with Special Reference to England and Locke,* Cork University Press, 1930, and C.B. Macpherson, *The Political Theory of Possessive Individualism: Hobbes to Locke,* Oxford: Clarendon Press, 1962, of which only the former has influenced the view expressed here.

39 *Cf.*R.H. Tawney, *The Agrarian Problem in the Sixteenth Century,* London: Longmans, 1912 and G. Unwin, *Industrial Organization in the Sixteenth and Seventeenth Centuries,* Oxford: Clarendon Press 1904, two seminal works on themes whose essential interdependence is often forgotten.

40 J. Stot, *A sequel to the Friendly Advice to the Poor,* Manchester, 1756, p.19.

41 According to Hagen, *op.cit.* pp. 303–8, nearly half of the 92 inventors and entrepreneurs mentioned in T.S. Ashton, *The Industrial Revolution 1760–1830,* Oxford, 1948, were Dissenters, but though this was a larger proportion than in the population at large, of which the Dissenters, excluding the Methodists, claimed about a fifth in 1811 (*Political Register,* 22 May 1811, XIX, p.1264), it was not so much greater than in the middle ranks, where most of them were concentrated.

42 T.R. Malthus, *Essay on Population,* Everyman, ed., London: Dent, 1951, II, p.254.

43 T.R. Malthus, *Principles of Political Economy,* London, 1820, p.470.

44 S.T. Coleridge, *On the Constitution of Church and State,* London; 1839, p.25.

45 Arkwright became a knight and left estates to all four sons, the Peels baronets and owners of Tamworth and Drayton Manor, Edward Strutt in 1856 became Lord Belper, the Guests Lords Wimborne, the Wortleys Earls of Wharncliffe and the Hardys Earls of Cranbrook.

46 *Cf.*S. Pollard, *The Genesis of Modern Management,* Harmondsworth: Penguin, 1965, ch. V; and A. Reford, *Labour Migration in England, 1800–50,* Manchester University Press, 1926, *passim.*

47 T.S. Ashton, *An Economic History of England: the Eighteenth Century,* London: Methuen, 1955, p.214.

48 In the three crucial decades up to and including the 1780s production was expanding faster than foreign trade; throughout the Industrial Revolution by far the greater part – about four-fifths – of production was consumed at home; and even in the leading sector, cotton, in spite of 75-fold increase in the importation of the raw material, exports never exceeded more than half the total production – W. Schlote, *British Overseas Trade from 1700 to the 1930's,* trans. W.H. Chaloner and W.O. Henderson, Oxford: Blackwell, 1952, p.51, table II; A.H. Imlah, *Economic Elements in the Pax Britannica* Cambridge, Mass: Harvard University Press, 1958, pp.40–1; E. Baines, *History of the Cotton Manufacture in Great Britain,* 1835, pp.217–18.

49 *British Magazine,* IV, 1763, 417.

50 H. Fielding, *An Enquiry into the Causes of the late Increase of Robbers,* London, 1750, p.6.

51 Grosley *op. cit.,* I, p.75; P. Kalm, *An Account of his Visit to England . . . in 1748,* trans J. Lucas, London, 1892, p.52.

52 J.H. Meister, *Letters written during a Residence in England,* London, 1799, p.8.

53 Colquhoun, *A Treatise on The Wealth . . .,* p.51.

54 *Cf.* D.V. Glass and D.E.C. Eversley, (eds), *Population in History,* 1965, esp. pt. II;

and also P.E. Razzell, 'Population Change in Eighteenth-Century England: a Reinterpretation', *Economic History Review,* 2nd series, XVIII, 1965, 312 ff.
55  At the critical period of take-off, average wages lagged behind profits and rent, arguing a shift in distribution from the former to the latter, but aggregate wages and purchasing power were expanded by the rise in population – *cf.* Phyllis Deane. *The First Industrial Revolution,* Cambridge University Press, 1955, p.31.

# 3
# THE ORIGINS OF THE POPULAR PRESS*

No historical myth dies harder than the belief that the modern popular press grew up in direct response to the introduction of state education in 1870. In the words of Lord Northcliffe's biographer,

Forster's Education Act had made the acquisition of the hitherto privileged arts of reading and writing universally compulsory, and a Conservative Prime Minister, Lord Salisbury, had made them free of all costs to parents. So, by the time that Harmsworth began his adventures as a popular editor he had, ready and eager to be exploited, a vast reading public of youthful citizens who had learnt to read over the previous twenty years.

In 1880 (R.C.K. Ensor wrote) ten years after Forster's Education Act, a branch manager of a fancy-goods business, named George Newnes, became aware that the new schooling was creating a new class of potential readers – people who had been taught to decipher print without learning much else, and from whom the existing newspapers, with their long articles, long paragraphs, and all-round demands on the intelligence and imagination, were quite unsuited. To give them what they felt they wanted he started in that year a little weekly, well described by its name, *Tit-Bits*.

For the historian of *The Times*, '*Tit-Bits* at a copper fell exactly within the intellectual and financial reach of a generation new to reading.' For Newnes' assistant, Alfred Harmsworth, it was a short step, via *Answers* (1888), to the founding of the *Daily Mail*, and the inauguration of the modern 'yellow press'. The myth is especially dear to the rival 'quality press': the reviews of Richard Hoggart's book, *The Uses of Literacy*, all stressed 'the compulsory literacy of 1870'.

However attractive to intellectual *amour-propre* or the perennial nostalgia for an imaginary past before cultural standards were debased, the belief rests on very slender foundations. On the one hand, the origins of the popular press go back far beyond 1870. On the other, it took much longer than a generation for the cheap London dailies to become the staple reading at the levels occupied by the illiterate before 1870. The rise of the mass-circulation dailies was an important phase in the history of journalism; but it was not the complete revolution it is usually supposed. In the dramatic form in which it is traditionally stated, and from which it receives its supposed significance, the belief in a direct causal connection between

* First published in *History Today*, July 1957.

the 1870 Education Act and the 'Harmsworth revolution' is almost pure myth, without foundation in fact.

The belief implies that the working class who today form most of the readership of the cheap London dailies, were largely illiterate before 1870. The assumption makes nonsense of the history of the previous hundred years. As Professor Aspinall and Dr. R.K. Webb have shown, the fears of English governments from the anti-Jacobin to the Chartist period, from the younger Pitt to Lord John Russell, were grounded in the knowledge and that large numbers of working men could read, and had access to inflammatory propaganda. The stamp duty on newspapers was increased between 1789 and 1815 from 1½d. to 4d., making the final price 7d., for the express purpose of discouraging their circulation among the reading poor. The press and the poor found ways of circumventing the purpose. Unstamped journals, ostensibly containing no news, like Cobbett's *Twopenny Trash,* were widely read. Samuel Bamford, the 'weaver-poet' tells how in 1816 the writings of Cobbett 'were read on nearly every cottage hearth in the manufacturing districts of South Lancashire: in those of Leicester, Derby and Nottingham; also in many Scottish towns'. Artisans clubbed together to buy the *Black Dwarf* and other 'seditious' papers. Newspapers were read aloud in ale-houses and clubs. In 1831, according to the Attorney-General, Cobbett's *Political Register,* at a shilling, was widely read amongst the working classes. After the reduction of the stamp duty to a penny in 1836, the Chartists had their own journals, like Ernest Jones's *People's Paper* (1852).

Working-class Radicals were perhaps educationally superior to their fellows. The same cannot be said of the London street-folk described by Henry Mayhew in the 1850's. Though they had next to no schooling, and few of them could read,

> even costermongers have their taste for books. They are very fond of hearing anyone read aloud to them, and listen very attentively. One man often reads the Sunday paper of the beershop to them, and on a fine summer's evening a costermonger, or any neighbour who has the advantage of being 'a schollard', reads aloud to them in the courts they inhabit.

Mayhew found the very prostitutes literate. Three-quarters of the 42,000 'disorderly prostitutes' prosecuted in London in the 1850s could at least read.

Reading, then, if not writing, was by no means a privileged art before 1870. Though the State did not itself provide instruction until then, elementary education was of much older date. Leaving aside older and less formal developments, the hundreds of charity schools founded in the eighteenth century did much to spread the three R's amongst 'the lower orders'. The early nineteenth century saw a great expansion, chiefly through the agency of the rival religious bodies, the Society for the Education of the Poor according to the Principles of the Church of England, and the British and Foreign Schools Society. For those children who could not attend day-schools, Sunday schools expanded rapidly from 1780. With their emphasis on Bible Study as the main foundation of moral conduct, they had a considerable influence on literacy. Some of them even taught writing, though against opposition. In 1833 a group of cotton operatives in Glossop, Derbyshire, unable to persuade the existing Sunday schools to teach their children to write, founded their own, and met, for lack of other accommodation, in the largest local public house.

By 1818, it is estimated, there were 675,000 children attending day-schools, and nearly half a million attending Sunday schools in England and Wales, though, of course, they overlapped. By Horace Mann's educational census of 1851 there were over 2 million and nearly $2\frac{1}{2}$ million respectively – that is, about one child in three under the age of fifteen was attending a day-school. Since few working-class children attended for more than one or two years, a much larger proportion received some instruction. In the twenty years before 1870 the numbers expanded still further as the state increased its financial aid until it bore a larger share of the costs than the voluntary bodies and the parents together. The 1870 Act was not a beginning but a point on a steadily rising scale. If the average attendance at public elementary schools almost quadrupled between 1870 and 1901, only part of the increase represented children not previously educated. Apart from the growth of the child population, most of it was due to the longer school-life of most children – six or seven years instead of two or three.

Those who attended neither day-school nor Sunday school were not always illiterate, for they were not necessarily mentally backward, and in an age of self-help might teach themselves with the help of parents or friends. It is not surprising, then, to find that, as early as 1841, two-thirds of the bridegrooms and more than half the brides could sign the marriage register. By 1871, before the board schools could have affected them, four-fifths of the men and three-quarters of the women could do so, while in Scotland the figures were even better. This is not proof that they could read, but it is circumstantial evidence. It is reinforced by contemporary surveys, like that of the

Manchester and Salford Educational Aid Society in 1865 in New Cross and St. Michael's wards: 'half the youthful population were unable to write, and about one-quarter unable to read' – in other words, three-quarters were literate. Dr. R.K. Webb who, in *The British Working Class Reader, 1790–1840*, has made the most exhaustive study of the subject, concluded that in the 1840s, though with great local variation, between two-thirds and three-quarters of the working class, and possibly more of the men, could read. It is clear that in the mid-nineteenth century, a generation before the school boards appeared, there was a reading public large enough to have supported a popular press of considerable size.

The myth that a generation of new readers called forth the popular press thus reduces itself to the improbable claim that the early halfpenny London dailies were chiefly supported by the third or less of the population which became literate between 1870 and 1900. It is reasonable to assume that most of these belonged to the lower strata of the working class. It is just these levels that Charles Booth and Seebohm Rowntree found living in poverty. In Booth's London in the early 1880s over 30 per cent of the population belonged to the poor and the very poor. In Rowntree's York, in 1899, very nearly the same proportion were in primary or secondary poverty. It is extremely improbable that the purchasers of the Edwardian halfpenny dailies came mainly from among those who could not afford enough food to keep them in health, and had nothing to spare for inessentials. If they read them in ale-houses or at second hand, they could hardly have had much effect on the character and circulations of the new papers.

Again, if the new dailies were already reaching so low for their subscribers, whence came the huge subsequent increases in newspaper circulations? Earlier estimates of total circulations are unreliable, but since 1920 the national dailies have increased in circulation from less than 5½ million to over 16 million. At the earlier date less than two families in three purchased a national morning paper. It was not until the Second World War that the sales of national dailies overtook the number of households in the country. Sunday circulations, significantly, did so by the First World War; but theirs is an older story to which we must return. It took up to half a century for the popular daily press as created – or remodelled – by Harmsworth to absorb the new readers produced by State education.

Without universal education, of course, the mass-circulation press could not exist. To that extent a causal thread, beginning long before 1870 and ending long after 1896, runs through both Forster's Act and the founding of the *Daily Mail*. Reduced to these terms, the connection between the two becomes a truism of egregious triviality. For all the significance left in it, the myth collapses under the weight of the evidence.

Its collapse, however, leaves us with two further problems. Where, if not in 'the Harmsworth revolution', are the origins of the popular press to be found? Secondly, allowing that the rise of the mass-circulation dailies was an important stage in the history of the press, to what causes must it be attributed?

The origins of the popular press go back long before Northcliffe. They are to be found, in part at least, where the most casual reader of nineteenth-century newspapers would expect to find them – in the press itself. The belief that all or even most newspapers before the *Daily Mail* were uniformly high-toned, serious and unbiased will not survive even a cursory reading of them. Long articles, long paragraphs, few headlines and fewer illustrations they may have had; but their demands on the intelligence and the imagination are easy to exaggerate. The *Report of the Royal Commission on the Press* (1949), the most considered critique of the modern popular press, has two major criticisms to make of its performance: that devotion to truth and absence of political bias were not maintained by most papers at the highest possible standards, and that they contained too much triviality and sensationalism, resulting from the desire to provide excitement and to 'minister to the imaginative gratification of the readers'. The same criticisms were, with justice, made of the nineteenth-century press.

The historian W.E.H. Lecky, writing in 1882 before 'the Harmsworth revolution', saw a very few men in control of the press acquiring a greater influence than most responsible statesmen.

They constitute themselves the mouthpiece and representative of the nation, and they are often accepted as such throughout Europe. They make it their task to select, classify and colour the information, and to supply the opinions of their readers, and, as comparatively few men have the wish or the power or the time to compare evidence and weigh arguments, they dictate absolutely the conclusions of thousands. If they cannot altogether make opinion, they can at least exaggerate, bias, and influence it'.

Their success came from writing down to the level of their readers:

A knack of clever writing, great enterprise in bringing together the kind of information which amuses or interests the public, tact in catching and following the first symptoms of change of opinions, a skilful pandering to popular prejudice, malevolent gossip, sensational falsehood, coarse descriptions, vindictive attacks on individuals, nations, or classes, are the elements of which many great newspaper ascendancies have been mainly built.

These strictures, with their familiar ring for modern ears, are fully borne out by the evidence. Lack of political bias was rare, even in the most reputable papers. Comment on political opponents was frankly partisan. 'Mr. Babbletongue Macaulay', said *The Times* of the early 1840s, was 'hardly fit to fill up one of the vacancies that have occurred by the lamentable death of Her Majesty's two favourite monkeys.' In a Corn Law debate in 1842, according to the *Manchester Chronicle and Salford Standard*, 'Lord John Russell, whether from mere presumptuous imbecillity [sic] or from *treachery*, ignominiously broke down in the midst of his argument.' For the *Manchester Courier and Lancashire General Advertizer*, Mr. Gladstone, 'stumping it at Chester' in support of his son's candidature on Derby Day, 1865, when every gentlemanly statesman was at Epsom, was 'the prince of the humbugs of the present day; and . . .we never knew a time in which humbug was so rampant as it is at present'.

Headlines, though restricted to a single column, could wring every drop of sensation out of the news. A random sample from the local press around mid-century reads as follows: HORRIBLE MATRICIDE NEAR BIRKENHEAD; RAPE BY AN EX-LOVER, FRIGHTFUL BOILER EXPLOSION; MELANCHOLY LOSS OF LIFE; THE MYSTERIOUS FRUITS OF SECRET LOVE; and MELANCHOLY DESTRUCTION OF A CHILD BY ITS MOTHER, WHILE FRANTIC WITH PAIN.

The verbatim reports of sensational legal cases, which today form the Sunday reading of a large part of the population, were a Victorian staple at a higher level of society. In an attack on the 'attractive and lucrative indecency of *The Times*' in 1864, the *Saturday Review* remarked,

We want a Moral Sewers Commission. To purify the Thames is something, but to purify *The Times* would be a greater boon to society . . . The unsavoury reports of the Divorce Courts, the disgusting details of the harlotry and vice, the filthy nauseous annals of the brothel, the prurient letters of adulterers and adulteresses, the modes in which intrigues may be carried out, the diaries and meditations of married sinners, these are now part of our domestic life.

Working men rarely read *The Times*. What did they read? Local papers were more in touch with what they knew. Published usually once or twice a week, they could be read and passed on before they were out of date. When penny morning papers appeared about the time of the repeal of the stamp duty in 1855, most working men had neither the time nor the money for them. In some areas, an attempt was made to reach them with the halfpenny evening paper, the first being *The Events*, 'A Daily Newspaper for the MILLION', which appeared in Liverpool in 1855. It was not a success; but others in Liverpool, Manchester, South Shields and elsewhere did succeed; and in many places a halfpenny press was available to the working class long before the *Daily Mail*.

Without doubt, the preferred reading of the Victorian working classes was the Sunday press. Published once a week at a moment when, if at all, the working man had both leisure and money, the Sunday paper was the true progenitor of the popular press. In 1828, when newspapers were at 7d., Toby Tims, the barber, quoted in *Blackwood's Magazine,* got *Bell's Weekly Messenger* 'from a neigh-bour, who has it from his cousin in the Borough, who, I believe, is the last reader of a club of fourteen'.

The Royal Commission found that the events which had the greatest news-value for the modern popular press were 'those concerning sport, followed by news about people, news of strange or amusing adventures, tragedies, accidents, and crimes, news, that is, whose sentiment or excitement brings some colour to life'. *Bell's Weekly Messenger,* according to Toby Tims, was

a most entertaining paper, and beats all for news. In fact, it is full of everything, sir – every, every thing – accidents – charity sermons – markets – boxing – Bible societies – horse-racing – child murders – the theatres – foreign wars – Bow-street reports – and Day-and-Martin's blacking.

By 1854, before they brought their price down to a penny at the repeal of the stamp duty, *Lloyd's Weekly News* (1842) and the *News of the World* (1843) had achieved circulations of 100,000, and *Reynolds' News* (1850) was not far behind. Over the next half-century *Lloyd's,* the prototype of the modern popular newspaper, outclassed all the rest, rising to 900,000 in 1890, when *Reynolds'* had little more than a third the circulation, and the *News of the World* had sunk to 30,000. In 1896, when the *Daily Mail* began to appear, *Lloyd's* reached a million, the first newspaper to do so. In popular appeal the Sunday press always led the way. In 1920 the total circulation was 13½ million – more than one for every family in the country. The new readers created by state education, like most working–class readers before them, turned first to the Sunday press.

Even the Sunday press does not exhaust the favourite reading of the Victorian working class, or the origins of the popular press. Until surprisingly late in the nineteenth century there was, at the lowest levels of society, a thriving indigenous literature of street-ballads, broadsheets and chapbooks. Sold in the countryside by pedlars or chapmen and in the towns by itinerant street-singers, they were the natural vehicle for the information and entertainment of a lively, inquisitive people for whom the sung or spoken word meant more than the written. They were a complete literature in themselves: 'cock-crows' or romances, nursery rhymes, songs sentimental like the often-printed 'Drink to me Only', or humorous like 'Pretty Polly Perkins of Paddington Green'. In 1856 Jemmy Catnach's successor at the Seven Dials Press stocked more than four thousand different titles. The most popular were the gallows-sheets, which had been known to sell 40,000 copies at an execution: execrable, moralizing verses on the murderer – Palmer the Rugeley poisoner, Mrs Maybrick, Burke and Hare, and others whose fame still lives. Sporting events, especially prize-fights, were favourite topics. News of any kind was a bestseller. Every notable event produced its crop of ballads: the Nore mutiny, the battles of Trafalgar, Waterloo, Navarino, Inkerman, and the rest, the various coronations, the 'Happy Reform' of 1832, Queen Victoria's marriage and the birth of every royal baby, Corn Law Repeal, the Great Exhibition, and so on. Peel's Income Tax in 1842 provoked a ballad of Gilbertian measure:

> 'Oh! poor old Johnny Bull has his Cup of Sorrow full,
> And what with underfeeding him, and leaching him, and bleeding him,
> Though overdrained before, he must lose a little more,
> He'll now be bled again by the Income Tax'.

The standard of comment was hard-hitting and uninhibited. The rhymers thought nothing of advising the Queen in the interests of the Exchequer to 'do it no more'; of accusing 'little Al, the royal pal', thought to oppose the Crimean War, of being a Russian; or of spreading malicious gossip about 'Margaret Slack and the Prince of Wales'. The 'human angle' was the basic approach; 'And my love fell with Nelson upon that very day' is a fair example. Sex, violence and crime were the most favoured ingredients and the moral tone grew shriller as the prurience increased. But what gives the street-ballad an even stronger claim to the ancestry of the popular press is the eye-catching, sensational lay-out. Black headlines and garish illustration begin with the ballads. A villainous woodcut is captioned by SHOCKING RAPE AND MURDER. Another has SELF DESTRUCTION OF FEMALE BY THROWING HERSELF OFF THE MONUMENT. THE IRISH NEW POLICEMEN shows a prisoner being bludgeoned in a Dublin police station, while PENAL SERVITUDE FOR MRS MAYBRICK: She Will Not have to Climb Golden Stairs' needs no illustration. The street-ballad beats the modern 'yellow press' in vulgarity, sensationalism, moral indignation, outspokenness and, above all, robustness.

Apart from the similarity of interests, style and audience, it is possible to show something like a continuity of readership from the street-literature to the Sunday paper, and so to the modern popular press. The link is provided by the penny serial novels. Romantic or heroic, lush or violent, and garnished with a woodcut, the serial novel showed that the market could be more continuously exploited. Illiterate costermongers, Mayhew was told, would go mad if they could not learn 'about the picture'. 'What they love best to listen to – and, indeed, what they are most eager for – are Reynold's periodicals, especially the 'Mysteries of the Court,' he was told by the men who read to them; 'They've got tired of Lloyd's blood-stained stories, and I'm satisfied that, of all London, Reynolds is the most popular man among them.' Edward Lloyd and G.W.M. Reynolds are a personal link between the street-literature and the popular press. Having learnt their trade and their audience with the serial novel, they developed the Sunday papers named after them.

The line runs back, then, from the modern popular press, through *Lloyd's Weekly* and *Reynolds' News* and the penny novels to the street-ballads. And the street-ballads themselves have an ancestry almost as old as printing. Before newspapers existed, the sixteenth-century ballads, full of monstrous births, lewd romances, popish plots, famine, war and pestilence, and the accessions and deaths of princes, were an established tradition. News-ballads threw up news-pamphlets, and they in their turn, by publishing under a continuing name and date-line, the *corantos* of the 1620s. The ballads were thus the progenitors not only of the popular but of all the newspaper press. When in the mid-nineteenth century they finally threw up the popular Sunday paper to cater for the last and lowest layers of society, they cut off their own blood-supply. By the 1870s they had withered, by the 1880s almost disappeared – but *Lloyd's* and *Reynolds'* were selling by the hundred thousand.

There still remains the problem of 'the Harmsworth revolution'. If a flourishing popular press existed before the advent of Harms-worth , to what can we attribute his achievement, the inauguration of the mass-circulation daily? For it was an achievement, marking a major turning-point in newspaper history. It has been flagrantly misrepresented. Neither the *Daily Mail* nor the *Daily Mirror* – nor, for that matter, even *Tit-Bits* – lowered the standards of popular journalism. If anything, they raised them. *Tit-Bits* and *Answers* may have been put together with scissors and paste; but they were putting together snippets of wholesome, edifying information. Newnes, Pearson and Harmsworth were working for a public as restless and self-improving as themselves. Samuel Smiles is their godfather. The *Mail,* the *Express* and the *Mirror,* in their early days at least, were purveyors of daily news and comment of a scope and quality hitherto unavailable at less than twice the price. Superficial, biased, trivial, sensational perhaps, they were none the less paragons by the side of the street-literature and many earlier news-sheets – not to mention some of the newless newspapers of today.

The achievement of Harmsworth is that he did for the newspaper what Leverhulme did for soap, or Ford for the motor-car. He found a product ripe for exploitation by mass-production methods. The Sunday press had shown its possibilities. He raised its quality to a uniform level, cheapened it, and sold it by the million. In the process he built himself, like them, a great commercial empire, to be imitated by others. He could only do so because of the enormous economic opportunities created by the social changes going on around him. For half a century before 1896, and with increasing speed in the great price-fall of the last twenty years, real income had been rising for the lower middle and working classes. For many of them, though not yet for the poorest, that meant a larger surplus after meeting necessities. This was an opportunity for the supplier of mass-consumer goods – soap, groceries, haberdashery, and the like – which made more than one millionaire's fortune. Part of the surplus was spent on a daily newspaper, as well as the Sunday and the local press. The early readers of the *Daily Mail* were the lower middle and the 'respectable' working classes. As layer after social layer rose out of poverty in the twentieth century, so the London morning press expanded to meet it, and adjusted its appeal.

The modern popular press is a phenomenon grounded in social and economic fact. It was not so much state education as the expansion and redistribution of the national income, which at every stage has fed and nourished it. If the morals, taste and truthfulness of this wayward mistress of the public are no better they they should be, that is not because they have declined. Rather is it because, since the days of the broadsheet ballads, the penny novels and the Victorian Sunday press, they have not progressed enough.

# 4

# INDIVIDUALISM VERSUS COLLECTIVISM IN NINETEENTH-CENTURY BRITAIN: A FALSE ANTITHESIS*

THE critical transition in social policy in nineteenth-century Britain, it is still generally believed, was the change from individualism to collectivism. Yet since Dicey came under fire in the late 1950s, there has been no accepted consensus about how and when this transition came about. Dicey himself, who was not strictly a historian but a theorist of jurisprudence, held a naive view of how things happen, how policy changes and is translated into law: a great thinker thinks, and converts disciples, who in turn contrive to turn the master's thoughts into the dominant wisdom or accepted common sense of the age, which then finds its way on to the Statute Book. In this way he arrived at his famous tripartite division of the nineteenth century into three periods of public opinion, government policy, and legislation: the first, up to 1825, or 1830, the period of Old Toryism, legislative quiescence, or Blackstonian optimism, dominated by Sir William Blackstone; the second, from about 1830 to 1865 or 1870, the period of Benthamism or Individualism, dominated by Jeremy Bentham and his disciples; and the last, from 1865 or 1870 to the time of his lectures on *Law and Opinion* published in 1905, the period of Collectivism, dominated, it seems, by no great thinker of powerful mind and principle, but merely by the pragmatic need to propitiate the emerging and increasingly powerful working-class voter.[1] It is surprising that Dicey could not find a great thinker on whom to serve an affiliation order for fathering collectivism. He was perhaps groping in the right direction in his famous, if much too brief, chapter on 'The Debt of Collectivism to Benthamism'. If he had pursued this line far enough, he might have fastened it on John Stuart Mill, who ended by calling himself in his *Autobiography* a 'Socialist', or on Edwin Chadwick, who ended by saying that *laissez-faire* meant 'letting mischief work, and evils go on which do not affect ourselves'.[2] But to complete the line for him is to accept the fallacy on which his model is based; and Mill and Chadwick no more *invented* collectivism than Blackstone did Old Toryism or Bentham individualism.

Since the Second World War, historians of policy and administration have thrown doubt on Dicey's interpretation. The first was

* First published in The Journal of British Studies, XVII, Fall 1977.

J.B. Brebner in a famous, if somewhat isolated, paper in 1948, in which he claimed that Adam Smith and James Mill were responsible for the *laissez-faire* elements in nineteenth-century thought, and that Bentham, in his devotion to administrative solutions to social problems, was really the father of collectivism.[3] In this he was followed by Werner Stark in his Introduction to *Bentham's Economic Writings*, who claimed him as the grandfather of the Welfare State.[4] But this is merely to turn the Dicey model on its head, without any lessening of its essential naivety.

From 1958 onwards, David Roberts, Oliver MacDonagh, and the Kitson Clark 'organic' school of autonomous administrative history – what Jenifer Hart calls the Tory interpretation of history[5] – repudiated the Dicey model altogether, and substituted one of their own. According to this, great thinkers and 'intellectual' opinion play no part whatever in forming policy: 'Broadly speaking, so far as the administrative matters with which we are concerned go, Benthamism had no influence upon opinion at large or, for that matter, upon the overwhelming majority of public servants . . .' – most of whom had 'not read Bentham or even heard of his name' (a most surprising claim, incapable of proof). In the MacDonagh model, the prime mover is the appearance (through industrialism, urbanization, and other concomitants of social change) of new or greatly enlarged social problems, such as child labour in factories, cholera in slums, or appalling conditions in emigrant ships, which present themselves as 'intolerable facts' against which ordinary, unstructured, humanitarian public opinion forces corrective legislation. Legislation, minimal at first, generates a process of further and increasing state intervention. New civil servants, inspectors, and assistant commissioners expose the unexpected size of the problem or uncover new and unsuspected problems underlying it, and show the inadequacy of the first tentative solution. 'Statesmen in disguise', they recommend by a process of 'feedback' in a sequence of reports, minutes, and memoranda a series of closer and closer approximations to a solution, which inevitably means more and more government intervention and machinery. The 'internal dynamism' of the process of reform takes over; the 'vital and neglected factor is the momentum of government itself'.[6]

Such a violent swing in interpretation was bound to provoke reaction, and Henry Parris and Jenifer Hart came to the defence of Dicey, though with rather more sophistication than he, and showed not only that a great many conscious Benthamites, such as Chadwick and Nassau Senior, did play a considerable part in the process, but that they played the critical role in the MacDonagh model itself, the injection of the vital X-ingredient, the appointment of the enforcement officers who were the chief link in the recurring chain of feedback.[7] For example, if it was the humanitarians – Ashley, Sadler, and company – who agitated for the key Factory Act of 1833, it was the Benthamites, Chadwick and Nassau Senior, who suggested the critical device of enforcement by professional government inspectors without which the 1833 Act would have been no more effective than earlier ones.[8]

Now, there is much to be said for both sides to this controversy. They are, in a sense, both right. We all know the classic examples of Benthamite social reforms: factory inspection, the new preventive police, the New Poor Law, the first General Board of Health of 1848-55, the education grants and school inspection from 1833 and 1839 onwards, the control and improvement of safety on the railways, the mines in 1842, and steamships in 1846, the reform of the civil service itself from 1855 to 1870, the Adulteration of Foods Acts from 1860, and so on. We also know the classic examples of non-Benthamite reforms: the Passenger Acts and the inspection of emigrant ships, the Alkali Acts from 1863, the prevention, chiefly by powerful property owners, of the scorching of the countryside by acid gases, and the policies of Sir John Simon at the Privy Council Medical Department and Tom Taylor at the Local Government Act Office. We know, too, that the process of 'feedback', the influence of inspectors and administrators on subsequent legislation, worked through both Benthamites and non-Benthamites, believers in a 'forward' policy of government intervention like Chadwick and Horner, and opponents of it like Tom Taylor, who, according to Royston Lambert, approved more schemes for drainage and water supply than ever Chadwick did.[9] Still further, we know how the confrontation of the real facts of various social problems and the experience of the failure of the first tentative solution converted both Benthamites and non-Benthamites, sometimes in conscious theory, nearly always in legislative and administrative practice, from believers in minimal government to exponents of government intervention, at least in their own particular sphere.

Thus both sides to the controversy are also wrong, in not allowing for what is right in their opponents' case. On the one hand, MacDonagh and company fail to explain why so many conscious, deliberate Benthamites took a leading role in particular reforms; and, apart from allowing Bentham to have been a shrewd if non-influential forecaster, why practically every cycle of reform and feedback followed the classic Benthamite model of 'inquiry, report, legislation, execution, inspection'. On the other hand, Parris and company fail to explain *why* their reformers were Benthamites, what attracted them to the writings of the garrulous old sage – or, more commonly, to those potted versions produced by his disciples – rather than to the large number of other pundits who offered themselves, and why they were listened to and became influential.

The answer, it would appear, is that the process of reform is never a one-way influence of ideology upon practice, or of the empirical 'pressure of facts' upon ideology, but a continuous interaction between the two, in which both are continually modified. Ideology itself is not conceived in a vacuum, but is a crystallization in one or more minds of the accepted wisdom or hitherto unvoiced assumptions of considerable bodies of people. At any one time, indeed, there will be a number of theorists offering such crystallizations. Which of them gets accepted by large numbers of followers will depend on which of them says what most people want to hear, what chimes best with their assumptions and interests, who 'speaks to their condition'. For example, John Locke in his *Essays on Government* crystallized the peculiar concept of property which the English landed class had been evolving, and fighting for, for three centuries or more; it was not altogether surprising that the victors of the Glorious Revolution should have accepted him rather than Sir Robert Filmer or Thomas Hobbes as their favourite philospher. Adam Smith crystallized the *laissez-faire* policy which had, for purely empirical reasons, been the internal practice of the English government since 1660, and merely tried to extend it to foreign trade, against 'the mercantile system'; it is only superficially surprising that he, rather than the few remaining 'mercantilists', should have been accepted by aristocratic politicians like the younger Pitt, Lord Liverpool, Lord Sidmouth, Peel and Huskisson even before the merchants and industrialists themselves. Similarly, Ricardo and the classical economists in the 1820s and 1830s 'spoke to the condition' of a new generation of merchants and industrialists who were now strong enough to stand on their own feet without government protection and saw great benefit to themselves in denying protection to others; the protectionists and paternalists like Samuel Gray, Michael Thomas Sadler, and the *'Blackwood's* economists – David Robinson, John Galt, W. Stevenson, W. Johnstone, and John Wilson – who opposed free trade and supported welfare measures, and understood the problems of slump and their solution by such Keynesian means as a managed currency and reflation better than Ricardo *et al.,* were ignored or laughed out of court.[10] In our century J. A. Hobson was ignored and even persecuted by the Marshallian economists for advocating precisely the same solutions for which Keynes was applauded only a generation later, when Marshallian solutions became manifestly inappropriate to our condition.

Conversely, ideology does not stand still, but adjusts continuously to practical experience. When, for example, ideology makes an egregious error, as in the New Poor Law of 1834, the theory is not instantly abandoned – it takes time for the error to sink in – but the practical experience of searching for an effective solution modifies the assumptions of the operators until their ideology is transformed from within. The pure doctrine of the workhouse test and less eligibility proves impossible of application, and is replaced by 1842 and 1852 as far as the industrial population is concerned by the labour test and 'outdoor relief regulation'. More significantly, the process of reform uncovers other causes of poverty, other social problems requiring solution, notably slum housing and disease, and the reformers in the front line, Chadwick, Southwood Smith, Arnott, and Kay-Shuttleworth, are converted from Benthamite individualists to Benthamite collectivists. In a similar way, a non-Benthamite individualist and anti-centralizing King Log like Tom Taylor could be converted by the experience of thirteen years in the Local Government Act Office into an active interventionist who browbeat local vestries through tumultuous and often violent inquiries into installing clean water and drainage. The Benthamites were attracted to Bentham and his remedies because he spoke to their condition, to their professional concern for systematic solutions to complex administrative problems, and because his model of the reform process – inquiry, report, legislation, execution, inspection – offered a short cut to getting things done. The non-Benthamites reached the same conclusion the hard way, by trial and error: they often began at the back end, with *ad hoc* inspection leading to dissatisfaction with the original legislation which set it up, and their inquiries and reports instigated a fresh round of legislation and execution. Either way, *laissez-faire* individualism was eroded and collectivism progressively took its place.

Yet there is still a problem: why did so many reformers and administrators, whether Benthamites or learners by experience, change sides so radically, from individualism to its supposed opposite, collectivism, in the course of their careers? The answer is that individualism versus collectivism is a false antithesis. They were not opposites but adjacent steps in a progression. Individualism was not a simple antonym to collectivism; both were in fact complex concepts. Those like Dicey who have treated them as opposites, two poles between which social policy could swing but, like north and south in magnetism, could not point both ways at once, have created for themselves a dilemma which does not exist. The answer to the problem does not reside in a paradox, like Dicey's 'debt of collectivism to Benthamism', or like Brebner that Bentham was really a collectivist, or like Lord Robbins that the classical economists were committed to *laissez-faire* only as an expedient not as a principle, or like Arthur Taylor that *laissez-faire* was becoming predominant in *economic* policy (free trade and internal industry) at the same time as collectivism was beginning to infiltrate *social* policy (the employment of women and children, public health, education, and so on).[11] The answer lies in the analysis of individualism and collectivism to determine whether they were antithetical and therefore incompatible with each other, or whether they were not in fact continuous entities lying along a gamut or scale on which the most critical difference might not fall between them but at some other point along the line.

There were in nineteenth-century usage at least two kinds of *laissez-faire* individualism and at least seven kinds of collectivism, and several kinds of collectivism overlapped and were perfectly compatible with one kind of individualism, if not both. The same overlap and ambiguity ran through the concepts of 'liberty' and 'liberalism', also key notions for an understanding of nineteenth-century society and politics, help to explain why they could appeal to such different interests and classes. If we can unravel them we shall be well on the way to understanding not only the drift of nineteenth-century party system and especially of the Liberal Party.

Individualism was the belief that the individual was best left to pursue his own interests without any more interference by the state than was necessary to ensure the same freedom for other individuals. From the beginning there were, as Halévy pointed out in *The Growth of Philosophical Radicalism,* two different versions of it.[12] The first, most typically represented by Adam Smith, held that the social harmony required, if the individual's interests were not to conflict to the point of social breakdown, would be provided by a 'hidden hand', meaning the natural tendency for men's self-interest to supply each others' needs. This *'natural* harmony of interests' operated ever when the interests were selfish or sinful, on the common Enlighten ment principle of Bernard de Mandeville's 'private vices, publi virtues' or Pope's Nature's God who bade 'that true self-love and social are the same'. The other version, which Halévy attributed to Bentham but which also has a longer ancestry going back to Hobbes's 'war of all against all', was that of the *artificial* harmony of interests': men's self-interests were not naturally harmonious. As the violent history of men in the state of nature and the tendency of criminals to dominate weakly-governed societies showed, they could only be made so by the contrivance of government. Unless the government protected the weak against the strong, property from thieves, and the 'haves' against the 'have-nots', and also 'held the ring' in non-criminal disputes between citizens, the self-interest of individuals would rapidly produce not harmony but anarchy. [13]

In practice, there was not so much difference between the two versions of individualism as might have been expected. As is well known, Adam Smith thought that the state was justified in interfering with, say, the corn trade in the name of defence and national survival in war, in providing free education if the poor could not provide it for themselves, or in supplying certain public works such as bridges or water supply which could not be profitably supplied by individuals. Conversely, Bentham and his followers thought that the onus of proving the necessity of state intervention should always lie on the interveners. J.S. Mill, down to the last edition of *The Principles of Political Economy,* which appeared when he had been privately converted by Harriet Taylor to what he called 'socialism', declared that 'letting alone should be the general practice' and placed 'the burthen of making out a strong case, not on those who resist, but on those who recommend, government interference'. [14] Yet there was, in theory at least, all the difference in the world between the two versions. The first was like Paley's clock: once having set it going, the Great Clockmaker could leave it to regulate itself. State intervention would not be necessary save in the most exceptional circumstances, such as war or natural catastrophe. The second assumed that state intervention was a continuing necessity, that indeed the state could not continue to exist and to guarantee the free pursuit of individual self-interest except by intervening. It is easy to see why the second should, and the first should not, lead easily and imperceptibly to more state intervention.

Yet the case for a *continuum* from individualism to collectivism does not rest primarily on this distinction. It rests much more directly on the ambiguity of 'individualism' and 'liberty' in both versions. Both Adam Smith and Bentham assumed that the state was necessary, albeit a necessary evil, to ensure the freedom of the individual to pursue his own interest. Interference with the free pursuit of self-interest could as easily come from other individuals – external invaders, internal marauders, fraudulent associates – from whom only the state could guarantee genuine protection. There was thus, even in the most minimal version of the *laissez-faire* state, the notion of *positive* freedom, i.e. not merely freedom *from* state control but freedom *to* enjoy rights and privileges, if only the right and privilege of enjoying one's property or income unmolested.[15] This positive freedom was explicitly invoked in English political thought by T.H. Green and D.G. Ritchie, who got it from Hegel, when they were consciously trying to tip the balance of liberalism towards collectivism, but it was implicit in both kinds of individualism from the beginning.

We could, perhaps, profitably introduce here a 'law' or principle which helps to put the claims and counterclaims of liberals, whether individualist or collectivist, into perspective. It is the 'law of the conservation of freedom', which states that there is always the same amount of freedom in any society; it differs only in its distribution. In some societies, Pharaoh's Egypt, Hitler's Germany, or Stalin's Russia, one man has it all: in others, the Athenian Republic, feudal Europe, America of the 'robber barons', it is shared by a few slave-owners, feudal lords, or capitalists; in yet others, more hoped-for than actual in the existing democracies of East and West, it is supposed to be equally shared by the whole populace. Those naive liberals of both *laissez-faire* schools who believed that they stood for the 'freedom of the individual' over against some abstraction called the state were in fact demanding a particular distribution of liberty, usually in favour of those landowners and capitalists who had a disproportionate share of it already. They were incensed when certain other members of society suggested a different distribution of liberty, more in favour of, say, women and children in factories and mines, or the tenants of slum property, or trade unionists, or even the consumers of adulterated food or drinkers of cholera-infected water, and labelled them 'collectivists'. But while this would be true of some liberals, it would be to oversimplify the transition from individualism to collectivism, which went on more effectively within some individual reformers rather than between rival groups. 'Collectivism' came to be used as a bogeyman by late Victorian intellectuals like Sir Henry Maine, J.F. Stephen, Lord Lytton, and Dicey himself, only when the transition had gone so far as to have riven the Liberal Party and alienated a large section of its membership.[16]

Once admit, then, that freedom can be positive, that the state can act to increase the freedom of the individual rather than limit it, or to redistribute freedom from those with too much towards those with too little, and it is easy to see how individualism could slide imperceptibly into collectivism. But what kind of collectivism? There were, it is suggested, at least seven kinds in use in nineteenth-century discussion. J.S. Mill and Dicey even produced an eighth, the 'collectivism' of the joint-stock company, which Dicey condemned but Mill used to justify the management of public utilities by government or local authority; which could not he said, be more careless or ineffective than joint-stock management.[17] Leaving 'joint-stock collectivism' aside as a semantic red herring, we might postulate a ninth, the intervention by police, either the amateur 'system of police' of the old, pre-industrial society or the new professional police from 1829 onwards, to protect life and property. But that would be to label *laissez-faire* itself collectivist, revealingly, but not in accordance with the usage of the age.

Let us come to the seven meanings in general use in the nineteenth century. The first was state intervention to prevent obvious moral nuisances or physical dangers not previously considered criminal, because not hitherto known to the public or thought immoral or dangerous: the overworking of women and children in factories and mines, the death by neglect of passengers on emigrant ships, the poisoning of food by adulteration, the scorching of crops, trees, and human lungs by acid vapour, the spreading of disease by water companies. To appoint a special police in each of these cases in the form of inspectors, assistant commissioners, or other enforcement officers was not different in principle from appointing a general police in a *laissez-faire* state. They might restrain the liberty of some individuals, but it was in the nature of law to restrain individuals, and the only question was whether the right individuals were restrained and whether the enlargement of the liberties of the rest was adequate recompense. Classical economists as devoted to the free market as J.R. McCulloch and Nassau Senior, for example, could see no breach of principle in restraining the right of millowners to work children and then women for unlimited hours, though they resisted it strongly for adult males.

It was a small step to the second form of collectivism, the enforcement of minimum standards of provision of certain services by some individuals for others: the education of factory children, the payment of wages in cash rather than truck, the enactment of housing by-laws. These might add to the costs and reduce the profits of the industrialists and landlords, and were certainly an infringement of their liberty, but a 'warrantable' infringement, since they enlarged the liberty of factory children, wage-earners, and tenants, which 'liberals' could think more important.

It was a further small step to the third form, state finance in aid of private provision of certain services: church building (1818), grants to the societies providing elementary education (1833), even those 'eleemosynary statutes', the Drainage Acts from 1846 in aid of farmers and their landlords – hardly an oppressed group with no one but the state to protect them.

State aid might grow by imperceptible degrees to the fourth form, direct state provision of a service for a part, albeit, a large part, of the population. Thus the elementary education grant grew so large in the 1850s and 1860s, and yet failed to complete the task, that the state felt impelled to 'fill in the gaps' by the public provision of board schools in 1870. Or the state might escalate from providing a service for a small section of the population, simply because it found it difficult to differentiate, to providing it for a large one, as the provision of dispensaries and infirmaries for the poor grew into a provision for non-paupers by the Medical Relief Disqualification Removal Act of 1885.

The fifth form of collectivism was the public provision of a service, on a voluntary basis, to the whole of a (usually local) population: the Manchester Police Commissioners in 1819 escalated from lighting the streets to selling gas to householders, thus inaugurating a 'municipal socialism' which ended in the public provision of water, electricity, trams and so on, in Manchester and many other towns.

Sixth comes the state monopoly of an essential service or public utility for the whole population. Leaving aside the armed forces, which could in theory be provided by private enterprise, the oldest in the Victorian age, the Post Office, dated from the age of state-chartered monopolies – the seventeenth century – and might be considered a throw-back to earlier, unenlightened times. But that did not stop it taking over the telegraph system in 1870, and most of the telephone system by the end of the century.

Nevertheless, a great gulf is fixed between that and the seventh and last, the nationalization of the means of production, distribution, and exchange. Apart from the Post Office and its ancillary communication this was only mooted, never enacted, during the nineteenth-century. The only time it reached the statute book was in the Railway Act of 1844, when the government reserved the right to purchase the railways, which of course was never exercised.

Curiously enough, with one exception, nationalization was not popular even with declared socialists in the nineteenth century, most preferring the 'gas and water' municipal socialism of the Fabians. Amongst the first to preach nationalization as a general panacea was Sir Leo Chiozza Money, the Fabian social surveyor, in 1905.[18] The one exception, of course, was land, to which was often added the mines and the railways as inseparable from land. Land nationlization has a long history and goes back at least to Thomas Spence's Plan for 'parochialization' of 1775 and Adam Smith's fellow Scottish professor William Ogilvie's *Essay on the Right of Property in Land* (1781). For most of the nineteenth century it was swamped under a mass of schemes for land reform, from 'free trade in land' (the abolition of primogeniture, entail, and strict settlement) to Henry George's 'single tax'.[19] The Land Nationalization Society, founded by Alfred Russell Wallace in 1881, was only one land reform association amongst many, and it did not consider itself the most extreme. Since it believed in compulsory purchase with full compensation, it deplored the 'confiscation' of Henry George's 'single tax' adopted by the breakaway English Land Restoration League in 1883.

In 1889 and 1891 National Liberal Federation Conferences adopted Georgist measures like the taxation of ground rents and mining royalties and the compulsory purchase of land for local purposes. This, as has been argued elsewhere, helped to give the Liberal Party the reputation of being on what Lord Salisbury called 'an inclined plane leading from the position of Lord Hartington to that of Mr Chamberlain and so on to the depths over which Mr Henry George rules supreme'.[20] It thus helped to alienate property owners, both landlords and capitalists, from the Party.[21] But the Liberal Party never at this or any other time crossed the boundary between the sixth and seventh forms of collectivism. It required an imagination more alarmist even than Lord Salisbury's to believe that the Liberal Party was really committed to a programme of collectivism which stretched all the way from factory and school inspection to full-blooded socialism.

Who had such an imagination? The answer is A.V. Dicey. Dicey was one of those Liberal Unionist intellectuals who had become disillusioned with the Gladstonian Liberals' threat to 'individualism' and 'liberty', by which they meant the liberty of individual property owners. We have seen how the two forms of *laissez-faire* individualism could shade imperceptibly into first one and then seven varieties of collectivism. But though the logical progression – which is not the same thing as the historical sequence, which was much more haphazard – was in theory continuous, there was a much greater leap from the sixth to the seventh than between any two previous steps, and certainly not excepting the step from individualism 2 to collectivism 1. The shortness and insignificance of that first step is shown by the fact that large numbers of contemporaries were unaware that they had taken it, and could straddle the boundary as far as different areas of policy were concerned with no consciousness of paradox or stress.

In other words, individualism versus collectivism was not the boundary line that mattered. The one that mattered, and mattered enough to drive men to abandon the political habits of a lifetime and change parties rather than cross it, was that between collectivism 6 and collectivism 7, between state provision of a few marginal services and state ownership of the whole means of production, distribution, and exchange. And yet no political leader in the nineteenth century, except a very few non-Fabian socialists like Hyndman, asked them to take that step. Why then did so many landowners and businessmen react as they did, and abandon the 'collectivist' Liberal Party for the by then hardly less 'collectivist' Conservative Party? The answer can only be the power of a myth, the false antithesis between individualism and collectivism. While British social policy had travelled eastwards, let us say, from Manchester as far as Sheffield, Dicey and his hearers were convinced that they were on their way (in modern terms) to Moscow or Peking. It has been suggested elsewhere how the Liberal Party came to fall into this trap, by a combination of ambivalent land reform and diluted social welfare measures.[22] Dicey did not invent the myth. Like so many other popularizers and propagandists – the nearest analogy is with Samuel Smiles and the self-made man – he came at the end rather than the beginning of the process of 'mythification'. But he stamped it so indelibly on the interpretation of social reform in the nineteenth century that it has taken the best part of this century to erase it. We forget that, like greater thinkers before him – John Locke, Adam Smith, Jeremy Bentham, and David Ricardo – he was a propagandist with a political purpose. He proves once again the wisdom of the adage that 'history is present politics'.

## Notes

1  A. V. Dicey, *Lectures on the Relation between Law and Public Opinion in England during the Nineteenth Century*, London: Macmillan 1905, *passim*. (Hereafter, *Law and Public Opinion*.)

2 J.S. Mill, *Autobiography*, London, 1873, 1958 ed., p.195; E. Chadwick, *On Unity*, London, 1885, p.99.
3 J.B. Brebner, *'Laissez-faire* and State Intervention in 19th-century Britain', *Journal of Economic History*, Supplement VIII, 1948, pp.59–73.
4 W. Stark (ed.), *Jeremy Bentham's Economic Writings*, Cambridge University Press, 1952-4, vol.I, Editor's Introduction.
5 J. Hart, 'Nineteenth-Century Social Reform: a Tory Interpretation of History', *Past and Present*, no. 31, July, 1965.
6 O. MacDonagh, 'The Nineteenth-Century Revolution in Government: a Reappraisal', *Historical Journal*, I, 1958; G. Kitson Clark, 'Statesmen in Disguise', *ibid.*, II, 1959.
7 H. Parris, 'The Nineteenth-Century Revolution in Government: a Reappraisal Reappraised', *ibid.*, III, 1960, and *Constitutional Bureaucracy: the Development of British Central Administration since the 18th-Century*, London: Allen & Unwin, 1969, Ch. 9. See also J. Hart, 'Nineteenth-Century Social Reform',
8 *Ibid.*, p.42.
9 R. Lambert, 'Central and Local Relations in Mid-Victorian England: the Local Government Act Office, 1858–71', *Victorian Studies*, VI, 1962.
10 See H. Perkin, *The Origins of Modern English Society, 1780–1880*, London: Routledge & Kegan Paul 1969, pp. 241–52.
11 Dicey, *Law and Public Opinion*, Lecture 11; Brebner, *'Laissez-faire'*, L. Robbins, *The Theory of Economic Policy*, London: Macmillan 1952, esp. pp.181–94; A.J. Taylor, *Laissez-faire and State Intervention in Nineteenth-Century Britain*, London: Macmillan 1972, Ch. 8.
12 E. Halévy, *The Growth of Philosophical Radicalism*, London: Faber & Gwyer 1928, 1959 ed., pp.15–18.
13 The authoritarian implications of Benthamite utilitarianism are well brought out by E. Stokes in *The English Utilitarians and India*, Oxford: Clarendon Press, 1959, especially pp.47–80, where in an imperial context they were unrestrained by the countervailing Benthamite principle of representative democracy.
14 J.S. Mill, *The Principles of Political Economy*, 6th ed., London, 1865, 1904 reprint, p.573.
15 The concept of positive freedom used here is not at all that criticized by Isaiah Berlin in his Inaugural Lecture, *Two Concepts of Liberty*, Oxford: Clarendon Press, 1958 which embraces the notion of self-mastery by a 'true' or higher self and paves the way therefore for authoritarian philosophers or regimes, like certain Benthamites and Hegelians or Fascist and Stalinist governments, to claim that they are liberating the higher self of the individual by enchaining the lower. It simply contrasts the positive freedom to fulfill one's self, whether labelled higher or lower, with the merely negative absence of constraint which was the core of the naive version of *laissez-faire* liberalism.
16 See J. Roach, 'Liberalism and the Victorian Intelligentsia', *Cambridge Historical Journal*, XIII (1957).
17 Dicey, *Law and Public Opinion*, pp.245–48; Mill, *Principles*, pp.580–81.
18 L.G. Chiozza Money, *Riches and Poverty*, London: Methuen, 1905; 1906 ed., pp.227–33, 250–56.
19 See H. Perkin, 'Land Reform and Class Conflict in Victorian Britain', Essay 7 below.
20 J.L. Garvin, *Life of Joseph Chamberlain*, London: Macmillan, 1932, I, 462.
21 See Perkin, 'Land Reform and Class Conflict', pp.121–26.
22 *Ibid.*

# 5
# THE 'SOCIAL TONE' OF VICTORIAN SEASIDE RESORTS*

THE class-consciousness of the Victorians, which showed itself in the segregation by class and sub-class in the social zoning of towns and suburbs, in the refined grading of schools, clubs and societies, and in the differential pew-rents within the churches and chapels, was nowhere more evident than in their pleasure resorts. People of different status might be forced to meet and mingle in factories and markets, city streets and even political meetings; some might still wish to in the surviving deferential society of rural village and country town. But most of the English in that age took their pleasures separately, in the company of their social equals, and each resort had its own 'social tone', finely adjusted to the exact status of its clientele. According to Dr A.B. Granville, F.R.S., in 1941, Bath was still the 'King of the Spas', there was 'a fragrance of aristocracy in the very air' of Buxton, New Brighton was 'the sea-bathing rendezvous, *par excellence,* of the Lancashire people of note: but the middle-classes, and the wealthy shopkeepers, have also their Brightons and Margates, in the sea villages of Bootle and Crosby Waterloo'. 'As the Manchester people', he went on, 'have their favourite sea-bathing at Southport, so have those of Preston at Blackpool. To Southport the Manchester factor and artisan – the rich and middling comfortable – repair during two months of the year, either for a week or two's residence or for a mere frolic.' But the 'superior classes' of the cotton towns avoided Blackpool and the other Lancashire resorts: 'None but such as cannot proceed farther south, or farther east, across Yorkshire, take up their abode here'.[2]

The social tone was not, of course, fixed and static. As John Walton has shown in the case of Blackpool, it changed within the same resort with the season of the year and from one area to another; above all, it could change over time, and the local authorities and the holiday trades in each went through agonies of debate down the century about the standing of their resort and how to keep or obtain the 'better class of visitor'.[3] Roles could even be reversed: Blackpool was 'a favourite, salubrious and fashionable resort' for 'respectable families' as late as 1835, while at Lytham in 1825, later to outshine it in social pretensions, 'if the company is less fashionable than at

*First published in Northern History XI, 1976 for 1975.

70

Blackpool, it is generally more numerous and usually very respectable'.[4] In 1900 a local newspaper was still arguing:

It is not mere numbers that Morecambe wants, but quality – a class of visitors who will do credit to the town, of the paying sort, and who will find their recreation in the natural beauties of the place rather than the attraction provided by enterprising public caterers.[5]

The social tone could be gauged in many ways: in the prices charged by the hotels and boarding houses (higher in Southport than Blackpool, higher in Brighton or Bournemouth than either); in the average rateable value of the residences; in the occupational structure of the town as shown by the Census returns (the percentage of 'gentlemen', rentiers and retired persons and the proportion of servant-keeping households); in the character and scale of the public buildings, parks, gardens and other amenities; in the types of entertainment provided, whether classical concerts, expensive indoor baths, art galleries and museums, or brass bands, donkey rides, beach entertainers and catchpenny amusements. Perhaps the most certain way to judge is with one's own eyes, from old paintings and photographs: contrast the elegant costumes, impressive buildings and invalid chairs of turn-of-the-century Southport with the cloth caps, close-packed boarding houses, and beach donkeys of Blackpool.[6] It would take a great deal more research to establish these differences, especially in quantitative terms, even for the leading seaside resorts of England, and the result would still be merely descriptive. This paper has a different question to ask and to attempt to answer. Why and how did these differences of 'social tone', which we can still recognize down to the present day, come into existence and change over time?

At first sight it would seem that geography played the largest part. Given that the Victorian resorts owed their rapid growth, though not always their origin, to the railways, those which were more accessible in terms of time and fares to the great cities and industrial towns were likely to be the more popular; and popularity with the lower strata of society would drive the higher further on, as it did in the residential areas of their home towns, to seek the more congenial company and psychological security of their own kind at greater distance and expense. Thus Brighton and Southend were more popular, and had a lower social tone, than Bournemouth and Torquay, which were beyond day-tripping distance. More than that: since the terminus for Southend was nearer the East End of London and that for Brighton in the West End, the former acquired a lower social tone than the latter. Similarly, when the Chester and Holyhead Railway opened up the north Welsh coast in 1850, 'It was like a gold rush',[7] and resorts sprang into existence along its whole length; the property speculation was more golden the further west you went, arguably because the higher fares from Lancashire and the Midlands graded the holiday makers by ability to pay. Certainly, the social tone, the quality of the public buildings and amenities, and the hotel and boarding house charges rose from Prestatyn through Rhyl and Colwyn Bay to 'the swagger Welsh resort', dignified Llandudno.[8]

Yet there are difficulties with this explanation. Even when they were nearly equidistant from their chief source of visitors, two resorts might have a very different social tone. Scarborough and Skegness are practically the same distance from the West Riding, but in social tone they were and are worlds apart. And what of the inland resorts, often much nearer like Harrogate or Buxton, which retained their aristocratic air down to recent times, and were never deluged by the 'vulgar mob'? Of course, the spas, centred on the bath and the pump room, the assembly room and concert hall, could never have accommodated the crowds of the railway age, while the seaside resorts could be as accommodating as the length of beach and promenade allowed. The railways turned Harrogate , Buxton and Leamington into high–class residential towns for the retired and suburbs for wealthy commuters. But why did some seaside towns, near enough to the industrial areas for commuters and therefore near enough for day trippers, become wealthy suburbs and high–class resorts, whereas the others next-door became day trippers' delights and, eventually, working-class resorts?

The north-west coast of England puts the whole theory to the test, since it was the nearest coast to any great industrial area and the whole of it was within day-tripping distance of the first area to produce large numbers of working-class holiday makers. For reasons connected in part with the early factory legislation, confined to cotton, but more with their early start in the new industrial society with its higher wages and more urgent need for a complete break not only from work but from the whole industrial environment, the cotton towns, both masters and workers, got the seaside habit long before the railways came. Catherine Hutton found at Blackpool in 1788 Lancashire gentry, opulent Liverpool merchants, Manchester manufacturers and 'a species called Boltoners. . . rich, rough, honest manufacturers of the town of Bolton, whose coarseness of manner is proverbial even among their own countrymen'.[9] Richard Ayton found there in 1813 'crowds of poor people from the manufacturing towns, who have a high opinion of the efficacy of bathing . . . Most of them come hither in carts, but some will walk in a single day from Manchester, distant more than forty miles'. At Poulton-le-Sands, later to be Morecambe, he found every house crowded with cart-loads of people, both middle-class and working, from nearby Lancaster and beyond, and had to sleep on 'a chaff bed in a hole at the top of the house'.[10] Blackpool and Lytham in August 1824 'never witnessed such crowds of visitors of various social classes as continued to flock to them in search of health, pleasure and relaxation. Cottages for six accommodated twenty or thirty, and no less than a hundred carts containing on an average eight persons each passed through Clifton Turnpike on Saturday and Sunday'.[11] Even Bootle, 'a pleasant marine village' three miles from Liverpool in 1825, 'much resorted to in the summer season as a sea-bathing place', had become by 1853:

A wholesale *Washing Station*; myriads of 'the unwashed' from the purlieus of Liverpool repair to this spot, and at high water boldly advance into the sea, male and female promiscuously, each supplied with a square piece of yellow soap fastened to the right hand by means of a piece of string, and set to work scrubbing themselves and each other in a manner truly gratifying to behold: – the mighty ocean is frequently tinged for miles, after one of these operations, with mud and soap-suds.[12]

Sea bathing had thus begun spontaneously all along the coast in the late eighteenth and early nineteenth century, and had been catered for just as spontaneously by local farmers, fishermen and inn-keepers, who opened their houses to visitors, built huts to shelter the bathers and later boarding houses, hotels and other amenities. In exactly the same way inn-keepers from the nearby villages of Poulton-le-Fylde and Churchtown had founded Blackpool in the 1750s and Southport in the 1790s.[13] Yet the one became, by the end of the next century, the most famous working-class resort in England, the other 'the Montpellier of the North'. Lytham, nearer to Preston and the cotton towns and originally more popular than Blackpool, became a select residential resort. New Brighton and Fleetwood, deliberately planned in the 1830s as high-class holiday and residential resorts, came to be working-class day trippers' delights. Morecambe, on one side of the great Bay, tried to become a select resort and commuter terminus for West Riding business men, but became instead the Yorkshireman's Blackpool; Grange-over-Sands on the other side, just as accessible by rail from Yorkshire, remained the smallest and most select of the north-west resorts of note.

The railways are not the explanation, since they arrived at all the resorts except New Brighton, served by the Mersey ferries, and Grange-over-Sands, which had to wait until 1857, in the 1840s, most of them between 1846 and 1850. They certainly brought more visitors and residents, and a population surge much larger in some resorts than others, but they carried both middle- and working-class visitors, wealthy commuters and impecunious day trippers with equal alacrity. Nor does the explanation lie in the intentions as distinct from the methods of the founders or original community of holiday traders; in every case they set out to attract as high a class of visitor as they could, since the rich paid more and stayed longer. The residents of Blackpool, Lytham, Southport and Morecambe in the early years all successfully petitioned their local railway companies to stop Sunday day trips not purely from sabbatarian motives but because they thought that rowdy day trippers, bringing their own 'baggin' (eatables) and spending little except on drink, would drive away 'the better class of visitor'. And everywhere, including Blackpool, Morecambe and New Brighton, the local authorities strove to regulate and restrict the 'anti-social' behaviour of working-class visitors and the street-traders, stall holders and amusement purveyors who catered for them.

The explanation lies, in each resort, in the social character of the resident community which came into existence there, and in the nature of the élite which dominated it; or, rather, of the competing élites, for in every case there was conflict over what sort of provision, especially of amusements and amenities, should be made for visitors, and it was the kind and quality of these which determined what social level of visitors and settlers would be attracted. Each resort has its own peculiar history and evolution, but in general the most important factor in determining the social tone was the competition for domination of the resort by large, wealthy residents, hotel keepers and providers of 'genteel' entertainments such as concert halls and bathing establishments; by small property owners, boarding-house keepers, and purveyors of cheap amusements; and, later in the century, by large, capitalist enterprises, usually financed from outside, providing cheap, spectacular entertainment for a mass public. The last element can usually be explained in terms of the first two: outside capital did not invest in largescale developments like the Blackpool Tower complex, the New Brighton Tower and Recreation Company or the Morecambe Winter Gardens until there was a reliable mass clientele, by which time the social tone was already established. The primary distinction, therefore, is between those resorts with predominantly large hotels, grandiose public buildings, genteel gardens and entertainments, and a high proportion of residents of independent means or business commuters, and those with predominantly small hotels and cheap boarding houses, a great variety of catchpenny amusements and, eventually, mass entertainment complexes. And this takes us back a surprisingly long way, to the origins of each resort, the original distribution of the land and the terms and conditions under which it was sold or leased.

The point can best be made in relation to Blackpool and Southport. Both began spontaneously, as we have seen, with the provision of sea-bathing accommodation by local innkeepers. But whereas the South Hawes sand dunes where William Sutton erected his wooden bathing house in 1792 and the original South Port Hotel in 1798 were unenclosed and owned by the joint lords of the manor, the related Bold and Fleetwood Hesketh families, Layton Hawes where Blackpool's half-dozen innkeepers provided accommodation for bathers was enclosed by an Act of 1767, and shared out between 108 proprietors the biggest of whom were the Cliftons and the same Fleetwood Heskeths as had a half share in Southport.[14] Sutton and other squatters at Southport quickly made their peace and took leases from the lords of the manor, who obtained a private act in 1825 to redistribute the land between themselves in two compact blocks and at the same time laid out Lords Street (as it then was) as a spacious avenue, 88 yards wide, with large leasehold plots on either side, chiefly to accommodate the higgledy-piggledy buildings erected by the original squatter-leaseholders. By this accident, and the policy of the ground landlords in enforcing covenants against industrial or offensive commercial development, Southport became a resort of large hotels, residential villas, genteel public and large private gardens. Its leading citizens, who in due course took over the control and development of the resort from the Fleetwood Heskeths and Sir Charles Scarisbrick, who bought out the Bold-Hoghtons in the early 1840s, were gentlemen of independent means and substantial traders and hotel-keepers. The Improvement Commissioners under the 1846 Act included five 'gentlemen', five clergymen, eight substantial traders and two doctors. Under their guidance and that of their successors on the Local Board and Borough Council from 1852–94, Southport became a high-class resort, a residence for retired cotton manufacturers, coal-owners and other successful business men, and from the arrival of the two railways in 1848 and 1855 a commuter suburb for Liverpool and Manchester.[15] And since middle-class residents and visitors long remained more profitable than working-class, Southport grew much faster than Blackpool, from 4,243 in 1851 to 18,176 in 1871 (as compared with 2,503 and 7,092) and was still ahead in 1901, with 48,046 (as against 47,348).

Blackpool, on the other hand, began as a community of small freeholders, and became more so as time went on. In the tithe award of 1838 there were only 24 holdings over 25 acres, and most of these inland, away from the sea front. Thomas Clifton, engaged in developing Lytham as a high-class resort, sold his Blackpool lands in the late 1840s. Sir Peter Hesketh Fleetwood, hard-pressed by the founding of his new town of Fleetwood, got rid of his small estate there between 1834–45; one notorious area, Bonny's Estate, to John Bonny, a hotel-keeper and farmer, who carved it up into small building plots for sea-front boarding houses and back-street cottage property. By such development the whole central area of Blackpool became an ill-planned mass of small properties, boarding houses, small shops, working-class terraces, and so on, with no space for the grand public buildings, broad avenues and gardens of Southport. Not that this meant that Blackpool welcomed working-class trippers and visitors with open arms. On the contrary, even the small hoteliers and boardinghouse keepers saw their main clientele, down to the 1870s and beyond, as coming from the lower middle-class, and regarded working-class day-trippers, who brought them no trade, and even the 'padjamers', working-class overnight visitors, who came during the brief Lancashire Wakes, with abhorrence. They successfully petitioned the railway company to cease Sunday excursions, though not trips by regular trains, from 1856 until the 1870s. The Local Board of Health from 1853 and the Borough Corporation from 1876 obtained by-laws to control and restrict the behaviour of rowdy, drunken and 'immoral' (nude-bathing) visitors and the activities of the street and beach traders, amusement and donkey proprietors, and cab and boat hirers who catered for them.[16]

But the working-class trippers and 'padjamers' continued to come, and increased enormously between the 1870s and the 1890s, when the great price fall brought a corresponding rise in real wages and a disproportionate rise in disposable income for pleasure trips and holidays. With them expanded the numbers and relative proportion of holiday traders catering for them, the cheaper boarding-house and café proprietors, the beach entertainers, the street vendors, the gypsies and fairground operators. As John Walton has shown, when the Corporation drove the traders from the promenade they took to the beach below the high-water mark; when it bought the foreshore and drove them from the beach they hired the front gardens of the sea-front boarding houses for their stalls and booths, thus originating the famous 'Golden Mile'. By the late 1890s enough local ratepayers had acquired an interest, direct or indirect, in catering for working-class holiday makers to defeat any further attempt to halt or reverse the evolution of central Blackpool into a working-class playground.

Outside the central area, protected by distance from the trippers and the noisy amusements, the South and North Shores maintained a quiet and decorous middle-class tone and even a share in the lucrative year-round provision for retired residents. The North Shore especially was aided in this by well-tried devices operated in the more select resorts, the use of covenants in sales and leases forbidding commercial or other noisome development, as in Claremont Park, and the closing of a residential area to the unwelcome poorer classes by the charging of tolls, as in the North Shore estate developed by the Land, Building and Hotel Company of 1863.[17] Blackpool thus retained a stake in the middle-class holiday and residential market, but its main social tone was set by its exuberant, irresponsible working-class heart.

From its early popularity and nearness to Preston and the central Lancashire cotton towns one might have expected Lytham to develop on the same lines at Blackpool. But the Thomas Clifton who sold his Blackpool acres in the 1840s did so to invest in his main estate at Lytham where, after obtaining a branch line in 1846, he began to develop a high-class residential resort. He leased most of the area to a land company of which he remained the principal shareholder, which leased out only large plots for villas and hotels under the strictest covenants against industrial or commercial usage. At St Annes, still nearer to Blackpool, his neighbour J.T. Talbot did the same a generation later, leasing his land in 1875 for 1,100 years to a similar land company.[18] At Lytham St Annes, as the two became, the residents of independent means and the well-to-do commuters became more powerful in the local community than the holiday traders, and it remained a small, select residential resort with a few genteel amenities, chiefly gardens and concerts, for middle-class holiday makers, and from when the trams arrived in the late 1890s, parasitic for more exciting amusements upon Blackpool.

Fleetwood, on the other side of Blackpool, had the reverse evolution, from a would-be St. Leonard's to a sort of poor man's Blackpool. It began from Sir Peter Hesketh Fleetwood's grandiose project for a new town which would be at once a high-class resort, a ferry port for Ireland and Scotland and a fish dock at the terminus of his Preston and Wyre Railway. The Prospectus of 1837 proclaimed:

It has long been a matter of surprise that Lancashire, with its immense wealth and population, should not possess any Watering Place of the character of those in the South . . . It has been determined by Mr Hesketh Fleetwood to have that portion of his estate at Rossall on Morecambe Bay laid out in the style of Brighton and St. Leonard's.

Decimus Burton, son of the designer of St Leonard's, was engaged to plan the model resort, and laid out the residential area with wide streets and large plots for imposing villas. Zenon Vantini, proprietor of the Victoria and Euston Hotels in London, opened a first-class hotel, the North Euston. 'Handsomely furnished dwelling houses' on Queen's Terrace were let by the month or season to 'fashionable arrivals'. For a few years, from 1840 to 1846, Fleetwood was the only resort on the coast with a railway, and until the Carlisle-Glasgow line was opened in 1848 was part of the main route to Scotland, via the steamers to Ardrossan, which Queen Victoria used in 1847. For that brief period Fleetwood was a fashionable resort.[19]

From then onwards, however, its status began to decline, and much of the planned resort was never completed. The branch lines to Blackpool and Lytham from 1846 took the working-class trippers and middle-class visitors to more exciting or less industrial places, and Fleetwood concentrated on its port and fisheries. By 1861 only about one in 25 of the heads of households were in the holiday trades, compared with one in 5 or 6 in Lytham, and there were only 17 lodging-house keepers. The local authority only emphasized the holiday trade when the port and the fishing were depressed, as in the 1890s when a *Guide* extolled the 'many natural advantages which make it an excellent and enjoyable seaside resort especially for those who require a quiet and undisturbed sojourn by the sea without the turmoil and buzz of the busy throng of more pretentious watering places' – in other words, without their amenities, too.[20]

After the tramway from Blackpool was opened in 1898 Fleetwood received some overspill visitors and day sightseers, and began to offer more attractions, such as concerts in the Mount Pavilion, amusements in Warrenhurst Park, and the long-awaited Pier. But the welcome for the holiday maker, and especially the day tripper, was always grudging, the shopkeepers refused to open on Sundays or Bank Holidays, and a scheme for a marine lake, recreation grounds and public baths costing only £2,000 was turned down in 1900 on the grounds of expense. When the fishing industry improved again in 1907 Fleetwood forgot its pretensions to be a holiday resort until the inter-war depression.[21]

Morecambe was a similar, though later and less successful, case to Blackpool. Until 1850 it consisted of the fishing village of Poulton-le-Sands, where a few fisherman, farmers and inn-keepers provided accommodation for the bathers who came in ephemeral crowds at the August spring tides. In 1850 the only large landowner, Roger Taylor, died and his estate was sold by auction in small lots, the largest, about 200 acres, going to the 'little North Western' Railway Company which had opened a branch to Poulton in 1848 and now planned a harbour for shipping out Carnforth pig iron and for the Irish ferries. It also built a hotel with a protective sea wall and began to advertise 'eligible building land at Morecambe' – thus transferring the name of the Bay to what was to become a town centre of the new resort.[22] The development was to be tightly controlled to maintain a high standard, and 'Houses will be immediately erected on a uniform plan laid down by the company'.[23] But the attempt to establish a company town reckoned without the small farmers and fisherman of Poulton, which one of the Railway Company directors was to call 'one of the most ill-regulated and dirty villages in the neighbourhood'. When the next 250 acres of the Taylor estate came up for auction in October, it was bought in small parcels by a group of local men, none of them major landowners, who proceeded along with other leading ratepayers to petition for a Local Board of Health, which they obtained in 1852, ostensibly because of 'the filthy state of the township' but mainly to wrest control from the Railway Company.[24]

In this they succeeded, partly because the 'little North Western' was taken over in the early 1860s by the Midland Railway, which moved the pig iron export and Irish ferries to Barrow. Since they regarded working-class holiday-makers as at best 'birds of passage whose residence does not extend over more than two or three days', they naturally set out , like the Railway Company, to attract their 'betters', and as early as 1853 the Lancaster Gazette was reporting that 'the middle class of people have erected comfortable and substantial houses for the reception of visitors'.[25] The line through Skipton to the West Riding offered a hinterland more accessible to Morecambe than to the rest of the south Lancashire resorts, and this connection, both for people and for capital investment, led Morecambe to be known as 'Bradford by the Sea'.[26] Besides visitors and retired residents the railway began in 1875 to carry commuters by a two-hour daily service to Bradford and Halifax.

Yet Morecambe grew much more slowly than Blackpool or Southport, from 1,301 in 1851 to 18,783 in 1900, and despite all the efforts of the Local Board and local and Yorkshire business men in providing gas, water and electric light, two piers, two miles of promenade, and Summer and Winter Gardens, they could not maintain the social tone they wanted, or keep away the day trippers, 'a disorderly and riotous mob' as the *Lancaster Guardian* described them in 1868.[27] As at Blackpool, from the 1870s the 'back houses' began to take 'their usual numbers of the working class'.[28] In Morecambe's age of expansion, the 1880–90s, a prolonged debate occurred between the champions of 'respectability', who wished to restrict the street traders, beach entertainers and others who catered for the working-class trippers, and those who benefited by their custom, notably the licensed victuallers and the entertainment companies.[29] The debate was never quite resolved. As one local newspaper put it in 1898, in 'catering for the public fancy':

There was a happy medium . . . it was certainly unwise to make the quality so good as to be over the heads of three-quarters of the people; neither was it right to minister to those least refined, and in some cases also to the vulgar.[30]

Morecambe tried to sit on the fence but leaned unwillingly to one side. The *Daily Telegraph* summed it up in 1891: 'It may be that, to the fastidious, rough honest-hearted Morecambe is a little primitive, and slightly tinged with vulgarity. But it is never dull'.[31]

Grange-over-Sands also developed spontaneously from a coastal village with a wide distribution of small landholdings: in 1832 three-quarters of the land tax assessments were under 10s. But the effect was utterly different from Blackpool and Morecambe. Grange developed chiefly by the immigration of retired industrialists looking for small estates in the mild climate and splendid scenery on the Lake District side of Morecambe Bay, beginning perhaps with John Wilkinson, the famous ironmaster, who bought Castle Head in 1786. By 1866 the largest group of names in the local directory, 21 out of 49, were of 'esquires', 'gentlemen' and others of unspecified occupation, who drew to them as time went on the service trades catering for such a wealthy group.[32] The Lancaster and Ulverston railway arrived in 1857, more concerned with Furness iron than visitors, and cut off the water from the growing resort, so that the usual promenade boarding houses and amusements were frustrated.[33] Outside the three large hotels and private residences the sanitation and amenities were primitive. A visitor noted in the 1870s that 'Grange was shunned by many who will not give up the ordinary conveniences of life for beauty of site and serenity of climate'.[34] The railway company might provide 'a splendid station, capacious waiting room with every convenience, good refreshment rooms . . . [and] grounds well laid out and planted',[35] but its high-class inhabitants ensured that Grange, still with under 2,000 population in 1901, would never become a miniature Morecambe.

New Brighton is perhaps the greatest paradox, and the best test, of all. No resort could have started with better qualifications for a high-class residential resort or have ended the century with better for a day trippers' paradise, but it managed to succeed as neither, and eventually became a distressed gentlewoman of a Liverpool suburb. After Liverpool Corporation obtained an Act in 1829 to build a sea wall at the end of the Wirral to prevent the sea from breaking through to Wallasey Pool and endangering the safe Mersey anchorage, John Atherton, a speculative builder of Everton, and his son-in-law, William Rowson of Prescott, bought 170 acres of sandhills on the corner of the peninsula, on which to develop an 'attractive and fashionable watering place'. In 1832 they set up a land company whose prospectus, 'Eligible Investment at New Brighton, Cheshire', proposed to build a hotel and ferry and lay out a planned resort which would be the Brighton of the north, with large detached villas, a church, market place, reading room, baths, billiard room and post office.[36] By 1841 Granville noted 'the few clusters of houses and villas that have since been erected in this perfect desert . . . [like] a modern village overwhelmed in ashes after some dreadful catastrophe', but there were three 'superior' hotels and the better villas were 'not unlike some of the best houses at Brighton'. The steam ferry to Liverpool, at 6d. each way, kept out all but the wealthy classes.[37]

New Brighton came under the Local Board of Health set up for Wallasey in 1853, and thus became part of an urban district which shaded from the select watering place through the pretty suburb of Egremont to the working-class district of Seacombe, hard by the growing docks of the Pool, which cut off Wallasey from the ship-building town of Birkenhead. This was later to exacerbate New Brighton's schizophrenia, but for half a century the Local Board worked hard to provide gas, water, lengthening promenade, a succession of improved landing piers and all the facilities of a select resort, and even municipalized the ferries.[38] When the elegant Promenade Pier was opened in 1867 the *Illustrated London News* described New Brighton as 'a kind of marine suburb of the town of Liverpool' which 'also enjoys with Blackpool a fair share of the health-seeking visitors from Manchester and other manufacturing towns'.[39]

But the land company did not control the whole area. On the

corner of the peninsula where the Mersey met the sea, squatters built a collection of driftwood shacks housing beach entertainers, donkey and horse hirers, gypsy fortune tellers and cheap cafés, which became known as 'Devil's Nest' or 'Teapot Row', catering for the inevitable day trippers. In the 1870s a Manchester syndicate added to this a brick-built row of small shops and refreshment kiosks with boarding houses over, Aquarium Parade, which from its staple menu was nicknamed 'Ham and Egg Parade' and became notorious for its rowdiness, insobriety and prostitution. To this in 1880 was joined the Palace and the Pavilion, entertainment centres fronted by lock-up shops. Finally, the New Brighton Tower and Recreation Company was launched with Manchester and Blackpool capital to open in 1898 the tallest tower in Britain, a great wheel of the Earl's Court variety, and a huge amusement park.[40]

The local residents and competing traders were furious. One Liverpool newspaper condemned the investment: 'What is obtained in return, except possibly the added risk of attracting hordes of savages from the backwoods of Lancashire, who would invade and depreciate its residential value'.[41]. The local authority and the magistrates made life as difficult as possible for the Tower Company, refusing to license its bars beyond 10 p.m. when the pubs outside were open until 11 p.m., refusing joint cheap tickets for the ferry and amusement park which they offered for the Promenade Pier, overcharging for electricity, and other petty annoyances.[42] As a Blackpool visitor remarked in 1914, 'It looks to an outsider as though a certain section of the "great unpaid" in this locality were determined to stifle enterprise in the amusement business'.[43]

A more positive element in the opposition, the New Brighton Improvement Association founded in 1889, tried to beautify the resort with gardens, tree planting and an improved promenade, and to advertise it as a restful residential resort. But the Town Council did not issue its first official *Guide* until 1911 and in the next ten years spent only £1,000 on advertising compared with the Tower Company's £20,000. Its most drastic action was to purchase and demolish 'Ham and Egg Parade' in 1906 and replace it by a new Marine Promenade and Gardens. But it continued to harry the day trippers with by-laws against smoking, alcohol, foul language, running or even games in the parks and gardens.[44] As a satirist put it in 1912, 'Our aim . . . is to make New Brighton a place of restful gardens and sweet music, a sort of threshold to Paradise, where candidates for celestial glory could come and exercise their embryonic wings'.[45] There was, however, a real dilemma, as the next issue of the other local paper pointed out: 'The class of trippers doesn't do a lot to cheer the heart of the shopkeeper. What are we going to try to make New Brighton? Is it to be a Blackpool or a Bournemouth? It cannot be both'.[46] That was in fact New Brighton's epitaph: it could not be either. The two competing élites stultified each other. The Tower lost money and was demolished in 1921.[47] After a spirited advertising campaign between the wars, which still brought in more trippers than residential visitors, it became 'a dormitory for Liverpool and as much a suburb of that city as any on the Lancashire side of the Mersey'.[48]

The social tone of Victorian seaside resorts in the north-west, and by extension elsewhere, was a product of the competing elements in the social structure of the communities which created and were created by them. This in turn was, oftener than not, a product of the original pattern of land distribution, the type and size of the landowners and the policies they pursued in selling or leasing land for development. The resulting social tone was determined by the dominant élite, though it was not always quite what they intended; or, where there were competing élites, it was a compromise, by 'splitting the difference', by social zoning, or by sharing out the season between different types of holiday maker. But where, as in New Brighton, the élites would or could not compromise, the result was disastrous and the resort eventually failed completely.

## Notes

1 This paper is the product of joint research by M.A. students in Modern Social History at the University of Lancaster in 1971–2 and 1972–3. Credit is due in particular to the following who wrote their short dissertations on north-west holiday resorts: J. Gill, 'the Origin and Development of Grange-over-Sands as a Watering Place'; J. Grass, 'Morecambe: the People's Pleasure. The Development of a Holiday Resort, 1880–1902'; L. Gregory, 'The Role of Sea Bathing in the Development of Southport'; M. Hutchinson, 'The Catering for Holiday Makers at Fleetwood, 1840–1973'; A. Neil, 'Local Government and the Middle Classes in Southport, 1824–67'; B. Sandham, 'The Municipal Politics of a Mid-Victorian Seaside Resort: Southport, 1867–75'; C. Widdowfield, 'The Local Board of Health of Poulton, Bare and Torrisholme and the Development of Morecambe, 1852–94'; K. Wilson, 'Social Leaders and Public Figures in the Rise of Morecambe, 1880–1914'; M. Winstanley, 'Conflicting Responses to New Brighton's Role as a Popular Seaside Resort, 1896–1914'. Acknowledgement is also due to two other Lancaster University theses: J.H. Sutton, 'Early Fleetwood, 1835–47: a Study in the Genesis and Early Development of the new Town, Port and Holiday Resort of Fleetwood-on-Wyre, Lancashire' (M.Litt., 1968); and to draft chapters of J. Walton, 'Social Development of Blackpool in the 18th and 19th centuries' (Ph.D., 1974). While grateful for their help, I must not blame them for the interpretation which is entirely my own.

84   *The Structured Crowd*

2  A.B. Graville, *The Spas of England*, 2 vols. London, 1841, reprinted 1971, I, pp.346, 351; II, pp.14, 24, 376.
3  J. Walton 'Residential amenity, respectable morality, and the use of the entertainment industry: the case of Blackpool, 1860–1914', urban History Conference Bristol University, April 1974; and *The Blackpool Landlady*, Manchester, University Press, 1978.
4  *Preston Chronicle*, 20 June 1835; Edward Baines, *History Directory and Gazetteer of Lancashire*, Liverpool, 1825, II, p.53.
5  *Lancaster Observer and Morecambe Chronicle*, 9 March 1900.
6  Compare two booklets of contemporary photographs, J. Tarbuck, *Southport as it was,* Nelson: Hendon, 1972) and K. Eyre, *Bygone Blackpool,* Nelson: Hendon, 1971).
7  *Britain and the Beast,* (ed.) C. Williams Ellis, London: Dent, 1937, p.166.
8  *Wallasey News*, 9 September 1909: 'One may do things at New Brighton which one would not dream of doing at dignified Llandudno . . . Fancy a joy wheel at the swagger Welsh resort!' (quoted Winstanley, dissertation, p.23).
9  C.H. Beale, *Reminiscences of a Gentlewoman of the Last Century*, Birmingham, 1891, pp.56–7.
10  Richard Ayton, *A Voyage round Great Britain, undertaken in the summer of the year 1813*, 8 Vols, London, 1814–25, Vol 5.
11  *Lancaster Gazette*, 21 August 1824.
12  Baines, op. cit., II, p.712; H. Glazebrook, *Lights along the line,* Liverpool, 1853, p.8.
13  W.J. Smith, 'Blackpool: a Sketch of its Growth, 1740–1851', *Transactions of the Lancashire and Cheshire Antiquarian Society*, LXIX, 1959, pp.70–3; F.A. Bailey, *A History of Southport*, Southport: Angus Dolonie 1955, pp.29–30.
14  Bailey *ibid.*, pp.30, 36; Smith *op. cit.*, pp.74–5.
15  Bailey, *op. cit.*, esp. chaps 5 and 8; Neil, dissertation, passim; Sandham, dissertation, passim.
16  Smith, *op.cit.*, pp.98–101; Walton, Ph.D. thesis.
17  Walton, Ph.D. thesis and conference paper.
18  J. Porter, *The History of the Fylde of Lancashire,* Fleetwood and Blackpool, 1976, reprinted Wakefield: E.P. 1968, pp.429–53.
19  Sutton, thesis, pp.121–7, 222–3, and passim.
20  Hutchinson, *op.cit.*, pp.9–14, 17–18; *A Pictorial Guide to Fleetwood,* Fleetwood, 1893, p.3.
21  Hutchinson, *op. cit.*, pp.17–37.
22  R.G. Armstrong, 'The Rise of Morecambe, 1822–62', *Transactions of Historic Society of Lancashire and Cheshire,* c, 1948, pp.147–75; Widdowfield, dissertation, pp.1–4.
23  *Lancaster Gazette,* 27 July, 7 September 1850.
24  Widdowfield, dissertation, pp.4–6; William Lee's Report to General Board of Health, 1851, p.5.
25  *Lancaster Gazette*, 3 June 1860, 11 June 1853.
26  For the role of 'Yorkshire money' in the development of Morecambe, see Grass, dissertation, chap. 3 and appendix 1.
27  Widdowfield, dissertation, pp.18–20; *Lancaster Guardian,* 22 August 1870.
28  *Lancaster Observer and Morecambe Chronicle,* 25 July 1873, commenting on a fall in the 'usual numbers of the working class'.
29  For the whole 'respectability' debate, see Grass, dissertation, chap. 4.
30  *Lancaster Observer and Morecambe Chronicle,* 15 July 1898.
31  Reprinted in *ibid.*, 11 September 1891.

32 Gill, dissertation, pp.33–5.
33 A. Harris, 'The Seaside Resorts of Westmorland and Lancashire North of the Sands in the 19th century', *Transactions of Historic Society of Lancashire and Chesire*, CXV, 1963, pp.154–6.
34 Dr Amos Beardsley, Scrapbook, 1968–76, I, p.69, quoted Gill, dissertation, p.38.
35 *Ulverston Advertiser*, 20 January 1876.
36 Winstanley, dissertation, pp.6–8.
37 Granville, *op.cit.*, II, pp.10–14.
38 Winstanley, dissertation, pp.8–10.
39 *Illustrated London News*, 7 September 1867.
40 Winstanley, dissertation, pp.11–12, 17–21.
41 *Liverpool Shipping Telegraph*, 13 June 1898.
42 Winstanley, dissertation, pp.29–36, 43–4.
43 *Wallasey and Wirral Chronicle*, 24 June 1914.
44 Winstanley, dissertation, pp.36–8, 41–9.
45 Letter in *Wallasey News*, 3 August 1912.
46 *Wallasey and Wirral Chronicle*, 7 August 1912.
47 Winstanley, dissertation, p. 41.
48 N. Ellison, *The Wirral Peninsula*, London: Hale, 1973, p.9.

# 6

# SOCIAL CHANGE AND THE NOVEL, 1840–1940*

AT first sight, the changes which took place in Britain between 1840 and 1940 were no less than the making of modern industrial society. Of course, the Industrial Revolution of the previous 60 years or so had laid the foundations: the first factories, the new smokey industrial towns, the first few railway lines, the first steamships, the first real trade unions and class-based political movements – the first Parliamentary Reform Act (1832), the Chartists (1836), the Anti-Corn Law League (1838) – and so on. But in 1840 there were far more people working in agriculture that in any single industry, even in cotton, the only industry in which the factory predominated (and only just); and there were far more people in domestic service (the second occupation in size) than in factories of all kinds. The factory system had still to conquer woollens, silk, linen, hosiery and lace, engineering and the metal trades, even the making of clothes, and it took most of the nineteenth century and a good part of the twentieth to take over most industries. Factory-made dresses for 'ladies' and suits for 'gentlemen', for example, only came in after the Second World War. Agricultural workers did not begin to decline in total numbers until after 1851, domestic servants until after 1891 – and then only slowly in both cases – and, curiously enough, factory workers (even if we include miners as being in a sort of underground 'factory') never did become a majority of the occupied population.

Again, in 1840 the railways had only just begun. The first modern passenger railway, between Liverpool and Manchester, opened in 1830, the London to Birmingham and the Grand Junction on to the Liverpool and Manchester in 1837, the Glasgow to Edinburgh in 1838. Most of the cities of Britain had still to be linked by rail, and the enormous social effects of rapid communication of *The Age of the Railway* were still to come: the nationalization of politics with national leaders addressing local meetings, the growth of a national press, cheap 'railway editions' of novels and other books, the growth of the 'railway suburbs' and the increasing segregation of the social classes, the growth of national trade unions, national employers' associations, national professional bodies, national reform movements like the temperance movement or the university exten-

* Given as the opening lecture at the Scottish Universities' International Summer School, University of Edinburgh, 1977, 1978 and 1979.

sion lectures, even the new, reformed public boarding schools, all depended on the railway.

In 1840, too, the rise of democracy was still a dream to the Chartists and other radicals. Only about one adult male in seven (and no woman) had the Parliamentary vote (even though the 1832 Act doubled the numbers), and it would take the Acts of 1867, 1884 and 1918 to give every man over 21 the vote, and the Acts of 1918 and 1928 every woman over 21. Not surprisingly, the welfare of the working class was not the first thing on the government's mind, and when it was, as in the New Poor Law of 1834, it was to deny poor relief to the able-bodied poor (what we call the unemployed) except in the dreaded workhouse. The first major Factory Act (the Ten Hours Act, 1847), the first Health of Towns Act (1848), the first Adulteration of Foods Act (1860), the first Housing Act (1875), laying down minimum standards for working-class houses, the first state hospitals and dispensaries for non-paupers (1885), and of course the whole rise of the Welfare State from the Liberal reforms (Old Age Pensions and National Insurance) of 1908–11 to the Beveridge Report of 1942, were all in the future.

True, industrialism had already made Britain the richest and most powerful country in the world, with the highest average standard of living, the largest export trade, the most powerful navy and, as a by-product of that wealth and power, the largest empire the world had ever seen. Moreover, Britain's power and wealth extended far beyond that formal empire, the parts painted red on the map, to the informal trading empire which included North and South American, China and large parts of Southern Asia and Africa. Yet at home many Britons did not feel wealthy or powerful: by our standards the majority were distinctly poor, and even by the standards of the 19th century probably between a third and a half of the population lived below the poverty line. Indeed, in 1840 the British economy was in the middle of the worst depression of the century, which reached its trough in 1842, and helped to give the name to the 'hungry forties'. In fact, the name was invented by a free trader in the early years of this century, Cobden's son-in-law, T. Fisher Unwin who published a collection of contemporary letters and accounts in 1904, *The Hungry Forties: Life under the Bread Tax,* to counter Joseph Chamberlain's campaign for imperial preference and tariff reform. The 1840s we now know, were less hungry than earlier decades and after 1842 began the rise of 'mid-Victorian prosperity'. Still, the depression of the early 1840s was bad enough to make both the working and middle classes very discontented and support the mass meetings of the Chartists and the Anti-Corn Law League.

By contrast, in 1940 – or rather in the 1930s, since in 1940 we were within 21 sea-miles (34 kilometres) of defeat by Hitler – Britain was a much richer and more compassionate country, if in comparative terms a much less powerful one. Average living standards had more than trebled in real terms (from less than £20 a year at 1913 prices to about £60), and this could be seen in the better food, better clothing, better houses with better furniture, radios, carpets, gas and electricity, more and better schools, shops, parks, the new cinemas, holiday camps, cars for the few, bicycles and buses for nearly everybody, described in my *Age of the Automobile*. It is true that there was, especially in the early 1930s, the worst slump of the 20th century and record unemployment, but because of the new state insurance even the unemployed of the inter-war years were better off than many of the employed labourers before the First World War. Wages were higher, prices were falling, families were smaller (two children instead of five or six) and wages went further, working hours were shorter, holidays were longer and mostly with pay from 1938, the expectation of life had doubled, and more than doubled for women, and infant mortality was much less than half that of the Victorian age.

There was still poverty, of course, even by Victorian standards: about 4 per cent of the population of York in 1936, about 9 per cent of the population of London in 1929, but this was less than half the percentage of the late Victorian age, and the degree of poverty was not so harsh. Moreover, there were now the makings of a Welfare State, at least for the working class: old age pensions since 1908, health insurance since 1911, unemployment insurance for some since 1911 and for most since 1923, widows' and orphans' pensions since 1925, and the Poor Law itself had been abolished in 1929 and replaced by local government Public Assistance. By 1942 Sir William Beveridge could say in his *Report* that the state provided for most of the varieties of need arising from the interruption of earnings in modern industrial communities. The old Poor Law infirmaries had become county and city hospitals, the next step in a national health service which began with the panel doctor service for insured workers in 1911. Housing Acts from 1909 but especially after the First World War had begun to provide subsidized 'council houses', with bathrooms and indoor lavatories, for many working-class families. State education, universal since 1870, free since 1890, with scholarships to the grammar school for bright working-class and other children since 1907, still did not provide 'secondary education for all' until 1944, but did allow a few working-class children (more than in Europe) to go to university. To pay for all this, income tax, introduced in 1841 at 7d (3p) in the £, had risen to 4s.6d – 5s. (22½p – 25p) in the 1930s and 7s.6d (37½p) in 1940, plus a surtax on high incomes which could rise to 10s (50p) in the £. Though the term Welfare State was not coined until the Second World War and not consciously put into practice until 1948, the four main pillars, social security, a health service, educational opportunity and graduated taxation, were all in place by 1940.

True, Britain was no longer the only workshop of the world, and for the first time since Napoleon was no longer piling up enormous balance of payment surpluses on foreign trade every year, but we still had very large currency reserves, and *less* unemployment than the US, Germany and most other industrial countries, and we were second only to the US in average standard of living. We still had the empire, which was even larger in theory than in the Victorian age, covering about a quarter of the world's land area and population, though in practice the white Dominions were already independent, and the major colonies were being slowly prepared for a distant independence. The Royal Navy was no longer the most powerful: since the Washington agreement of 1922 it was ostensibly equal to the American and 40 per cent bigger than the Japanese, but compared with its world-wide tasks it was weaker than the American and in the Far East inferior to the Japanese. Moreover, Britain, a small offshore island, was thought to be more vulnerable to the aerial bomber than any other major country: nearly two million casualties (one-third of them killed) were expected in the first 60 days of a European war – which explains why Neville Chamberlain was ready to appease Hitler at Munich.

In brief, by 1940, or its eve, Britain was still a major power, head of the world's largest ever empire, still the leading financial centre, the third largest industrial producer, the second richest country measured by average living standards, one of the leading countries in the evolution of a Welfare State, and a far, far more comfortable place to live in than the Britain of 1840.

Yet it might be argued from another point of view that, fundamentally, very little had changed. To a social historian who looks below the superficial improvements in living standards, social welfare and the parliamentary franchise at the underlying realities of the social structure, the most striking fact is the extraordinary unity of the period 1840–1940. From start to finish it was a class society, based on crude and extreme inequalities of wealth, status and power. What society, especially what industrial capitalist society, is not, you may ask? In degree at least, the societies which came before 1840 and after 1940. In 1840, as I have shown in my book on *The Origins of Modern English Society*, Britain had only just evolved into a full-blown class society. Pre-industrial society, I argued there, was an unequal society intensely conscious of differences in wealth and status, but it was not *class*-conscious, as is clear from the absence of trade unions, employers' associations, class-based political movements, and the like. These came into existence during the Industrial Revolution, with the growth of industrial capitalism (not all of it in the factory system), with the expansion of towns free from the paternal guidance and discipline of the traditional aristocracy, and with the breakdown of the landowners' paternalistic control even in the countryside.

From about the end of the Napoleonic Wars, the landed ruling aristocracy came to be consciously challenged, over control of Parliament, over taxation and the Corn Laws, over the Church and its tithes, and even, ineffectually, over the laws by which they held their property, by the emerging capitalist and working classes. The turmoil, occasionally rising to violent conflict in the streets between rioters and troops, was still going on in the 1840s, but what I have called the viable class society of Victorian Britain, a society in which conflict was settled by negotiation (including industrial strikes) rather than by violence, was already coming into being. Its main feature was that each class, the landed upper class, the capitalist middle class and the wage-earning working class (there was no peasant class in Britain, outside the Scottish and Welsh highlands at least) accepted the other classes' right to exist and to bargain over their share of the national income and political power. Their bargaining power, of course, was very unequal, though the two lesser classes gradually levelled it up on the political side by successive reforms of Parliament and central and local government and on the economic side by the evolution of a powerful trade union movement. Indeed, on the political front they slowly wore down the monopoly of the landed aristocracy, who lost their majority in the House of Commons from 1886, in the Cabinet from 1905, the veto powers of the House of Lords in 1911 and especially their ability to prevent unpleasant taxes like supertax and death duties. But their decline on the economic front was more apparent than real. The big landowners, contrary to popular opinion, grew richer rather than poorer, they joined the boards of capitalist companies, they diversified their investments into mines, railways, urban property development, colonial land, steel, shipping, motor engineering, banking, and other commercial enterprises. Some recent research I have done on top people in British society since 1880 shows that the successors of John Bateman's great landowners of 1879 are still amongst the richest and most successful of all the élites in Britain. (See Essay 9, especially appendix).

Since 1945, British society has changed greatly. The various classes, and especially the working class, no longer accept their place in an immutable class society. They do not take it for granted that 'the rich man in his castle, the poor man at his gate, God made them high and lowly and ordered their estate'; or even the capitalist in his villa or the office worker in his semi-detached. The manual wage-earners no longer accept that anyone should be rich, that the manager should have a much larger income, a free car and three hours for lunch, or the office worker shorter hours and longer holidays; they are demanding the *same* hours, the *same* holidays, pensions, canteen and restroom facilities, and even security of tenure and guaranteed earnings, which look very like a permanent salary. In fact, equality has gone so far that the skilled workers are complaining that the unskilled are *too* equal, and that their differential earnings and privileges must be restored. The reasons for all this are fascinating, and it may be that Britain, as it was the first country to go the work-oriented industrial society, is the first to break through to the leisure-oriented anti-work society, in which we all expect to live by exploiting each other. But that is not strictly relevant to literature and history, 1840–1940.

What it does mean for literature and history however, is that the century from 1840 to 1940 marks the zenith of the mature industrial class society in Britain. You can see it in the novels of the period, which are obsessed by class and the inequalities of wealth and power from beginning to end. At the beginning, the novels of Dickens, Mrs Gaskell and Disraeli are full of the shocked discovery of the brutal inequalities of class. Dickens' *Oliver Twist* (1837–8) or *Great Expectations* (1860–1) show the desperate importance of money and the cruel ways in which those with it treat those without it; *Hard Times* (1854) displays class conflict in all its naked violence (based on the Preston cotton strike of 1853). Mrs Gaskell, who lived in Manchester, describes in *Mary Barton* (1848) the vast gulf between the mill-lowners and the factory operatives, and the dire consequences of trying to bridge the gulf by love instead of marrying within your own class. Disraeli, who believed in the alliance of the aristocracy and the workers against the capitalists, tries in *Sybil, or the Two Nations* (1845) to prove the opposite and show that the Chartist's daughter can marry the landowner's brother, Charles Egremont, across the gulf of class, but then cheats by making her the real heiress of the land on which the town of Marney (Manchester) stands. It is very like Dickens' solution in *Oliver Twist,* where the lower-class hero turns out to belong to the propertied class after all, and happiness lies in being restored to your own class.

'Hypergamy' as Geoffrey Gorer called marriage across the barriers of class, or other relationships which cut across them, are what so many of the novels of the Victorian age are about. As Trollope says in *The Three Clerks,*

a man from the ordinary ranks of the upper classes, who has had the nurture of a gentleman, prepares for himself a hell on earth in taking a wife from any rank below his own – a hell on earth, and, alas! too often another hell elsewhere also. He must either leave her or loathe her . . . he will have to endure habits, manners, and ideas, which the close contiguity of married life will force upon his disgusted palate, and which will banish all love.

But at least he *could* marry her. A woman who married beneath her class was at best a laughing stock, at worst a social outcast and pariah.

Later novelists are just as obsessed with class, but explore it in greater depth and with more realism. George Eliot is concerned in *Middlemarch* (1871–2) with the varieties of social levels and values within the middle class, and, despite her emphasis on suffering and self-sacrifice, the plot turns on money again, and Dorothea's forfeiture of Casaubon's fortune if she marries Will Ladislaw – significantly, a maverick of Polish extraction who therefore rises above the English class system and its petty snobberies. Thomas Hardy is more pessimistic: *Tess of the D'Urbervilles,* his heroine of the people and true heiress (like *Sybil*) of the landed estate, wins only seduction, misery and a tragic death on the gallows from her attempt to recross the class barriers. Robert Louis Stevenson is apparently more concerned with individual psychology, and *Dr. Jekyll and Mr. Hyde* is a remarkable anticipation of Freudian schizophrenia; yet is it too fanciful to see in it a paradigm of the two increasingly opposed middle classes, the highly moral, caring unselfish professional class and the wicked, grasping, selfish capitalist? Kipling and Conrad chronicle the export of the English class system overseas: Kipling the stern, resourceful, paternalistic, empire-building public schoolboy of the 'white man's burden' and the rough but golden-hearted common soldiers (*Stalkey and Co.* and *Kim*); Conrad the broken characters and moral detritus of English class society (*Lord Jim* and *An Outcast of the Islands*), – in that age of imperialism it took a foreign observer, a Polish sea-captain, to see the seamier side of British empire-building.

At the end, the novelists are still more obsessed by class, but in a different way. H.G. Wells moves between humorous or sad chronicles of the lower middle class of clerks and shop-assistants (*Kipps*, 1905, and *The History of Mr Polly*, 1910), descriptions of English society in dissolution with the advent of the new rich (*Tono-Bungay*, 1909), and fantasies like *The Time Machine* (1895), which look like attempts to escape from modern capitalist society but culminate in its self-destruction (*The Shape of Things to Come*, 1933). D.H. Lawrence in his early and late novels (*Sons and Lovers*, 1913, *The Rainbow*, 1915, *Women in Love*, 1920, and *Lady Chatterley's Lover*, 1928) returns to the theme of marrying or loving across the class barriers – 'hypergamy', marrying above yourself – and explores not merely the social difficulties but the psychological tensions it causes.

These are writers from the lower side of the abyss. From the other side comes a new breed of desperate men, appalled at the decadence of their society and the decline of their own privileged class, and relieving their insecurity either in mocking, bitter satire (James Joyce, Evelyn Waugh, Aldous Huxley) or in strained concern (T.S. Eliot, W.H. Auden, J.B. Priestley, Richard Llewellyn, George Orwell) – or (in the last case) both. The mature class society between the wars had reached a neurotic, insecure, self-regarding, menopausal late middle age, by fits nostalgic for the supposed golden age of the Victorians and Edwardians – golden only for the few – guilty about the privileges and comforts of the few and coping with that guilt through the hedonistic escapism of the 'bright young things' and Martin Green's *Children of the Sun* (1977) (Evelyn Waugh, Harold Acton, Charles Cockburn) or the utopian escapism of the fashionable middle-class left (Auden, Spender, Hugh MacDiarmid, Christopher Isherwood, John Strachey), or apprehensive about the emerging materialism, totalitarianism and destructive militarism which might destroy their world *without* putting anything better in its place (Huxley, Wells, Orwell). Mature class society in short, had its young, middle-aged and elderly phases.

So there was social change between 1840 and 1940 after all. If the great social changes – the rise of industry, living standards, consumerism, democracy, the Welfare State, destructive militarism in the world outside – are superficial in comparison with the stability and persistence of the mature class society of Britain between 1840 and 1940, that does not mean that that class-ridden society did not vary at all.

For one thing there were important regional and indeed national variations. It was *English* society which was most snobbish and class-ridden, and the metropolitan society of London and the home counties most of all. Scotland and Wales were always different, more open and democratic, and national pride acted as a counterbalance to upper-class metropolitan (which they oversimplified as merely English) arrogance and snobbery. Snobbery is not a passive prejudice; it is an active device for 'putting people in their place', operated by the self-confident English public-school product against his 'inferiors', whether *petit-bourgeois* and working-class Englishmen or foreigners and colonials of all classes. It worked with the *petit-bourgeois* Englishmen and still more with their suburban wives. It worked less well with the English working class, who took it with a pinch of salt and a deflating mockery of 'la-di-da' accents and social pretensions, and sometimes with resentment, but they took it all the same. It worked much less well with the Scots and Welsh (and not at all with the Irish), who had their own culture, their own self-respect and, most important, their own education systems, which placed great emphasis on educational opportunity, on social mobility and on beating the English at their own game.

Consider the importance of Welsh and Scottish accents. One of the cruellest forms of snobbery perpetrated by the public school English was the use of a 'cut-glass' accent to put down their social inferiors. Until recently (until the 'Angry Young Men' of the late 1950s introduced real working-class actors onto the London stage in place of 'stage cockneys' and comic caricatures of working men, and until the Beatles and other pop stars of the 1960s made Liverpool 'scouse' and other regional accents superior assets), any English working-class boy or girl who did manage to get to university was forced to conform to the upper-class pattern of speech – Joan Bakewell tells a story of going into the lavatory in an Oxbridge college with a Yorkshire accent and coming out with a public school one, just in order to make her life there bearable.

Not so the Welsh or the Scots: they kept their accents however high they rose – consider Lloyd George or Ramsay MacDonald – and they were the more respected for it. The accent was a symbol of their national identity and relative freedom from the English class system, which indeed they manipulated to their own advantage: it was always easier for a Scot or a Welshman to climb the ladder of the London establishment than for any grammar schoolboy from the

English provinces. But even in Wales and Scotland the *upper* class conformed: they sent their sons to public schools and Oxbridge, they spoke with an English upper-class accent (Balfour, Macmillan, Douglas-Home), and they were treated at home as if they were English. (In a Welsh village I know well, the squire was an architect of national renown, with the very Welsh name of Clough Williams-Ellis, but he spoke with an English accent, married into the metropolitan left-wing establishment – the sister of John Strachey – and despite his paternalistic socialism was rejected as an agent of English culture by his Welsh nationalist villagers.)

By contrast, an English provincial accent was a handicap, and a Lancashire man or Midlander was more foreign to the English upper class than a European or an Asian. The image of the Englishman abroad, on the Continent, in America, in the ex-colonies, is an out-of-date caricature of the public school educated, reserved, 'effortlessly superior', overconfident man with a loud voice, used to giving orders. I remember finding myself at a party once with an American, a New Zealander, an Irishman and assorted Europeans, who began criticising 'the English' in these terms, expecting me to be provoked. In the end I said, 'The English you are describing are just as foreign to me as they are to you. To them you are, in Arnold Toynbee's terms, external barbarians. I am an internal barbarian.'

More important than regional differences were changes over time, since they would ultimately do more to undermine the stability of class society. One of these changes in the underlying structure I have already mentioned, the transformation of the landed aristocracy into an integral part of the capitalist plutocracy, which took place mainly between 1890 and 1920 when a quarter of the nobility acquired directorships of big companies. Many small landowners began to sell up, long before death duties began to bite, and there was a veritable 'flight from the land' between the wars, though not, as often supposed, into bankruptcy and poverty. Their independent political power certainly declined, and their party, the Conservatives, became chiefly the organ of business, big and small. But it would be wrong to underestimate their influence down to and beyond 1940. In 1940 itself Britain turned in her darkest hour to an offshoot of the ancient aristocracy, Winston Churchill, and since his two governments every Tory Prime Minister until Heath and Thatcher – Eden, Macmillan, Douglas-Home – came from or married into the landed aristocracy. But the decline of the political power of the landed class and its absorption into the capitalist plutocracy and the high professions was one of the most important social changes in the whole of British history.

At the other end of the social scale, another decline was occuring, little noticed but immensely important, which ran clean contrary to Marx's forecasts. Far from becoming larger and larger (and growing poorer and poorer), the manual working class was actually shrinking (and becoming more affluent). As a proportion of the occupied population it declined from 82 per cent in 1881 to 70 per cent in 1931 (and it would decline to 58 per cent by 1966). The reasons for this decline, at the very time when the working class was becoming far more organized in terms of mass trade unionism and the Labour Party, are complex, but it was chiefly because of the shift in a mature, late industrial society from manufacturing to services: commerce, banking, insurance, local and central government, education, medicine and other professions, shopkeeping, the hotel and catering trades, and the entertainment industry (music hall, theatre, cinema and radio).

This does not mean that the manual working class was becoming less influential. On the contrary, it was becoming more so. Organized labour in the form of trade union membership rose from 1.2 million in 1874 to over 8 million in 1920 (though it declined to 5 million or less between the wars), and the Labour Party rose from no MPs in 1900 and 29 in 1906 to form minority governments in 1924 and 1929–31. But all the time sons and daughters of the working class were quietly rising into the middle class and becoming clerks, secretaries, salesmen, foremen and managers, teachers, nurses, and professional people of all kinds. This upward mobility no doubt helped to stave off discontent, make class inequality more bearable for the able and ambitious, and reinforced the support for the Conservative Party, which held office for most of the period from 1886 to 1940. But in the longer term it was moving towards a different sort of society, what is now called post-industrial society, based on services rather than manufacturing, and on an educated, qualified, intellectual or at least non-manual labour force which would feel little or no solidarity with the manual working class.

Because of this shift in the economic and occupational structure of society, the people in between, the vaguely labelled and immensely variegated middle class, were changing most of all. Apart from the enormous growth of middle-class occupations, especially of the lower middle class of office workers, lower managers and lesser professions, it was becoming increasingly specialized and differentiated. In spite of the apparently simple tripartite model of industrial society, always divided, e.g., by Marx (aristocracy, *bourgeoisie,* proletariat) or Matthew Arnold (Barbarians, Philistine, Populace), into three broad classes, it was always far more complicated than that, and the complexity went deepest in the chief growth area, the middle class – important to us because it both produced and consumed most of the literature, much of it centred around middle-class life and the relations of middle-class characters with those from other classes. Leaving aside the enormous range of wealth, status and power between the top and bottom of the middle class, from the rich industrialists, bishops and judges down to the poorer shopkeepers, clerks and teachers, there had always been two parallel but distinct middle classes, which became more separate as that society aged. One was the traditional *bourgeoisie* in the Marxist sense of the capitalist business men, from rich bankers and millowners down to small shopkeepers and independent tradesmen. The other was the non-capitalist or professional middle class, from bishops, judges, medical consultants and high civil servants down to the teachers, nurses, and local government and other office workers. The rise of large-scale industry and commerce was reducing the first, the number of capitalist employers, and squeezing out the small business man and the self-employed, as Marx had forecast. But the second, the professional and salaried occupations, were expanding and proliferating like fruit flies in a genetics laboratory.

It was to this class that most of the social commentators of the period belonged: from John Stuart Mill, Carlyle, Matthew Arnold and Marx himself to John Strachey, G.D.H. Cole and H.N. Brailsford. Yet they all left themselves out of their mainly tripartite models of society. That is why I have called them the forgotten middle class. Marx, in so far as he thought of them at all, bracketed them either with the *petite bourgeoisie,* who would be ground between the upper and nether millstones of the capitalist and working classes, or with the 'workers by brain' whose role, as in Lenin's world, was to lead the masses to revolution. In fact, they did neither. Some joined the Labour Party (and a few the Communist Party) in that uneasy coalition of trade unionists and intellectuals in which the middle-class intellectuals told the genuine workers what to think, and accused them of 'false consciousness' if they did not; but the overwhelming majority increasingly voted Conservative. Far from becoming the spearhead of revolution they became the featherbed of complacent reaction.

It would be foolish to underestimate them, however. They are so easy to despise and to satirize in their suburban complacency that the left has always underestimated them. They were not only the main bulwark against revolution, they were also the wave of the future. It was they who pioneered the consumerism and the smaller family – 'man, wife and baby car' – of the inter-war period, but also the emphasis on education and qualifications, on expert service and the 'caring professions', which was to characterize post-war post-industrial society. The organized working class may not like it, but the unorganized have since voted with their feet and their wage packets for the same privatized, suburban life style. If the seeds of a new society grow within the body of the old, then the most important social change going on in the mature class society of 1840–1940 was the enormous expansion and differentiation of an educated, qualified, service-oriented, professional salariat which, if America sets the pattern, will soon become the majority of the occupied population, in Britain.

If I am right – and I do not necessarily approve of what I see – the conclusion to this analysis is paradoxical. The class society of 1840–1940 was a fertile field for literature (less fertile towards the end) because literature thrives on conflict, particularly on the sort of personal conflict which arises from relationships which cut across the bias of the social fabric. In the new, sanitized world of post-industrial society where every sort of conflict, between the races, between the sexes, between the generations as well as between the classes, becomes a 'social problem' to be solved by the Welfare State, with its own particular institutionalized 'caring profession' to solve it – the Race Relations Commission, the Equal Opportunities Commission, youth leaders and the whole battery of social work professions – conflict is a disease to be cured, not an inescapable aspect of human relations to be explored. That is perhaps why post-war literature has had to invent fictitious/factitious conflicts at the superhuman/less than human level in star-trekked outer space (the adolescent literature of science fiction), in the degenerate public schoolboy spy stories of Cold War fantasy (Ian Fleming's James Bond), in the equally wishful, if more adult sexual fantasies, upper and lower-class, of Iris Murdoch (*A Severed Head*) and Anthony Burgess (*A Clockwork Orange*).

The sad declension would seem to be: real, especially class conflict – great literature; unreal, factitious conflict – poor literature; soon, no conflict - no literature. But perhaps there will always be conflict of some kind, between the sexes, between the generations, between the races, or between just ordinary 'crossomical' human beings, for the author of genius to work on. Nevertheless, we should be grateful to our predecessors of 1840-1940 for suffering so much class conflict in order that we might enjoy the superlative harvest of their suffering.

# 7.

# LAND REFORM AND CLASS CONFLICT IN VICTORIAN BRITAIN*

DISRAELI told the House of Lords in 1880:

If I were asked to mention the two subjects which most occupy the thought of the country at the present moment, I should say one was the government of Ireland, and the other the principles upon which the landed property of this country should continue to be established;

and he reminded them of his

conviction – and it is a profound conviction – that the politics of this country, so far as internal affairs are concerned, will probably, for the next few years, mainly consist in an assault upon the constitutional position of the landed interest.[1]

After the renewed agrarian violence of the previous winter, Ireland's troubles were manifest, but it would have been beyond even Disraeli's political prescience to have foreseen the campaigns of Henry George or the burgeoning of the socialist societies of the 1880s. He was merely expressing a feeling widespread at the time that a crisis was impending in 'the land question' which would not be confined to Ireland. The *Manchester Guardian* talked of 'the prominent position which the land question has now reached', and prophesied that 'the stirring of the national mind which is already visible on this subject will before long translate itself into a call for action'.[2] *The Times* observed, 'Among the many questions with which the Liberal Government will have to deal in the new Parliament, those connected with land are by far the most important', and advised extreme caution.[3] Gladstone, with that enigmatic waywardness which at once encouraged and confused his followers, had declared that the state was in principle perfectly entitled to buy out the landowners if it became expedient to do so.[4] Bright, whose venerable elder statesmanship no one could call revolutionary, told his Birmingham constituents that 'the time is near in my opinion when the great landed monopoly of this country will be assailed, and when it will be broken into and broken up'.[5]

The prospect of a general attack on the land system induced what Justin McCarthy called 'the landowners' panic'[6] – the first of the

*Written about 1958 and first published in J. Butt and I.F. Clarke, (eds) *The Victorians and Social Protest*, Newton Abbot, David & Charles, 1973.

100

resignations which would eventually carry most of the Whigs out of the Liberal into the Conservative party. It was not so much 'land quacks', in Lord Derby's phrase, that they feared. Land nationalization had been advocated for a hundred years, from Thomas Spence to Herbert Spencer, without result, and Henry George had not yet crossed the Atlantic. Rather was it 'a new thing, and one of much significance . . . that thoughtful men and good citizens see much to be amended in the land laws'.[7] The danger lay in the appeal of land reform to classes already well-represented in the Commons, amongst whom there were many who looked forward with enthusiasm to alterations in the land laws which they believed would produce far-reaching changes in the distribution of property, and therefore in the structure of society. The Lords, under Disraeli's strategical direction, prepared to choose the least unpopular ground on which to meet the challenge of the Commons.

In the event, of course, nothing came of it. Apart from the legis-lative spring-cleaning of 1925, designed to adapt the forms of land law to the realities of land-ownership, there has never been a fun-damental reform of the land system.[8] The collision between Lords and Commons – expected for a further five or six years – was averted by the break-up not of the 'landed monopoly' but of the Liberal Party over Irish Home Rule. The land reformer who said that 'the people of this country can only grasp one, what may be called first-class, political question at a time',[9] backed the wrong one. The importunate irrelevance of Home Rule dragged the Radicals and land reformers from the high road just as their Canaan came in sight, to pass another generation in the wilderness. By then it was too late. Yet the land reform agitation deserves a place in history larger than the footnote it is usually accorded. It is the aim of this essay to claim for it a place nearer to the centre of the socio-political development of Victorian Britain and to discover what light it can throw into the fog which still clings around two of its major themes, the relations between the aristocracy and the middle classes, and the fission and incipient decline of the Liberal Party.

# I

What were the reasons for the impending crisis in the land question in 1880? No doubt the example of Ireland and the 'great depression' helped to precipitate it. The Irish question was pre-eminently one of land, and Cobden had prophesied that the end of prosperity would revive discontent with the land system in Britain. The landlord made an accessible scapegoat, but though they gave the opportunity and provided some of the steam, Ireland and the depression were not the main drive behind the agitation. The main drive must be sought, where it has traditionally been found, in the hostility of the middle classes towards the landed aristocracy. The clash of interests between landlord and manufacturer was as familiar to Disraeli, Carlyle, Roebuck and their contemporaries as it is to the historian.[10] They saw its influence in all the political battles of a restlessly legislative age. The most celebrated actions were fought over the corn laws and factory reform, but the skirmishing can be followed, under their own banners or those of Church and Dissent, through the struggles over parliamentary reform, taxation policy, education, Church establishment, tithes, game laws, reform of the civil service, the universities and the army, and even rural squalor and the health of towns. Since every one of these touched on the land question or the influence of landowners, the land question was permanently in the field and might at any time become the centre of the battle. That it should do so around 1880 could be explained by the growth of urban democracy and the need of the middle classes for a louder drum to recruit the new electors. Its failure could equally be explained by the reluctance of the working-class voter to distinguish between landlord and capitalist, and the consequent abandonment of the attempt.

This has been the traditional view of both orthodox and Marxist historians; the land reform movement was an aspect – since it failed, an unimportant aspect – of the conflict between land and capital. As long as the conflict lasted, that is, until the rise of a politically aggressive proletarian movement forced land and capital into defensive alliance, land reform was charged with life and power. When the conflict ceased, land reform atrophied. For the traditional orthodox view, here is C.R. Fay:

The thing of which John Bright was persuaded, that landlordism is the common foe, was tenable only in the days of Bright. It was impossible in the days of Thomas Spence; for industrialism was then too young to be self-conscious. It was impossible in the days of Henry George; for by then socialism had passed beyond land reform altogether.[11]

For the traditional Marxist view, here is Marx himself: 'The whole thing [all land reform since Baron Colins] is . . . simply a socialistically decked-out attempt to save capitalist rule and actually re-establish it on an even wider basis than its present one.'[12]

The main difficulty about both these views is their conception of the middle class as a monolithic grouping around the capitalist manufacturers and merchants. This it was not. No class is monolithic in its reaction. The Victorian middle class was less monolithic than most, partly because many of its members were tied by birth, marriage or friendship to the landowning class, partly because many of them looked forward to acquiring estates and becoming themselves landowners, most of all because it was not one class but several. The assumption that the new, raw capitalists of the Industrial Revolution were the true middle class, and that all the rest were a *petite bourgeoisie* trailing along in their wake, lies behind both traditional views. Against it may be set the existence of two influential groups which originated and directed middle-class opinion quite as much as they. The first was a group of businessmen who belonged to an older and less radical commercial world — old-established merchants, especially in the East and West India trades, bankers, brewers, even some manufacturers. Superficially their incomes were of the same type as those of the newer capitalists, but, even before the spread of the industrial company, tended to be more stable, to give their earners more leisure, and to approximate more and more closely to the character of interest. Such men felt a close affinity with the *rentier* and the landlord, and could not be stirred into specious activity against them. Some of them, like most merchants of Liverpool and certain West Riding manufacturers, had a longstanding sympathy with the Tories, and though the rest mainly supported the Liberals, they were as a group a conservative rather than a radical force in politics. They were, moreover, a group which in the economic nature of things was bound to grow, since the development of larger units and the spread of the public company favoured the type of businessman whose income contained an apparently unearned element, as against the owner-manager. They were a nucleus around which middle-class conservatism could grow.

The other group was the professional class, a class which, though neglected by historians, has had an influence on the development of the last hundred years out of proportion to its numbers. The neglect is explained by the great diversity of social origin, family connection and political allegiance to be found amongst professional men. This in turn was reinforced by the peculiarity of their economic interest, which enabled them with greater ease to take up a wide variety of 'progressive' or 'advanced' political attitudes. It will be found that much in Victorian middle-class opinion which has been attributed to the industrialists was due to, or more consistently pursued by, professional men. In particular, they played a leading part in the later stages of the land reform agitation which goes far towards explaining its character, its temporary success, and its ultimate failure.

It is hoped that a study of the land reform movement will show how, beginning as a manifestation of general middle-class hostility, it became the catalyst which helped to resolve the middle-class into its elements, and to unite a large part of the business class in a new combination with the landowners. Far from being a strategem which the capitalists abandoned with reluctance when forced into alliance with the landlords, land reform was one of the most important factors alienating them from the Liberal Party. It was not socialism so much as capitalism itself which by the 1880s had passed beyond land reform altogether.

## II

The hostility of a large part of the middle-class towards the landowners was for most of the century real enough. The myth of middle-class rule had no foundation in contemporary middle-class opinion. The *Westminster Review*, observing in 1833 that 'the landed interest must always exercise great sway in public affairs, for that class alone have much leisure to meddle in them', had called the Reform Act 'an unreal mockery, if the power of the wealthy landowners be not clipped by depriving them of the means of living upon the public wealth'.[13] John Bright told the Commons in 1848: 'This House and the other House of Parliament are almost exclusively aristocratic in their character. The administration is therefore necessarily the same, and on the Treasury Board aristocracy reigns supreme'.[14] John Stuart Mill noted in 1871 that 'the landlords, and those who looked forward to being landlords, have had the command of Parliament up to the last Reform Act, and still wield enormous power'.[15] At all three dates the middle class was vociferously aware that the landowners were the ruling class, and most of them deplored it.

At the heart of their hostility lay the denial of the economic necessity of the landowning class. Brought up on the gospel of work and the horror of waste common to the Evangelical and the Benthamite, they could not separate unearned luxury from the idea of sin. It was the idleness rather than the wealth of the 'lounging class' that offended them.[16] 'We are literally nearly all workers,' boasted Edmund Potter, the world's leading calico-printer, of his little Pennine town, 'we have scarcely a resident amongst us living on independent means – leading a strictly idle life'.[17]

Capitalists worked, landlords did not. Chamberlain's jibe at those 'who toil not, neither do they spin' was the common coin of the age.[18] The classical economists from Adam Smith onwards – themselves professional men – have been accused of indecently exposing the landowners to the charge of uselessness. By drawing an arbitrary line between rent and profit, they justified middle-class prejudice against the 'land monopoly'.

Wages and profit (wrote Nassau Senior) are the creation of man. They are the sacrifice made, in the one case of ease; in the other, of immediate enjoyment. But a considerable part of the produce of every country is the recompense of no sacrifice whatever; is received by those who neither labour nor put by, but merely hold out their hands to accept the offerings of the rest of the community.[19]

In the unflattering role they gave the landowner the economists were merely expressing the instinctive opinion of the middle class. The typical landowner had inherited his estate. The typical capitalist, before the days of large unearned incomes from industrial shares, was the active entrepreneur without whose skill and energy, profit, rent and wages would all cease. Like the professional man, he did not need abstruse reasoning from the labour theory of value to convince him that he was contributing much to society, the landowner little. He knew that idleness for him meant bankruptcy, for the landowner nothing worse than boredom. In this conviction lay the moral superiority of the middle class.

Land reform offered the middle class the opportunity of prosecuting their hostility to the extreme point of abolishing the landowners as a class. Whereas the other reforms – parliamentary, fiscal, administrative, educational, ecclesiastical – aimed at the superstructure of aristocratic power and privilege, land reform aimed at the foundations, at the great estates themselves. Break up the great estates, the argument ran, and the whole edifice of idle wealth and luxurious privilege would crumble away. This was the test of how far hostility was prepared to go. Though the middle class might agree that the power of the landed class ought to be diminished, they were not unanimous in seeking its liquidation. Rather were they deeply divided, between those, a small minority, who prescribed for the great estates a swift death, painless or otherwise; those who wished to remove all the obstructions to a gradual death from natural causes; and those who, though often hostile to landed pretensions, did not wish them to die at all. The land question became critical because it appealed to the deeply rooted prejudices of the middle class. It failed to achieve political effect because the only practical programme of reform to achieve wide popularity, 'free trade in land', was one which promised, what it could doubtfully perform, the silent and painless erosion of the great estates.

## III

What all land reformers, and indeed most of the middle-class, could agree on was simple enough: land had got into too few hands. How few was not at first clear. The figure of 30,000 landowners given currency by the 1861 Census of England and Wales was patently wrong, if only because more than half of these were women. It was to scotch this absurdity and quieten the 'great outcry raised about what was called the monopoly of land' that Lord Derby called in the House of Lords in 1872 for the returns which came to be known as the New Domesday Book. They showed that there were rather more than a million proprietors in the British Isles (excluding the metropolis) of which about 300,000 owned more than one acre.[20] Low as these figures were compared with most European countries,[21] reformers were not convinced. They examined the returns, which had been prepared on a county basis by the poor law officials of the Local Government Board, and found them to be full of errors and duplications, a landowner being counted as many times as he held estates in different counties, and as many times in the same county as the officials knew him under different spellings of his name. Thus the Duke of Buccleuch counted as 14, 28 dukes as 158, and 525 peers as more than 1,500 owners.[22] Reformers therefore published their own estimates, deducting for errors, duplications, corporate owners, glebe lands and charities and favoured a figure of less than 200,000 individual owners of 1 acre or more. Even this, they claimed, understated the case, for it included large numbers of small, non-agricultural properties on the outskirts of towns. Sir Arthur Arnold calculated that 7,000 persons owned four-fifths of the United Kingdom, while G.C. Brodrick estimated that 4,000 proprietors of 1,000 acres or more owned more than one half of England and Wales, and that nearly half the enclosed land was held by an aristocracy of only 2,250 families.[23] Whatever the figures, Britain compared with most parts of the Continent was a country of large estates, where, except in isolated pockets like Cumberland and the Isle of Axholme, peasant proprietors were practically non-existent.

The concentration of property, it was asserted, was not fortuitous. 'The means by which large masses of property have been acquired in this world are principally two, force and fraud', the *Westminster Review* had declared in 1844.[24] Just as seventeenth-century parliamentarians used history as a weapon against the Crown, so nineteenth-century land reformers used it against the landlords. The peers and squires, they asserted, had once been mere tenants of the land, in which their royal overlord and the cultivating sub-tenants had enjoyed valuable concurrent rights. By a long and nefarious process they had turned lordship into ownership, and deprived both king and peasants of their rights. Feudal dues, the king's immemorial rent-charge in the land and the main source of taxation, had been systematically evaded over centuries and finally abolished between 1645 and 1660. The statute by which feudal tenures had been turned into freehold, 12 Charles II, c24, and vestigial feudal incidents exchanged for an excise on beer paid chiefly by the non-landed, became for reformers the symbol of the iniquity of landowners. The wrong had been aggravated by 'the great land tax fraud' by which, as Cobden put it, the people had been 'cheated, robbed and bamboozled upon the subject of taxation'.[25] On this view, the needs of war had in 1692 forced Parliament to restore the old burden in the shape of the four-shilling land tax. This in its turn had been evaded by legislative trickery and administrative chicanery until, instead of meeting most of the needs of the state, it bore a mere 4 per cent of its expenses.[26]

The peasants had been robbed by a parallel process. They had first had their ties with the soil loosened by the substitution of a spurious commercial freedom for the security of manorial custom. Then, when economic conditions were favourable, they were driven out by enclosures and the throwing together of farms, for wool at one period, corn at another. Thus had the English peasantry been divorced from the soil and millions of acres 'taken from the public property of the poor and added to the private property of the rich'.[27]

It was also agreed that the evils resulting from the maldistribution of land reached far beyond those immediately involved in its cultivation. 'The land laws of this country', wrote James Beal, the Radical estate-agent, 'are at once the root, the cause and the protector of the greatest social evils with which we are afflicted, and demand, far more than the Corn Laws, a public agitation in favour of their abolition.'[28] The least of these evils was the undermining of the family life and parental authority of the landowners themselves by the practice of settling the estate upon an unborn eldest son. The heir was tempted into extravagance and debt,[29] whilst the younger sons were either turned out to make their own living or provided for by the patronage system. As the veteran free trader, Colonel T.P. Thompson, put it,

> This is clearly the end and the aim of primogeniture, that £10,000 a year is to be concentrated in the hands of the eldest son, that it may act as a battering-ram for procuring £1,000 a year for each of the others . . . by entry into the public pantry, and appropriation of the victuals that is [sic] therein.[30]

The political and economic consequences were equally deplorable. In spite of two Reform Acts, the Ballot Act, and the reform of the civil service, Lord Derby in 1881 could still place political influence first amongst 'the objects which men aim at when they become possessors of land', and 'the money return' last of all.[31] It was still widely believed that bribery, tenant-bullying and place-hunting were the characteristic contributions of the landed interest to political life. The economic grievance lay in the indebtedness of the large estates and their alleged failure to improve agriculture. The Earls of Derby and Leicester were quoted to show that food production could be vastly increased. The land was allegedly under-capitalized since it was in no one's interest to invest in it: not the landlord's, since under the settlement system he was a mere life-owner without the means or the motive to improve; nor the tenant's, since outside Scotland few had even the limited security of a long lease, and to improve was to invite a rise in rent. It was admitted that some settlements provided exceptional powers to lease and mort-gage, and that in 1856 and 1877 Parliament had (subject to Chancery control) enlarged the powers and lightened the burdens of limited owners. But the reformers' logic was inexorable: in spite of the Settled Estates Acts, in spite of those 'eleemosynary statutes' the Drainage Acts (by which, it was said, a landlord could get the state and the tenant to improve his land, and make a profit out of the transaction), the land had not been improved.[32] As long as settlement remained, the needs of landowners' families would come before those of agriculture.

Most grievous of all were the social consequences. There was scarcely a social problem, from rural hovels and village pauperism to the slums, drunkenness and moral degradation of town life, which reformers did not place at the landlords' door. The landlords had divorced the people from the soil, and therefore they were respon-sible for the consequences: the loss of prosperity and self-respect, the dependence on an insecure wage, the lack of steps in the form of allotments and smallholdings by which the landless man could climb to a farm, and 'all the vast and unnumbered social sores connected with pauperism and rural degradation'.[33] Reformers were willing to except 'the *noblesse oblige* sort of property' and to agree that the worst slums were owned by small rather than large landlords. It was the system itself they attacked.

Finally, it was agreed that the need for reform was urgent. The maldistribution of land was, they believed, rapidly worsening, and the process of squeezing out the small owner accelerating. The growth of industry, commerce and population was inflating rents and with them the landlords' share of the nation's income. Unless the trend was reversed and the land more evenly distributed, nothing could prevent the landlords from achieving a stranglehold on the community.

## IV

On the diagnosis and prognosis of the disease all land reformers could agree. On the remedy there was the most profound disagreement which extended to the heart of the question, the principle of property itself. There was an unbridgeable cleavage between the minority who favoured some form of public ownership of land or rent, and the majority who clung to the principle of private property. Though there were schemes, such as Mill's for taxation of the unearned increment of rent or Chamberlain's piecemeal municipalization,[34] which aimed to attract both, they served rather to convince opponents of the dangerous connection between all land reform than to unite reformers. Nor was there much more agreement amongst those who favoured public ownership. They were divided into fragmentary groups seeking nationalization, municipalization, or the appropriation of rent: nationalization with or without compensation, at once or by stages lasting up to a century, of land alone with or without the 'improvements', or of land, mines, railways, and even indeed all the means of production – for at this point land reform shaded into socialism; municipalization with voluntary or compulsory purchase; and state appropriation of varying proportions of rent, from the four-shilling tax at valuation, through the unearned increment tax, to complete confiscation.[35] That means divide even more than ends is a commonplace amongst revolutionaries. If Marx rejected land reform as a capitalist deviation, the land nationalizers who followed Alfred Russell Wallace came to reject the Georgist single tax as confiscatory and unjust.[36]

On the other side was a deficiency rather than an embarrassment of means. The end was the replacement of the great estates by a wider distribution of property, ultimately perhaps by a nation of property-owners, home-owners and peasant proprietors. Given the rooted suspicion of state intervention and the firm attachment to private property general amongst the Victorian middle class, how was this end to be achieved? It might be possible to prevent further maldistribution by putting a stop to the enclosing of wastes and commons. Part of the re-awakening of the land agitation in the 1860s was the reaction to the attempts of London landlords to appropriate commons like Hampstead Heath, Clapham and Wandsworth Commons for building development. A public outcry led to the founding of preservation societies, a Select Committee, and to the Metropolitan Commons Act (1866) to prevent further encroachment. A ten-year battle ensued, in and out of the courts, until the veto was in 1876 extended to the rest of the country.[37] But the preservation of commons could not rectify the existing maldistribution. Nor could other schemes do more than mitigate its effects. Tenant right, or compensation for improvements unexhausted when the tenant quit his farm, had been advocated by Philip Pusey from 1847 onwards, and embodied in an ineffective Act (1875) fitted with an escape clause. Moved by the bad harvests of the later 1870s and taking advantage of the land agitation, the Farmer's Alliance sprang up in 1879 to demand an effective Act, and got it in 1883.[38]

Leasehold enfranchisement, a movement attracting such diverse figures as Cardinal Manning and the ex-stonemason Henry Broadhurst, aimed at giving the tenant the option of buying the freehold, so as to prevent at the termination of a lease the transfer to the landlord of the tenant's improvements, especially buildings. An association was formed, a Bill sponsored in 1885, and a series of Select Committees on Town Holdings obtained between 1886 and 1892, without legislative result. The complications of the system of building leases, with any number of intermediate lessees between the freeholder and the actual occupier, and the lack of sympathy for a scheme which in the view of other reformers transferred value created by the community from rich landlords to wealthy tenants in the West End of London and elsewhere, were against it.[39] The allotments and smallholdings movement had a wider appeal and a tradition of philanthropic endeavour going back to the 1830s. Jesse Collings' scheme in the 1880s, modelled on the Bright clauses of the Irish Land Act of 1870, proposed to substitute State-aided purchase for paternalism. It was the only sectional scheme offering much hope of substantially modifying the distribution of land but, like the others, it was subordinate to the main movement for land reform, and overlapped it both in aims and personnel.[40]

The only scheme which commanded wide support inside and outside Parliament was one which not only accepted the principle of private property in land but aimed to enhance it. At the same time it offered, without any state intervention beyond a few minor changes in the law, an ultimate redistribution of the land amongst a much larger proportion of the population. This ingenious programme was known as 'free trade in land'.[41] It was the one variety of land reform which attracted supporters from every class, even from amongst the landowners themselves. At no point was it inconsistent with free trade or *laissez-faire*. Indeed, it claimed Cobden's blessing as the essence of free trade applied to the land market. Far from depriving the businessman of his hope of purchasing an estate, it increased that hope by promising to cheapen the cost of acquiring it. Meanwhile, it promised painlessly to break up inefficient and unwieldy estates, and silently to erode the privilege and influence of the large landowners.

How was this paradox to be accomplished? By the abolition of the devices by which, it was claimed, the great estates were artificially held together. John Bright defined free trade in land as follows:

It means the abolition of the law of primogeniture, and the limitation of the system of entails and settlement so that life-interests may be for the most part got rid of, and a real ownership substituted for them. It means also that it shall be as easy to buy and sell land as to buy or sell a ship . . . It means that no legal encouragement shall be given to great estates and great farms, and that the natural forces of accumulation and dispersion shall have free play, as they have with regard to ships, and shares, and machinery, and stock-in-trade, and money. It means, too, that while the lawyer shall be well paid for his work, unnecessary work shall not be made for him, involving an enormous tax on all transactions in connection with the purchase and sale of land and houses. A thorough reform in this matter would complete, with regard to land, the great work accomplished by the Anti-Corn Law League in 1846.[42]

Primogeniture and entail were more the symbol than the substance of complaint. Few landed estates passed by intestacy, and entail, by which in theory an estate could be made to pass to a long though limited series of life-owners, could be barred by the cheap and foolproof method provided by the Fines and Recoveries Act of 1833. The villain was strict settlement, the device by which, through successive resettlements at the marriage of the eldest son in each generation, an estate could be kept out of the market ostensibly for ever. A sort of treaty between the families of the bride and bridegroom, it created or confirmed a life-estate in the land for the bridegroom's father and provided that it should pass on his death to the son, and on the latter's death to the eldest son of the marriage. Meanwhile the estate had to provide an income or a start in life for every member of the family, including jointures for the widows of the life-owners, dowries for the daughters, and portions for the younger sons, in each generation.[43] In this way, it was said, the estate would be kept together, at the expense of a large burden of debt, and in defiance of the natural forces making for its dissolution.

The system of conveyance by private deeds out of which settlement had grown was the chief obstacle to the cheap and speedy transfer of such land as did reach the market. To assure a good title and guard against secret transfers and charges a purchaser, mortgagee or long leaseholder had to investigate the title for sixty years past. This begot delays and expense. Since solicitors were, until 1881, paid by piece-rate, according to the searches they made and the length of the documents they examined or engrossed, the expense bore no relation to the value of the property, but only to the complications of the title. The legal cost of transferring small properties was disproportionately high and might, in some cases, exceed the purchase price. A premium was thus given to large transactions, and small purchasers discouraged.

The only complete solution was the abolition of private conveyance and its replacement by the public registration of title. This had been advocated by the 1829 Real Property Commissioners, and since then by a succession of eminent lawyers, Select Committees, Royal Commissions and Lord Chancellors. Registration of deeds, as in Middlesex, Yorkshire, Scotland and Ireland, and in the ineffective voluntary registration Acts of 1862 and 1875, was useless. What was needed was compulsory registration, the title to land inhering in an entry in the register, with its reference to a cadastral map, confirmed by a certificate in the owner's possession. Nothing less, it was urged, could provide an indefeasible, marketable title, and make land transactions as cheap, simple and speedy as those in other commodities. But ownership had to be a simple relationship, and settlement, with its countless concurrent and future interests in the land, stood in the way. As the celebrated conveyancer, Joshua Williams, admitted, 'I do not think that the registration of titles will succeed unless you please to abolish settlements altogether'.[44] The landlords, it was pointed out, could not have their cake in secret and binding dispositions of land and eat it in cheap transfer and ready mortgages.

The advocates of free trade in land had revolutionary expectations. If primogeniture, entail, settlement and private conveyance were abolished, 'land would be thrown open to free competition, the overgrown estates would soon be broken down, and a great portion of the soil would gradually come into the possession of the working classes'.[45] Such a belief could be held only by those who supposed the existing system of landholding to be incompatible with the laws of supply and demand operating in a free market, and the great estates to be contrary to nature and political economy, requiring the 'pressure of feudal law' to keep them in being. Over most of the world outside the British Isles, it was argued, the staying power of the peasant and his ability to wring more from the soil at less cost except in patient labour had left him in possession. The natural distribution of the land was the widest compatible with earning a modest family living from it, and only the political self-interest of the landlords prevented its realisation.

## V

In origin free trade in land was a by-product of that most characteristic political manifestation of the middle class, the Anti-Corn Law movement. In the words of the *Westminster Review* in 1846,

'Free trade in land' would be the boon demanded by the landowners, if they knew their own interest, in compensation for the repeal of the corn laws – a free unrestricted power of alientation, which would turn our overflowing commercial capital from foreign loans and railways into English farms – which would transform our nobility into a commercial aristocracy, and enable the farmer and the tradesman to become the proprietor, instead of the tenant, of his farm and of his shop.[46]

The land question was never far from the minds of the Leaguers from the start. The first Anti-Corn Law Tract ended with some 'remarks on the land tax fraud', and the exigencies of debate constantly forced the question of land to the front. When the repealers did not raise it, the protectionists did. It was Peel who justified the corn laws by the 'extraordinary burdens on land', and sent the repealers burrowing into history for the legendary sins of the landlords.[47] It was 'Dowry' Knatchbull who ineptly shone the limelight on strict settlement.[48] And it was the agriculturists' plea of the necessity for protection which the League met by demanding in the interests of agricultural efficiency a thorough reform of the land laws.[49] Indeed, as far as the middle class was concerned, land reform dated from the corn law agitation.[50] Earlier land reformers, Paine, Ogilvie and Spence, and even Cobbett, whose *Legacy to Labourers* (ironically dedicated to Peel) had appeared as recently as 1834, were ignored until resuscitated by the Georgists in the 1880s.

Whilst the campaign lasted, the Leaguers were almost as incensed about land laws as about corn laws. Many expected the League to develop into the party of the middle class, in whose programme free trade in land would have a prominent place. From their point of view repeal came too quickly and too easily. As James Beal put it, 'The sudden conversion of Lord John Russell and Sir Robert Peel to the policy of Free Trade prevented the development of the Anti-Corn Law League campaign to the broader area of Free Trade in Land, which was the next inevitable stage in the agitation'.[51] It rapidly became clear that victory had, temporarily at least, sated the middle class, and it was not prepared to press its advantage against the landowners. This was the measure of Peel's statesmanship. Land reform was a weapon held in reserve, and it had not been needed. The class which had so unstintingly supported the League was not united behind Bright's attempt to harness its motive power to a radical programme of free trade, smaller taxes, a cheaper foreign policy, a wider franchise, and free trade in land.[52] In spite of the efforts of Cobden and Bright land reform languished for nearly twenty years. It maintained a flickering interest only in the bills of Locke King against primogeniture and of Philip Pusey on tenant right. The reason, as Cobden clearly saw, was the apathy of the merchants and manufacturers, an apathy based on their ambivalent attitude to land. As he told Bright in 1851, 'Public opinion is either indifferent or favourable to the system of large properties kept together by entail. If you want a proof, see how every successful trader buys an estate, and tries to perpetuate his name in connection with 'that ilk' by creating an eldest son'.[53] Their indifference was likely to increase as commercial and industrial incomes grew larger, as their incomes assumed a more complex character, and the distinction between profit and rent grew more blurred.

Until his death Cobden continued to look to the merchants and manufacturers to lead the attack on 'feudalism'. 'With many faults and shortcomings, our mercantile and manufacturing classes', he wrote in 1862, '. . . are after all the only power in the State possessed of wealth and political influence sufficient to counteract in some degree the feudal governing class of this country. They are, indeed, the only class from whom we can in our time hope for any further beneficial changes.' He tried to wink at their 'timid and servile conduct towards the aristocracy', but he more and more despaired of galvanizing them into effective action:

We have the spirit of feudalism rife and rampant in the midst of the antagonistic development of the age of Watt, Arkwright and Stephenson! Nay feudalism is every day more and more in the ascendant in political and social life. So great is its power and prestige that it draws to it the support and homage of even those who are the natural leaders of the newer and better civilisation. Manufacturers and merchants as a rule seem only to desire riches that they may be enabled to prostrate themselves at the feet of feudalism. How is this to end?[54]

Then suddenly, in the last few months of his life, there were signs of resurrection in the land question. The revival may be dated from his own last speech at Rochdale in November 1864: 'If I were five-and-twenty or thirty, instead of unhappily twice that number of years, I would take Adam Smith in hand, and I would have a League for 'free trade in land' just as we had a League for free trade in corn.'[55] Land reform, we know from his letters, was never far from his mind. The previous year he had had to defend Bright and himself against *The Times'* attack on 'the two Gracchi of Rochdale'. Why did he choose so late a date to suggest a League? Perhaps he was responding to a new atmosphere favourable to land reform. The reviews of the middle 1860s suddenly rediscovered the land question and the merits of peasant proprietorship. Neither the ideas nor even the books reviewed were new: they included W.T. Thornton's *A Plea for Peasant Proprietors* (1848), J.S. Mill's *Principles of Political Economy* (1848), F.W. Newman's *Lectures on Political Economy* (1851), and Herbert Spencer's *Social Statics* (1851).[56] Perhaps the new interest was a belated response to Cobden and Bright's patient education of the public mind on the land question. At all events, from this time onwards a public opinion began to form around the land-reforming ideas of these men, and of Thorold Rogers, Henry Fawcett, Nassau Senior, Sir Henry Maine, Shaw Lefevre, Cliffe Leslie, and their fellows. Some of them, notably Fawcett and Shaw Lefevre, led the agitation of 1865 against the enclosure of commons, and founded the first preservation societies. It was men like these, professional authors, journalists, academics and lawyers, who were to play the leading part in reviving land reform and organizing the wave of public opinion which swept on to the abortive crisis of the early 1880s.

Professional men, of course, are society's intellectuals, and it is not surprising to find them producing the ideas which society discusses. They have, however, been too readily viewed as individuals or, if grouped at all, grouped into family connections without sufficient emphasis that such connections are normal in any social class. It is instructive to look at them as a class, and ask what it is that marks them off from their neighbours. They are as a class peculiar in one respect, that they are not tied by economic interest to any particular economic system. Whereas the landowner and the businessman see their incomes, their way of life and their very existence, tied to the economic system which produces them, the professional man is aware that in any organization of society, provided it does not fall below the moral and technical standards of existing civilization, his services will be necessary, valued and rewarded. He is not therefore under the same economic pressure to maintain the system, and is free to indulge in criticism and reform. Neither, of course, is he under pressure to change it. He is, compared with the landowner and the businessman, released from the narrower constraints of economic interest, and is freer to exercise his judgment according to other, non-economic criteria. What in others requires a considerable insight or effort of will, comes easily to him. He is apt, therefore, to see politics in moral terms rather than those of economic interest.[57]

The moralization of politics – the appeal in political questions to abstract justice and social ideals – is the characteristic contribution of the professional class to public discussion. That it should have become an important factor in Victorian political life is not unexpected. First, the professional class was growing rapidly and achieving a wider influence because of the changing character of society. Industrialism and urbanization did not merely increase the weight of the business and proletarian as against the landowning and cultivating classes. Together with the ensuing rise in living standards they increased the demand for the professional services of administrators, teachers, lawyers, doctors, architects, engineers, ministers of religion, journalists and authors. As the balance of population tilted decisively in favour of the towns, the professional class came into its own. Secondly, in its tendency to see politics in moral terms it was for a long time swimming with the tide of middle-class opinion. Hostility against the landowners was highly moralistic. Like any interest or group which feels excluded and aggrieved, the early Victorian business class was apt to seek comfort in moral condemnation of its opponents. As long as the tide of hostility flowed against the landlords uninterrupted by cross-currents deriving from the changed economic interests of businessmen, the moral view of politics prevailed. One of the functions of the professional class was to carry over this fruitful if exasperating attitude from an age in which it worked for the businessmen into one in which it worked against them. Land reform was one of the vehicles in which this was achieved.

It is not pretended that all professional men were land reformers, or all land reformers professional men. Land reformers were drawn from all classes, even from the landed class itself.[58] To see politics in similarly moral terms is not necessarily to reach the same position. Land reform itself had professional men amongst its opponents, the economist McCulloch, the historian Froude and the lawyer Underhill, for example. Others, like the lawyer-historians Pollock and Seebohm, saw small value in it and rejected the assumptions of free trade in land. The professional class was too small to affect politics by itself, and the moral attitude encourages proselytisation. Nevertheless, the professional class was strongly represented amongst land reformers, more strongly amongst land-reforming Members of Parliament than in the Commons as a whole, while amongst the Radicals they formed a substantial group and occasionally a majority.[59] Inside and outside Parliament professional men played a leading role in agitation, strikingly so in the more extreme kinds of reform. Mill's Land Tenure Reform Association, which went beyond free trade in land to advocate taxation of the unearned increment of rent, was founded in 1870 chiefly by professional men, in association with six members of the (first) International Working Men's Association. Amongst the moving spirits were Mill himself, Fawcett, Thorold Rogers, Cliffe Leslie and J.E. Cairnes, all academic economists, Alfred Russell Wallace the naturalist, and the journalist John Morley, the exceptions being Dilke the Radical landowner, and P.A. Taylor, of the well-known silk-manufacturing firm of Courtaulds.[60] Wallace founded in 1881 the Land Nationalization Society.[61] The Land Reform Union (later the English Land Restoration League) which split off from it in 1883 to organize Henry George's second lecture tour of Britain, exhibited a similar combination of professional and working men.[62] It was the same formula – in some cases the same men – which produced the Socialist societies of the 1880s and has since played so large a part in the origin and development of the Labour Party. The moral attitude to politics was apt to lead some professional men further left than land reform.

Free trade in land found support in every class: amongst working men, like George Odger and his friends of the first International and the Land Tenure Reform Association, for whom it was first of many steps; amongst some Whig landowners or their heirs, like Lords Carington, Lymington and Blandford, for whom it was the one step to prevent all others; it even found a sort of sympathy amongst some Tory landowners who favoured a modified form which would safeguard the principle of family estates while frustrating criticism.

Its main strength, however, lay in the middle class, and even there in the professional rather than the business group. The first body to inherit Cobden's legacy was the Cobden Club – that Fabian Society of progressive Liberalism. Its membership was so wide that its annual dinners looked like the Liberal party in conclave. But the majority were merely annual diners, and the burden of propaganda was carried by a small group of enthusiasts amongst whom professional men were predominant: dons like G.C. Brodrick, Warden of Merton College, Cliffe Leslie and Thorold Rogers, the lawyers Shaw Lefevre, MacDonell and Wren Hoskyns, and the agricultural expert James Caird. Mill, Rogers and Cliffe Leslie formed a link with the Land Tenure Reform Association. The Cobden Club published the handbooks of the movement: *Systems of Land Tenure in Various Countries* (1870), the main contributors, apart from foreigners, being Wren Hoskyns, Cliffe Leslie, Judge Longfield of the Irish Landed Estates Court and Sir George Campbell of the Indian Civil Service; Sir Arthur Arnold's *Free Land,* G.C. Brodrick's *English Land and English Landlords,* and W.E. Baxter's *Our Land Laws of the Past* – all except the last, a small pamphlet, by professional men.[63] Other leading publicists were the journalists Charles Bradlaugh and Justin McCarthy, Professors J.S. Blackie, E.S. Beesley and J.S. Nicholson, the lawyers Joseph Kay, T.E. Scrutton and Osborne Morgan, and the estate agent James Beal

This is not to deny the importance of the Radical businessmen: Bright, Chamberlain, Collings, Baxter, J.W. Barclay, William Fowler, and the rest. Indeed, the decisive step in the development of the agitation was the inclusion of free trade in land in the Radical programme of the seventies. In Chamberlain's attack on the Liberal leadership in 1873 Free Land took its place besides Free Church, Free Schools and Free Labour in 'the motto of the new party'.[64] From this point on, the history of free trade in land was bound up with that of the Radicals. Through them it achieved its footing in Parliament, and by its connection with them it unwittingly condemned itself to failure. Who then were the Radicals? According to a contemporary view they represented, like land reform, a reaction of capital against land. For Charles Mackay, a progressive political journalist, they were 'a narrow-minded and often uneducated plutocracy' sprung from the Manchester School of a generation earlier.[65] A French observer saw in them 'a campaign of the English *bourgeoisie* against a privileged class whose rights they covet'.[66] Such an over-simplification ignores the evidence of the Radicals themselves. From the beginning their rebellious anger was aimed not at landlords alone but at 'the power of wealth' in general. Chamberlain's broadsides were fired indiscriminately at 'wealthy landowners and millionaire manufacturers'.[67] If he were appointed Chancellor, the City, Gladstone thought, would be terrified of his views of 'ransom'.[68] Goldwin Smith's original complaint that the Liberal party was swerving from its proper aim 'to put an end to class government and establish a government of the nation' was provoked as much by 'the terrible influence of capital over labour' as by the pretensions of the aristocracy: 'These millionaires were in fact on the point of becoming, in conjunction with the landowners, our absolute masters'.[69] The conjunction was inherent in the Radical programme. The appeal to the working-class voter, the emphasis on welfare measures and State intervention, and the demand for 'ransom' in the shape of graduated taxation, were a calculated attack on the rich as such, irrespective of their source of income. Only 'free land' singled out the landlord for attack. The rest of the programme, with the possible exception of Church disestablishment and reform of the House of Lords, could be viewed as inimical to both landowner and businessman. Businessmen supporting the programme were clearly an aberration from the norm, and regarded by their fellows as cranks and demagogues. Chamberlain and his friends had – according to the point of view – betrayed or risen above the interests of their class. Their dictum, that 'politics is the science of human happiness',[70] was an explicit statement of the moral attitude. Such an attitude was natural to the professional men who formed the largest occupational group amongst the Radicals. To the businessmen it was a luxury afforded only at the expense of their immediate class interests.

## VI

In the later 1870s the increasing confidence of the Radicals was one of the causes converging to force a crisis in the land question. Depression and bad harvests combined to raise complaints from businessmen and farmers at the high level of rents at a time of falling prices. For the Irish peasant they meant not hardship but ruin, and landlord-tenant relations took an ugly turn. The land reformers in Britain and Ireland rose to meet their opportunity with a crescendo of public discussion in the press and on the platform. In this atmosphere the Conservatives, with an instinct which was part of their traditional equipment for dealing with reforms which had become inevitable, determined to forestall worse measures by bringing in their own. The Agricultural Holdings Act (1875) and the Settled Estates Act (1877) having failed to abate the rising storm, a bolder programme was attempted. The Lord Chancellor, Lord Cairns, had given notice of four land Bills when, in April 1880, the Conservative Government was defeated at the polls. The Liberal press demanded that Gladstone should deal 'first and boldly with the land question', and this he promised in the House to do, only asking time for the government to consider it fully.[71]

No comprehensive reform was attempted by the government. Gladstone had small faith in the efficacy of free trade in land to perform its promises, and his overriding concern was to prevent the defection of the Whigs. He had early warning before the end of the year in the resignation of the Duke of Argyll over Irish land policy. Apart from the Irish Land Act of 1881, the only government measures were marginal: the Ground Game Act (1880) enabling the tenant farmers to take hares and rabbits concurrently with the landlord, and the Agricultural Holdings Act (1883) to prevent the landlord from contracting out of his obligation under the 1875 Act to compensate the tenant for improvements. Instead, the government encouraged Lord Cairns to carry on with the Tory Bills already introduced, and these were enacted. Two of them were technical improvements in conveyancing and litigation, while the third introduced the modern system of remunerating solicitors by a maximum percentage of the price of the land transferred. The fourth was the Settled Land Act of 1882, which set out the main principles governing settled land ever since.[72] In effect it put the entire management of the land, as if it were his own freehold, in the hands of the tenant-for-life, subject to certain safeguards protecting the interests of other beneficiaries. It even allowed the outright sale of the land, provided that the purchase money, after meeting charges on the estate, was secured on the same terms and for the same purposes as the land it represented. It did not please the reformers, who were not to be satisfied with anything less than the complete abolition of settlement, primogeniture and entail, and regarded the Act as an attempt to encourage settlement by increasing its convenience.

Outmanoeuvred and frustrated, the agitation grew more strident and extravagant. The early 1880s saw the founding not only of the Land Nationalization Society and of the Georgist movement but also of a multitude of Socialist clubs and societies, from Hyndman's Social Democratic Federation to the Fabian Society, all including amongst their objects the public ownership of land. The less extreme reformers, through the Free Land League of 1885, intensified their demands, and leasehold enfranchisement grew from an idea into an organised movement. The 'advanced' Liberals, looking ahead to the rural labourers' vote, espoused Collings' scheme for allotments and smallholdings. By the 1885 election, with Hartington and Chamberlain taking opposite sides on most questions, the main division in politics was seen to be not that between Liberal and Tory, but between 'advanced' Liberals and the 'moderates' or Whigs. Chamberlain was confidently introduced as 'your coming Prime Minister'.[73] Hartington gloomily forecast that the future Liberal party would be Radical, and that there was nothing for the Whigs but to disappear or turn Tory.[74] The land question played a more prominent part than in any election before or since, and the Radicals claimed that 'three acres and a cow' had won the English counties. The election won, and the caretaker government turned out on Jesse Collings' smallholdings amendment – against which a significant group of Whigs voted with the Tories[75] – the Liberal Party seemed poised once more for a Radical advance and an attack on the land question. At this point Gladstone launched his Home Rule 'thunderbolt', and land reform was lost in the rift which split the party and unexpectedly left Chamberlain, Collings and their friends on the Whig side. From that landslip it was never to recover.

The 1886 split had the same significance for land reform as for the Liberal Party in general. Though both had triumphs still to come, for both it proved the real beginning of the end. Yet at the time it seemed to clear the way for a new advance, unhampered by the Whigs, and progressive Liberalism was now much freer to experiment with democratic and social reforms, amongst which land reform promised to occupy a prominent place. The loss of Chamberlain and his friends, though they continued to pursue moderate land reform, was regretted, but the defection of Hartington and the 'moderates' had been a calculated risk, and was not wholly unwelcome. The party could now continue its accustomed advance towards the left, its expected evolution into the party of the Radicals. At Manchester in 1889 the National Liberal Federation adopted a substantially Radical programme which included enfranchisement of leaseholders, security for tenants' improvements, increased powers for obtaining land for allotments, abolition of restrictions on the transfer of land, and even the taxation of ground rents and mining royalties along Georgist lines. The famous 'Newcastle programme' of 1891 went further still, embracing the abolition of primogeniture and entail, and the compulsory purchase of land for local purposes. The Tories were sufficiently sensitive of the electoral appeal of land reform to pass, in the Allotments Act (1887) and the Smallholdings Act (1892), modified versions of Collings' and Chamberlain's schemes – without, of course, the essential element of compulsory purchase. It seemed that once Irish Home Rule was achieved, comprehensive land reform would be the next legislative concern of a future Liberal government.

No such comprehensive reform was ever achieved, or even attempted. The harassed Liberal minority government of 1892–5 was too obsessed with Ireland to pay it much attention. When the Liberals returned to power in 1906, they had the means to achieve it, but the will was lacking. The Smallholdings Acts of 1907 and 1908 merely extended the provisions of the 1892 Act, though in a manner more offensive to property, since compulsory purchase for letting by local authorities was potentially more voracious of land than State-aided purchase by the smallholders themselves. The nearest the last Liberal government came to effective land reform was in the land taxation clauses of the 1909 Budget, which Lloyd George inserted under pressure from the Land Valuation Parliamentary Campaign Committee, formed in 1906 amongst Liberal M.P.s of Georgist leanings. More than any other Budget proposal, these taxes on unearned incremental land values and undeveloped land and minerals precipitated the collision with the House of Lords and so the constitutional crisis.[76] It was Lloyd George himself who, in 1922 at the insistence of the Conservatives in his Coalition, repealed the land tax clauses of 'the People's Budget'. Non-socialist land reform as a political possibility petered out with the First World War and the quarrel as to its conduct which began the final break-up and decline of the Liberal Party.[77]

## VII

Why did the land reform movement fail? Partly because in the only variants acceptable to the propertied members of the Liberal Party it came so near to success. The reforms of the early 1880s were a sufficient instalment of free trade in land to test its main assumptions and prove them false. Life-owners did not use their new powers to flood the market with estates. The 'natural drift' of property towards the small owner did not assert itself. Peasant proprietors did not triumphantly emerge as the fittest survivors of agricultural depression. State-aided purchase under the 1892 Act and leasing under those of 1907–8 were an admission that the free market was failing to produce smallholdings or to change significantly the distribution of property.[78] If in the twentieth century there has been a considerable increase in owner-occupation, it has been amongst existing farmers rather than new peasants from the working classes; and if a break-up of some great estates, it has been the fortuitous by-product of taxation policy rather than the deliberate result of land reform.

Ultimately, however, the failure of the movement was due to Liberal equivocation – a flirtation with land reform rather than a marriage, and one which was disastrous to other Liberal prospects. Equivocation was inherent in the indecision of the late Victorian Liberal Party as to its future purpose and appeal. It was both a symptom and a cause of the process by which the party was alienating many of its traditional supporters without permanently gaining new ones. It failed to answer with a clear voice the question, to whom was Liberalism, to whom was land reform, supposed to appeal? In the policies it pursued it increasingly asked its propertied supporters to rise above their economic interests, while not offering to meet more than part-way the economic aspirations of the working class. The tension between these two appeals was too great for the party's survival. It is not too much to say that equivocation over land reform was the most damaging example of the policies which undermined the Liberal Party and prepared the way for its decline. The agitation, which began in the class conflict between the businessmen and the landowners, ended by helping to bring about their *rapprochement* in the same political party and so had a profound if paradoxical effect on the social structure of politics.

However difficult it is to measure, it is clear that in the last quarter of the nineteenth century a geological shift was taking place in the political allegiance of the landed and business classes, and in the ability of the Liberal party to command their support. Sir Robert Ensor saw a symbol of this change in the transformation of the City of London from a Liberal into a Conservative stronghold.[79] John Roach in a stimulating article on the Liberal intelligentsia has said, 'In the history of Victorian politics more attention might be given to the change which converted a large part of the educated classes from the Liberal side to the Conservative'.[80] It is a change which demands explanation, all the more so since it runs counter to theoretical expectations both orthodox and Marxist. That it should have been the Conservatives, the traditional party of the majority of landowners, rather than the Liberals, the party (notwithstanding its landowning wing) of the majority of Victorian businessmen, which survived into the twentieth century as the party opposed to Labour, is one of the more surprising quirks of modern British history. The decline of the Liberal Party had its origins in the drift of landowners, businessmen and others to the Conservatives which began well before 1886, and of which the Unionist defections were only the most spectacular example.

Unfortunately, such a shift in the traditional allegiances of important social groups defies accurate statistical measurement. Both Ensor and Roach illustrate it by individual examples – Goschen, Henry Sidgwick, Sir Henry Maine, J.F. Stephen, Robert Lowe, and Lord Lytton. Such examples can be multiplied by anyone familiar with the period. The problem is how far they support inferences about the behaviour of whole classes. J.A. Thomas's statistics of the economic interests of M.P.s provide useful information about some of the most politically active members of the various classes.[81] There are considerable difficulties in using his figures, which are discussed in the Appendix to this paper, where a method of counteracting the effects of the electoral swing is developed. The resultant analysis shows that up to the early 1880s a Liberal government commanded the support of two-thirds or more of the businessmen in the Commons, and a Liberal opposition more than half. By the 1890s, the position was reversed: it was the Conservatives who had two-thirds of businessmen M.P.s when in office, and half when out of it. Over the same period Liberal landowning M.P.s shrank from a substantial minority to a negligible one. This analysis confirms the view that between the 1870s and the 1890s the Liberal Party was steadily losing ground in its share of the parliamentary representation of both landowners and businessmen, that the losses were greater amongst 'City men' than amongst, say, merchants, and that the only important group of which the Liberal share increased was the professional class.

Given that such a drift did occur, why did it come about? Ensor rightly rejected 'the fashionable Marxian answer', that the capitalists were forced by a proletarian challenge into the arms of the landowners and their party. 'In the political field,' he wrote, 'the working-class stirrings of the 'eighties came to very little all told; and if in the trade union field they were less negligible, they wore no revolutionary aspect.' Nor does there seem to have been any likelihood of the working class itself capturing the Liberal Party and driving out the businessmen. Ensor's own answer was that 'the source of alarm was agrarian, not proletarian; it was Irish, not British'. Irish agrarian violence evoked in the businessman's breast 'a moral horror at unprevented and largely unpunished crime'; a 'feeling that in Ireland justice had been overborne by force'; and 'a peculiar kind of patriotic impulse'. No doubt it did. But were businessmen so much more sensitive than other Liberals to morality, justice and patriotism? Were those who remained behind indifferent to these appeals? Did the Liberal Party condone Irish violence? And if the businessman was repelled by violence in the 1880s why did he remain unmoved by the threat of it in Ulster in 1912? Though Irish affairs indeed contributed to the defections, there is no need to rely for the explanation on such nebulous emotions.

May not the main cause be found in emotions much nearer the head and pocket: in fear for the power and influence of the propertied classes, and for the institution of property itself? Roach has laid bare the misgivings of 'old Liberals', like Sidgwick, Stephen, Maine, Lowe and Lytton, at the implications of Liberal policy: it seemed to them to be paving the way for a tyrannical, egalitarian democracy which would despoil the rich and abrogate national and imperial responsibilities in an orgy of selfish hedonism. It was not so much working-class stirrings which evoked this fear. As yet the new voters predominantly supported the traditional parties. The danger lay in what many considered those irresponsible middle-class politicians, inside and outside the Liberal Party, who played upon their greed and envy, and aimed to buy their votes with an insidious bribery which could only whet their appetites for more. 'Ransom' (graduated taxation) and 'socialism' (expensive welfare measures) would weaken the defences of property and open the breaches to more extreme egalitarianism. The Georgists and Social Democrats, the land nationalizers and Fabians, would not need to win a victory at the polls if their 'friends' inside the Liberal party could be persuaded to transform it into an instrument of their policies.

To many it seemed that the Liberals were caught up in a 'creeping conspiracy' against property which threatened landowner and businessmen alike. Land reform had a special place in this 'conspiracy'. It was the continuous strand linking the Liberals with the extremists to their left. It began with land reform for Ireland which by 1881 had begun to undermine the rights of property owners there. Who could say it would not spread to Britain, where free trade in land, leasehold enfranchisement, compulsory purchase, and the taxation of ground rents, would lead insensibly to the single tax, if not to outright nationalization? Home Rule itself could be construed as part of the conspiracy. Not only was it accompanied by a Bill to buy out the Irish landowners at twenty years' purchase for £120 million – a scheme which might have been drawn up by Wallace.

Gladstone himself admitted that the crucial problem was the position under an Irish Nationalist government of 'the minority', which in 1886 – whatever it became by 1912 – meant not so much Ulster as the landed class throughout Ireland.[82] As Salisbury put it, 'By the Land Act of 1870, by the Ballot Act of 1872, by the Land Act of 1881, and last of all by the Reform Act of 1884, the power of the gentry in Ireland is absolutely shattered'.[83] Their subjection without safeguards to a Dublin government of their enemies was to invite spoilation or worse. Home Rule was an instalment of the Radical plan 'to smash up the landowners'.[84] Salisbury put it succinctly: 'We are on an inclined plane leading from the position of Lord Hartington to that of Mr Chamberlain and so on to the depths over which Mr Henry George rules supreme'.[85]

For the plausibility of this view of the direction in which Liberalism was tending, Liberals themselves, and especially those on the left wing of the party, must bear some of the responsibility. The moral appeal in politics is apt to appear humbug to those whose interests are threatened. Many Liberals allowed themselves to be carried by it into arguments against the privileges of property which seemed capable of indefinite extension in the direction of egalitarianism. Land reformers especially were open to the temptation to press their arguments beyond what was necessary to support their moderate, unrevolutionary schemes. They could be accused of speaking with two voices, one for the upholders of private property, and one for its detractors. Mill himself was upbraided by the *Edinburgh Review* in 1871 for offering his schemes to land nationalizers and socialists as a step towards their goal, and to others as a bulwark of private property.[86] His Land Tenure Reform Association and its successors, as we have seen, seemed to act as a bridge, in doctrine and personnel, between the Liberals and the Georgists, and more extreme reformers beyond them. According to Hyndman, in 1885, the Radicals were doing the Social Democrats' work for them, and Chamberlain was 'too clever a man not to know that the very arguments which he uses against the landowners will be turned against himself as a capitalist and the class to which he belongs'.[87] Even though Chamberlain left the party, his programme and the arguments remained.

How were capitalists likely to react to such a danger? As we have seen, they ceased as a class to be interested in land reform when the Corn Laws were repealed. By the last quarter of the nineteenth century there were many reasons why their apathy should have turned into a more active revulsion. As the structure of industry and commerce changed with the growth of business units and the spread of joint-stock organization, the distinction drawn by the classical economists between profit and rent, between earned and unearned wealth, was no longer relevant. Arguments against the one were arguments against the other. Moderate land reform might lead to more extreme kinds, and these in turn to varieties of socialism. Other Radical measures, above all graduated death duties (introduced by Harcourt in 1894) and graduated income tax (introduced by Asquith and Lloyd George in 1907 and 1909), made no distinction between land and other property. The propertied classes would stand or fall together. The defection of the Whigs, whether over Ireland or the more general danger to property, was a danger signal to many businessmen. It deprived them of their surest anchor against a drift to port and the equalitarian rocks. Some of them preferred to abandon ship.

What of those businessmen and landowners who were left? There were enough of them to prevent a thorough-going land reform, the capture of the party by the left wing, or its transformation into a predominantly working-class party. Many remained out of loyalty, habit, or an attachment to free trade. But the hard core were believers in the high principles of Liberalism, with its concern for the under-dog, for social justice as they conceived it, and for a state of society in which hard work and enterprise were rewarded and privilege was not allowed to become gross exploitation. That is, they were motivated less by economic interest than by sentiment, generous impulse, personal ambition or eccentricity. Like the Radicals and land reformers before them, they stood out from their fellows as aberrations from the norms of the classes to which they belonged. They were becoming exponents of the moral view of politics. The increasing prominence of professional men in the Liberal Party was symptomatic of the trend. Only amongst this interest in the Commons did the Liberals maintain much more than their share of the representation. When last in office under Victoria the party could claim a majority only of this interest, and in the Cabinet professional men nearly equalled the rest. By 1906, for the first time in any Cabinet, they equalled the landowners and businessmen and could, with a trade unionist, outvote them.[88] It is significant for the evolution of the parties that when in 1911 the Conservatives came for the first time to choose a businessman, Bonar Law, as their leader, the Liberals were led by a barrister, Asquith, closely seconded by a solicitor, Lloyd George.

If this analysis is correct, the late Victorian defections left the

Liberal Party with its roots less firmly bedded in the sub-soil of economic interests. By the beginning of this century it had become that rare and noble political plant, a party mainly devoted to the moral view of politics, and dangerously isolated from the hard facts of economic motivation. Its subsequent history pathetically proclaims that such a rarefied idealism does not pay. It lost the permanent, solid support of the propertied classes without gaining that of the working class. Though in 1906 the cry of 'free trade in danger' temporarily rallied some traditional supporters, the great Liberal majority was from one point of view a dwarf standing on the shoulders of a giant. Working-class votes were lent, not given, for the moralist in politics (as the Labour Party intellectuals today) is never wholly trusted. When the Liberals ceased to serve working-class interests, working-class politicians were ready with an alternative allegiance. The Liberal Party, crumbling on both wings, decayed to a high-minded and admired but unsupported remnant. To its decline the agitation for land reform, which to Disraeli in 1880 had seemed to threaten the constitutional position of the landed interest and with it, perhaps, the extinction of the Conservative Party, had made a peculiar and perverse contribution.

## APPENDIX

## A MEASURE OF THE DRIFT OF BUSINESS AND OTHER MPs FROM THE LIBERAL TO THE UNIONIST PARTIES, 1868–1914

In his analyses of the socio-economic composition of *The House of Commons, 1832–1900* and *1906–1911* (Cardiff, 1939 and 1958), Dr. J.A. Thomas gives useful statistical tables of the economic interests of the M.P.s in each Parliament from the Great Reform Act to the First World War. These he tries to use to show, *inter alia,* when the business interests in the House of Commons began to outweigh the landed interest, which he takes to be as early as the 1850s. This conclusion does not follow from his figures which, being of 'interests' rather than M.P.s and not allowing for the overlap either between landowners and businessmen or between the various business interests (he gives only one category for landowners and eleven for business interests in the first book and no less than sixty-eight in the second), total far more than (usually more than double) the number of M.P.s in each Parliament. Whether or not we accept that, down to the First World War at least, most landowners were likely to be landlords first and businessmen second and certainly to come to the defence of land against any radical attack, the landed interest was in a clear majority amongst M.P.s until the Parliament of 1880, and in a minority only from 1885 onwards.

His figures can, however, be used for a more interesting purpose, to illustrate the drift of both landowners and businessmen from the Liberal to the Conservative and Unionist and Liberal Unionist Parties in the late nineteenth and early twentieth centuries. The difficulty in this analysis is that some method must be devised to counteract the effect of the electoral swing, which normally gave each party a larger number of M.P.s from every interest when in a majority in the House than when it was in a minority, the number increasing with the size of the majority.

The effect of the electoral swing can be eliminated by constructing an associative index (AI) on the following formula:

$$\frac{\text{Liberal members of interest}}{\text{Unionist members of interest}} \times \frac{\text{Unionist M.P.s}}{\text{Liberal M.P.s}}$$

The index, as it is greater or less than unity, shows by how much the Liberal share of each interest is greater or less than the Liberal share of the M.P.s of the two parties. (Liberal Unionists are included with Unionists. Other parties, notably Labour and the Irish Nationalists, are for simplicity's sake excluded from the calculation.) If the index for an interest is 1.0, the Liberals have the same share of it as they have of the combined Liberal and Unionist M.P.s; if it is 2.0, they have twice the share of the interest as of M.P.s, and so on. In Table 1, the first row of figures for each interest gives the Liberal percentage of the category, the second the associative index. (Working-class M.P.s have been omitted, since until the 1900 Parliament they were comparatively few and almost entirely Liberal, and from 1906 predominantly Labour. A small number of farmers, auctioneers and land agents and other miscellaneous occupations have also been omitted. Newspaper proprietors in the nineteenth century were still primarily journalists, and have been attached to the Professions. 1910 refers to the Parliament elected in December of that year.)

The table shows that the Liberals always had a minority of the landed M.P.s whether in or out of office, and that their share fell off sharply from 1886 onwards, becoming very small by the Edwardian age. Their share of the related category of military and naval M.P.s (a rather small category) was still smaller, and fell off earlier, from 1880 onwards, to become almost negligible before the end of the century.

TABLE 1

*Liberal Proportion of Each Interest in the House of Commons,
1868–1910*

|  |  | 1868 | 1874 | 1880 | 1885 | 1886 | 1892 | 1895 | 1900 | 1906 | 1901 |
|---|---|---|---|---|---|---|---|---|---|---|---|
| Land | % | 47.4 | 33.9 | 48.6 | 47.5 | 25.1 | 23.8 | 17.0 | 16.7 | 51.7 | 23.5 |
|  | AI | 0.63 | 0.72 | 0.66 | 0.67 | 0.69 | 0.36 | 0.48 | 0.43 | 0.37 | 0.31 |
| Business | % | 71.8 | 57.3 | 69.7 | 61.1 | 40.9 | 49.9 | 32.0 | 32.3 | 71.6 | 52.5 |
|  | AI | 1.73 | 2.05 | 1.58 | 1.22 | 1.39 | 1.15 | 1.09 | 1.03 | 0.93 | 1.11 |
| Professions | % | 72.7 | 61.5 | 77.2 | 68.7 | 45.6 | 56.0 | 40.8 | 44.3 | 82.1 | 57.7 |
|  | AI | 2.04 | 2.24 | 2.36 | 1.63 | 1.75 | 1.47 | 1.60 | 1.60 | 1.76 | 1.37 |
| Armed | % | 44.4 | 24.8 | 41.3 | 28.6 | 11.8 | 14.7 | 7.5 | 11.1 | 40.8 | 24.3 |
| Forces | AI | 0.56 | 0.46 | 0.49 | 0.30 | 0.28 | 0.20 | 0.19 | 0.27 | 0.26 | 0.32 |

Their share of the business M.P.s began as a large majority, more
than twice their share of combined M.P.s in the 1874 Parliament, and
fell steadily to the end of the century, when it was close to unity, and
remained so in the Edwardian age (but see the next paragraph). Only
in the case of M.P.s from the professions did the Liberals succeed in
maintaining a predominant share of the interest; omitting lawyers,
who were relatively equal in the two parties, the Liberal share was
overwhelming.

A more refined analysis of the business interest is still more
illuminating. If we take finance (bankers, insurance and finance
company directors) to represent the growing financial and corporate
end of the spectrum of capitalism, and merchants to represent the
declining traditional and more individualist end, we get the result
shown in Table 2.

It will be seen that the Liberal share of the financial interest began as
strongly as that of the wider business interest, but fell off sharply
from 1880, and by the end of the century reached levels approaching,
though not yet reaching, those of the landowners.[89] Their share of
the merchants, overwhelmingly predominant at the start of the
period, also declined to the end of the century, though it was still
much greater than unity in 1900, but recovered strongly in the era of

TABLE 2

*Liberal Proportion of Finance and Merchant Interests in the House of Commons, 1868–1910*

|  |  | 1868 | 1874 | 1880 | 1885 | 1886 | 1892 | 1895 | 1900 | 1906 | 1910 |
|---|---|---|---|---|---|---|---|---|---|---|---|
| Finance | % | 71.7 | 51.1 | 61.4 | 54.0 | 31.1 | 38.0 | 21.7 | 20.9 | 64.1 | 42.1 |
|  | AI | 1.77 | 1.47 | 1.11 | 0.87 | 0.93 | 0.70 | 0.65 | 0.57 | 0.66 | 0.74 |
| Merchants | % | 82.9 | 72.7 | 81.0 | 77.4 | 57.2 | 66.2 | 46.8 | 39.3 | 87.1 | 66.7 |
|  | AI | 3.39 | 3.74 | 2.97 | 2.55 | 2.75 | 2.25 | 2.04 | 1.40 | 2.50 | 2.00 |

the Tariff Reform movement, to reach levels greater than the Liberal share of the professions. Table 2 illustrates how liberalism continued to hold attractions for the traditional businessman of the owner-managing phase of capitalism – a declining breed by the twentieth century – while it increasingly alienated the newer corporate businessman of high finance capitalism – the breed fittest to survive in the twentieth-century economy.

## Notes

1 *Parliamentary Debates*, 3rd Series, vol 256, 619 and 618.
2 13 February and 31 March 1880.
3 5 May 1880.
4 Speech at West Calder, 27 November, *The Times*, 28 November 1879.
5 *Manchester Guardian*, 25 March 1880.
6 *The Nineteenth Century*, August 1880.
7 J. MacDonell, *The Land Question*, London, 1873, p.2.
8 The abolition of the law of primogeniture and the virtual assimilation of the law of real property and that of personalty in 1925 were, however, amongst the aims of the largest group of Victorian land reformers.
9 W.E. Baxter, *Our Land Laws of the Past*, London, 1881, p.3.
10 Cf A. Briggs, *Victorian People*, London: Odhams, 1954, p.29.
11 C.R. Fay, *The Corn Laws and Social England*, Cambridge University Press, 1932, p.143. The quotation continues the argument that 'between socialism and land reform there is no natural affinity', but this does not alter its implication concerning the failure of land reform.
12 K. Marx and F. Engels, *Selected Correspondence*, Moscow: Foreign Languages Publishing House, 1956, p.416: Marx to F.A. Sorge, 20 June 1881.
13 January 1833, 'Causes of the Distress of the Landed Interest'.
14 G.M. Trevelyan, *Life of Bright*, London, 1913, p.166.
15 *Dissertations and Discussions*, London, 1875, vol IV, 251: Speech on Land Tenure Reform, 15 May 1871.
16 Cf G.C. Brodrick, *English Land and English Landlords*, London, 1881, p.355.
17 E. Potter, *A Picture of a Manufacturing District* [Glossop] Manchester, 1856, p.24.
18 J.L. Garvin, *Life of Chamberlain*, London: Macmillan, 1932, vol I, p.392. It was applied for example, nearly twenty years earlier, to the same class in the same way by the *Westminster Review*, July 1864, 'The Tenure of Land'.
19 *Political Economy*, 1872 ed., p.89. Cf A. Smith, *The Wealth of Nations*, 1776, book I, chap XI.
20 Parliamentary Papers, 1876, vols 335 and C.1492. Owners of land outside the metropolis total as follows (owners of one acre and over in brackets): England and Wales 972,836 (262,986); Scotland 132,131 (19,104); Ireland 68,758 (32,164). These total for the United Kingdom 1,173,725 (314,704), but allowance must be made for duplications. Deducting for these and for corporation, charity and glebe lands, George Shaw Lefevre arrived at totals of 1,153,816 (301,378) in a population (1871) of 27,431,000 – *Freedom of Land*, 1880, p.10.
21 Cf *Parliamentary Papers*, 1869, vol C.66: 'Reports . . . respecting the Tenures of Land in the Several Countries of Europe': the report on France (Part I, 59) gives an estimate of 5,300,000 owners, 5 million of whom average 6 acres each, in a

population of 38 million; that on Prussia (Part I, 217) 1,111,117 proprietors, and only 60,739 tenants in a population of 19.7 million.

22  A. Arnold, *Free Land*, London, 1880, p.4.

23  *Ibid*, p.7; Brodrick, *op cit*, p.165. Cf J. Kay, *Free Trade in Land*, London, 1879, pp.14–17; Shaw Lefevre, *op cit*, p.9–13.

24  March, 1844, 'The Land Tax'.

25  R. Cobden, *Speeches on Questions of Public Policy*, London, 1870, vol I, p.344.

26  Speech in House of Commons, 14 March 1842, reprinted as *The Land Tax Fraud*, 1842.

27  T.E. Cliffe Leslie, 'The Land System of the Country a Reason for a Reform of Parliament', in *Fraser's Magazine*, February 1867. Cf *inter alia*, Anti-Corn Law League, *The Constitutional Right to a Revision of the Land Tax 1 (1842)*; *Westminster Review*, January 1870, 'Land Tenures and their Consequences', and October 1870, 'The Land Question in England'; Leslie, *Land Systems and Industrial Economy of Ireland England and Continental Countries*, London 1870, p.207; J. Fisher, *History of Landholding in England*, London and Edinburgh 1876.

28  J. Beal, *Free Trade in Land*, London 1876 ed., p.v.

29  Ironically, the few spectacular examples of such behaviour, eg in the second Duke of Buckingham and Chandos or 'mad' George Wyndham, ended in sales of part or all of the land.

30  Quoted by Beal, *op cit*, p.24.

31  'Ireland and the Land Act', in *The Nineteenth Century*, October 1881.

32  Cf MacDonell, *op cit*, p.118.

33  Beal, *op cit*, p.vi.

34  Cf Mill, *op cit*, vol IV, p.239. 'Explanatory Statement of the Land Tenure Reform Association' (1870); Garvin, *op cit*, vol II, p.191.

35  Cf H.M. Lynd, *England in the 1880s*, London and New York: Oxford University Press, 1945, pp.124–32. For contemporary schemes for public ownership of land, *see inter alia*, G. Odger, 'The Land Question', in *Contemporary Review*, August 1871; MacDonell, *op cit*, p.72; G.B. Clark, *A Plea for the Nationalisation of Land*, London, 1881; A.R. Wallace, *Land Nationlization*, London, 1882; and the publications of the Land Nationalization Society, by Wallace, F.W. Newman, Rev W.R. Fletcher, F.L. Soper, and others. For attacks on such schemes by moderate land reformers, see H. Fawcett, 'The Nationalisation of Land', in *Fortnightly Review*, December 1872; J.S. Nicholson, *Tenant's Gain not Landlord's Loss*, Edinburgh, 1883, p.75; S. Smith 'The Nationalisation of Land', in *Contemporary Review*, December 1883; F. Pollock, *The Land Laws*, 1883, p.184. The special taxation of land was a familiar idea in Britain before the arrival of Henry George: cf the ideas of Spence, Paine and James Mill. MacDonell, *op cit*, p.74, fore-shadows the Georgist single tax in a scheme, alternative to nationalisation, for progressively confiscatory taxation of rent

36  Cf J. Hyder, *The Case for Land Nationalization*, London: Simpkin & Marshall, 1913.

37  Cf Lord Eversley, *Commons, Forests and Footpaths*, London, 1910. Commons were not completely safe from encroachment by lords of manors until the virtual repeal of the Statute of Merton (1236) in 1893 – *ibid*, p.211.

38  Cf J. Howard, *The Tenant Farmer: Land Laws and Landlords*, London, 1879; *Programme of the Farmer's Alliance* [Broadsheet, 1879]. The principal leaders of the movement were Howard, agricultural implements manufacturer and freehold farmer, J.W. Barclay, shipowner and freehold farmer, and W.E. Bear, agricultural journalist; they were all strong supporters of free trade in land, leasehold enfran-

chisement, and the campaign, led by P.A. Taylor and J.B. Grant, of the Anti-Game Law League.

39 Cf MacDonell, 'Some New Aspects of the Land Question', in *Fortnightly Review*, May 1872; J.T. Emmett, 'The Ethics of Urban Leaseholds', in *British Quarterly Review*, April 1879; J.S. Rubinstein, *The Enfranchisement of Leaseholds* (1884); H. Broadhurst, 'Leasehold Enfranchisement', in *The Nineteenth Century*, June 1885; *Reports, etc., of Select Committees on Town Holdings*, 1886–92, Parliamentary Papers, 1886, vol XII 367; 1887, Vol XIII 41; 1888, Vol XXII 1; 1889, Vol XV 1, 1890, Vol XVIII 1; 1890–1, Vol. XVIII 15, 1892, Vol XVIII 613, and of *Royal Commission on Housing of Working Classes*, Parliamentary Papers, 1884–5, Vol XXXI 1. For a reasoned attack by an eminent lawyer, see Sir A. Underhill, *Leasehold Enfranchisement* (1887).

40 Cf J. Collings and J. L. Green, *Life of Collings*, London: Longmans, 1930, chaps XVIII ff.

41 It was in no way a specifically Irish movement as might be inferred from W.L. Burn 'Free Trade in Land: An Aspect of the Irish Question', in *Transactions of Royal Historical Society*, 4th series, vol XXXI, 1949.

42 Baxter, *op cit*, p.4.

43 Cf H.J. Habakkuk, 'Marriage Settlements in the 18th Century', *Transactions of Royal Historical Society*, 4th series, XXXII, 1950.

44 Arnold, *op cit*, p.126.

45 'G.R.', article in *National Reformer*, May–June 1862, reprinted as *The Land Question* (1863).

46 March, 1846, 'Registration of Landed Property'.

47 *Anti-Corn Law Tract No. 2: Sir Robert Peel's Burdens on Land* (1842).

48 Sir Edward Knatchbull, Paymaster of the Forces 1841–5 – cf Fay, *op cit*, p.93.

49 *Anti-Corn Law Tract No. 2*, p.103.

50 Cf *Westminster Review*, March 1844, 'The Land Tax'.

51 *Op cit*, VIII.

52 Cf Briggs, *op cit*, p.219.

53 Morley, *Life of Cobden*, 1903 ed., p.561.

54 *Ibid*, pp.860 and 945.

55 Coben, *op cit.,* vol II, p.367.

56 Cf *National Reformer*, *loc cit*; *Morning Star*, December 1863 and January 1864, letters from Thorold Rogers and others; *Fraser's Magazine*, March 1864, 'The Land Tenure Question'; *Westminster Review*, July 1864, 'The Tenure of Land'.

57 Cf my *Origins of Modern English Society, 1780–1880*, chap VII, section 4, 'The Forgotten Middle Class'.

58 Of the 62 M.P.s mentioned in Dod's *Parliamentary Companion, 1880*, as land reformers or Radicals (excluding Irish members) 15 were primarily landowners or their relatives, 43 engaged in industry, commerce or finance, 15 professional men, 3 working-class representatives, and 2 army or naval officers. It should be noted that these figures do not exhaust the number of 'advanced' Liberals interested in some reform of the land laws.

59 J.A. Thomas, *The House of Commons, 1832–1901* Cardiff: University of Wales Press, 1939, p.16.

60 M. Beer, *A History of British Socialism*, London 1929 ed., vol II, p.240.

61 Other prominent members were the economists F.W. Newman and P.H. Wicksteed, and Mill's step-daughter Helen Taylor; Land Nationalization Society, *Annual Report, 1887*.

62 Cf H. George, jr, *Life of Henry George*, London, 1900, p.422.

63 Other handbooks were S. Lefevre's *Freedom of Land*, London, 1880, written at

Chamberlain's suggestion and published by the National Liberal Federation; and J. Kay's *Free Trade in Land*, 1879, a posthumous reprint of articles in *Manchester Examiner and Times*, December 1877 – September 1878. After the founding in 1885 of the (Liberal) Free Land League (later the Land Law Reform Association), the Cobden Club itself concentrated on the defence of free trade against the 'fair trade' movement.

64 'The Liberal Party and its Leaders', in *Fortnightly Review*, September 1873.

65 C. Mackay, *The Liberal Party, its Present Position and Future Work*, London, 1880, p.18; Mackay favoured universal adult suffrage and a United States of Europe.

66 *Radicalism: its Effects on the English Constitution*, translated from *Journal des Débats* by T.L. Oxley, London, 1880.

67 Garvin, *op cit*, vol II, p.392.

68 *Ibid*, vol II, p.178

69 'The Aim of Reform', in *Fortnightly Review*, March 1872.

70 Garvin, *op cit*, vol II, p.67.

71 *Daily News*, 5 May 1880; *Manchester Guardian*, 25 May 1880.

72 It was replaced in 1925, but the principles remained unaltered.

73 Garvin, *op cit*, vol II, p.59.

74 *Ibid*, p.104.

75 *Ibid*, p.169.

76 D. Lloyd George, *The Lords, the Land and the People*, London, 1910. The taxes were a duty of 20 per cent on the enhanced value of land to be paid when it changed hands, and ½d in £ on the capital value of undeveloped land and minerals. The root of the objection to them was not their size but the fact that the valuation they involved could form the basis of indefinitely extended taxation or even nationalisation.

77 Similar land taxes to Lloyd George's were, however, included by Snowden in his 1931 Budget, and repealed by the National Government of 1934.

78 Smallholdings provided under the Liberal Acts up to the end of 1914 totalled 18,484, only about 2 per cent of which were purchased, and two-thirds of which were said to be taken by village tradesmen rather than full-time agriculturalists. In January 1949 the total stood at 22,449, of which 9,288 were part-time holdings – Board of Agriculture and Fisheries, *Annual Report of Proceedings under the Small Holdings and Allotments Acts of 1908 and 1910, etc., for 1914* (Cd. 7851 and 7892, 1915), 4, 22; W.H.R. Curtler, *The Enclosure and Redistribution of Our Land*, Oxford: Clarendon Press, 1920, pp.300, 304; Ministry of Agriculture and Fisheries, *Smallholdings*, London: HMSO, 1949, p.50.

79 R.C.K. Ensor, 'Some Political and Economic Interactions in later Victorian England', *Transactions Royal Historical Society*, 4th series, XXXI, 1949.

80 'Liberalism and the Victorian Intelligentsia', in *Cambridge Historical Journal*, XIII, 1957.

81 J.A. Thomas, *The House of Commons, 1832–1901*, Cardiff: University of Wales Press, 1939, p.14–17, tables 1–6 (1868–1900), and *1906–1911*, Cardiff: University of Wales Press, 1958, pp.28–31, 44–5, tables IA, IIB, IVA.

82 Cf Morley, *Life of Gladstone*, London, 1903, vol III, 236.

83 *Ibid*, 256.

84 Cf H.D. Traill, 'The Allies: A Political Dialogue', in *The Nineteenth Century*, June 1882.

85 Garvin, *op cit*, vol I, p.462.

86 October 1871, 'Essays on the Tenure of Land'.

87 'The Radicals and Socialism', in *The Nineteenth Century*, November 1885.

88 The 1892 Cabinet contained 6 landowners, 1 rentier, and 2 representatives of commerce and industry, as against 8 legal and professional men; that of 1906, 8 landowners and 1 from commerce and industry as against 9 legal and professional men and 1 trade unionist – of H.J. Laski, *Studies in Law and Politics*, London: Allen & Unwin, 1932, chap VIII, and W.L. Guttsman, *The British Political Elite*, London: McGibbon & Kee, 1963, chap IV.

89 An equally illuminating test would be that of the railway directors who, beginning in 1886 with their opposition to Mundella's Bill to control railway freight rates, increasingly transferred their allegiance from the Liberal to the Conservative Party – cf W.H.G. Armytage, 'The Railway Rates Question and the Fall of the Third Gladstone Ministry', *English Historical Review*, LXV, 1950.

# 8

# THE PROFESSIONALIZATION OF UNIVERSITY TEACHING*

THE title of this essay ought to be the re-professionalization of university teaching, since the original medieval university was a professional training school for theologians, that is, for the professional thinkers and problem-solvers of medieval society. Its founders, Peter Abelard, Duns Scotus , William of Occam and the rest of the 'Schoolmen', were professionals to the core: they invented, or adapted from the Arabs and Greeks, the major tools of thinking which we still use – the dialectical method (thesis, antithesis, synthesis), the economy of hypothesis (Occam's razor), linguistic analysis (grammar), persuasive reasoning (rhetoric), and so on. They soon took on board the other vocational professions as they emerged, notably medicine and the several varieties of law, by the simple device of adding postgraduate faculties. And they rapidly adopted a form of professional organization, to segregate them from the unqualified and protect them from interlopers, which has remained effective down to the twentieth century: the chartered body with its monopoly of awarding degrees. The very words which they used to describe the organization – *universitas, collegium, societas* – were professional words, adapted from the commercial and industrial guild system; and the degrees were simply the levels of professional status, derived also from the guilds – undergraduate or apprentice scholar, bachelor or journeyman scholar, master scholar licensed to practise independently, and doctor or elder scholar, an alderman of the guild or *universitas*.[1]

The medieval universities, then, to which we should add their secular equivalent, the inns of court – graduate schools for secular lawyers – were training schools for all the learned professions – those requiring the ability to read and write the Latin language of learning – and, since such learning was necessary for many aspects of government, increasingly for the service of the state as well. This last function saved Oxford and Cambridge from the fate of the monasteries under Henry VIII, who said in their defence:

I tell you, sir, that I judge no land in England better bestowed than that which is given to our Universities, for by their maintenance our realm shall be well-governed when we be dead and rotten.[2]

---

* First published in T.G. Cook, (ed.), *Education and the Professions*, London: Methuen, 1973.

Why the universities and inns of court declined into mere finishing schools for young gentlemen, mainly during the sixteenth century, is not my concern here. It has been admirably dealt with by Professor Charlton in his book *Education in Renaissance England*.[3] Their popularity with the sons of the aristocracy and gentry increased as lecturing and examining diminished almost to the point of vanishing – a thought for today's campaign against them – so that by Queen Elizabeth I's day gentlemen's sons at Oxford outnumbered the lower orders by six to five.[4] They seem unlikely to have learned much of a professional kind: most professors did not profess, most readers no longer held readings, most lecturers refused to lecture, and the student who read a book and wrote a paper was lucky if he could find a tutor to hear him read it. At Cambridge, according to William Harrison in 1577, the colleges

were erected by their founders at first only for poor men's sons, whose parents were not able to bring them up to learning; but now they have the least benefit of them, by reason the rich do so encroach upon them . . . being placed, most of them study little other than histories, tables, dice and trifles . . . Besides this, being for the most part either gentlemen or rich men's sons, they oft bring the university into much slander. For standing upon their reputation and liberty, they ruffle and roist it out, exceeding in apparel and banting riotous company (which draweth them from their books into another trade), and for excuse, when they are charged with breach of all good order, think it sufficient to say that they be gentlemen, which grieveth many not a little.[5]

The final stage in their decline came after the Civil War and Restoration, when their popularity even as finishing schools – or drinking, gaming and wenching schools – began to sag, and the colleges turned into tiny property-owning oligarchies of leisured fellows – landed gentlemen by appointment, as it were, instead of inheritance – most of them spinning out a reluctant bachelordom while waiting for a college living in the church to fall vacant. Edward Gibbon found the 'monks of Magdalen', Oxford, 'decent, easy men, who supinely enjoyed the gifts of the founder'.[6] The undergraduates can be typified by Jack Egerton, heir to a Cheshire estate, who went to Magdalene, Cambridge, for a year or two without taking his degree. His mother wrote to him in 1729:

Your promises aided by my strong affections prove powerful enough to make me give in to what you desire [more money], even to forget past miscarriages if you'll be serious and make the best use of your time you possibly can for the future and study as much as in you lies to retrieve the precious time you have unhappily lost. In order to that you must drop all the Idle part of your acquaintance and they'll not care to trouble you if they find you intent upon a Book. Don't make much of your Self in a bad way.

No philosopher in Cambridge will find occasion for more than four-score pound a Year.[7]

By the eighteenth century, then, university teaching had reached the nadir of its fortunes as an occupation. One of its leading lights, Adam Smith, blamed the low pay and status of what he called 'that unprosperous race of men, commonly called men of letters', on the overcrowding of the market for teachers by cheap, subsidized education, only mitigated by the job opportunities of a still more inferior market, for Grub Street journalists:

The time and study, the genius, knowledge and application requisite to qualify an eminent teacher of the sciences, are at least equal to what is necessary for the greatest practitioners in law and physic. But the usual reward of the eminent teacher bears no proportion to that of the lawyer or physician: because the trade of the one is crowded with indigent people who have been bought up to it at the public expense; whereas those of the other two are encumbered with very few who have not been educated at their own. The usual recompense, however, of public and private teachers, small as it may appear, would undoubtedly be less than it is, if the competition of those yet more indigent men of letters who write for bread was not taken out of the market. Before the invention of the art of printing, a scholar and a beggar seem to have been terms nearly synonymous. The different governors of the universities before that time appear to have often granted licences to their scholars to beg.

He goes on, still more topically, in a way which would gladden Mrs Thatcher's heart:

This inequality is upon the whole, perhaps, rather advantageous than hurtful to the public. It may somewhat degrade the profession of a public teacher; but the cheapness of literary education is surely an advantage which greatly overbalances this trifling inconveniency. The public too might derive still greater benefit from it, if the constitution of these schools and colleges, in which education is carried on, was more reasonable than it is at present through the greater part of Europe.[8]

It is often claimed that Scottish education in general and Scottish universities in particular were not so moribund and amateurish as the English, and certainly the movement for reform of the profession was to begin there, amongst the friends and pupils of Adam Smith at Glasgow and at Edinburgh. But their superiority has been misunderstood and exaggerated, since they were primarily engaged in providing the secondary education which in England was provided by the endowed grammar and public schools. As late as 1823 *Blackwood's Edinburgh Magazine* remarked of the largest of them:

The University of Glasgow is composed of two things; first, a school where boys from twelve years of age up to sixteen or seventeen, are instructed in the elements of Classical learning – for they do not know even the *alphabet* of the Greek tongue when they are matriculated – and also, in the first elements of Mathematics, Logic, Ethics, etc.; and secondly, of an institution in which lectures are delivered on Medicine, Law and Theology for the benefit of those of rather riper years . . . The boys who attend the school wear red frieze gowns – and miserable filthy little urchins the far greater part of them are. To dream of comparing them with the boys of Eton, or Westminster, or Winchester, or Harrow, either in regard to appearance, or manners, or what is of higher importance than all, in regard to SCHOLARSHIP, would be about as absurd, as it would be to compare a Spouting Club in Cheapside with the British House of Commons.[9]

In Adam Smith's day, however, the social revolution which was ultimately to lead to the professionalization not only of university teaching but also of most of the non-manual occupations of modern society had already begun. The Industrial Revolution was undoubtedly the main driving force behind the reform of the old universities and the founding of new ones, as it was behind the reform of the old professions like medicine and the law and the founding of vast numbers of new ones, from engineers of every kind, through architects, surveyors, dental surgeons, pharmacists, chemists, physicists and the like to chartered company secretaries, accountants, insurance officials, and even interior decorators and photographers. These have been admirably chronicled by Geoffrey Millerson in *The Qualifying Associations*.[10] Industrialism operated very indirectly on the universities, since at first the universities were totally irrelevant to industrialism. Their function was the conservation of ancient scholarship, not the discovery of new knowledge, and scarcely one of the great inventions and discoveries that made the modern world was made in a university, until at least the closing decades of the nineteenth century. The Hunter brothers in surgery, Jenner in medicine, Priestley in chemistry, Bentham in law and government, Malthus in population studies, James Mill and Ricardo in economics, Davy and Faraday in physics, Darwin in biology, Sir George Cayley in aeronautics, Thomas Wedgwood in the discovery of light-sensitive chemicals which led to photography and, it goes without saying, the whole gamut of practical inventors in textiles and metallurgy, from Arkwright and Crompton to Nasmyth and Bessemer, operated entirely outside the universities. Two exceptions prove the rule: James Watt was given laboratory space in Glasgow University to prevent his eviction by the City Corporation – but this was by the individual patronage of Professor Joseph Black, and Watt was in no sense a university don or research assistant; and the Rev. Edmund Cartwright, inventor of the power loom, a wool-combing machine, a quadricycle and an alcohol engine (forerunners of the bicycle and the internal combustion engine), was sometime fellow of Magdalen College, Oxford – but he resigned to marry an heiress long before he took to inventing.[11]

Yet these inventions and discoveries, so remote from the ivory towers of the dons, were destined so to transform society that it would come to demand a totally different university system and a new kind of university teaching profession to service it – or rather, two systems, one completely new and one a reformed version of the old, with two almost incompatible professions to staff them. Both systems were to fuse in the twentieth century into a single one, with important elements contributed by each to a single profession.

The new system was new only for England. It had its roots in the Scottish universities, and, through them, in the main European tradition of university education. It was the professorial tradition of scholarship and research, of the dedicated scholar who found time to share his abundance of learning and discovery with a small band of student apprentices. It was oriented towards the real world and its problems, whether scientific, technological or social, and it stressed the vocational element of education, both in a sense of a serious call to the life of scholarship and in the sense of being relevant to the student's particular career. The tradition, never quite dead in Scotland, was revived in the eighteenth century, by Adam Smith and his teachers and pupils of the 'Scottish historical school of philosophy' – Adam Ferguson, Dugald Stewart, William Robertson, John Millar and the rest – who in effect founded the modern social sciences, notably economics, historical sociology, the statistical analysis of society, and that economic interpretation of history and government which so influenced Marx.[12] There was also a very practical school of applied science, characterized by Watt's patron, Joseph Black, professor of Glasgow and later at Edinburgh, where he laid the foundations of the modern schools of medicine and chemistry.

Into England the new system was imported by graduates of Edinburgh University, led by Thomas Campbell, James Mill and Henry Brougham, who with their Whig and dissenting friends founded University College, London, in 1826. This was a response to the demand by the expanding middle class for a university education, cheaper and more relevant to their needs than the ancient learning of Oxbridge. The first chairs, half of them filled by Scots, included medicine, law, political economy, logic, philosophy, modern languages, chemistry, natural philosophy (physics), engineering (not filled till 1841), mineralogy, industrial design and education – the whole spectrum of a modern university curriculum with the deliberate exception of theology. James Bryce began the first training of teachers there in 1836. The medical school was the lynch-pin of the enterprise – three out of four students (347 out of 469) in 1834 were medicals – showing the direct pressure of the demand of the new industrial society for professional service. Medical schools were in fact the leading shoot of the new growth, and no less than 60 of them were founded in various towns, as against 29 general colleges, down to 1851. The more important of these medical schools and local colleges evolved, often by amalgamation, into the new civic universities of later Victorian and Edwardian England, notably in Manchester, Liverpool and Leeds (the Victoria University, 1880), Birmingham (1898), Sheffield (1905), Newcastle (1908) and Bristol (1909), and the University Colleges of Nottingham (1881), Reading (1892), Exeter (1893) and Southampton (1902). All these followed in the professorial steps of Scotland and London.[13]

So too did the foundations of the Tory-Anglican counter-movement. King's College, London, opened its doors in 1831 with even lower fees than the rival 'Godless college in Gower Street', and with equally professional and vocational courses, including by 1840 medicine, engineering and architecture, and with an impressive staff of professors which included J.F. Daniell, inventor of the hygrometer and constant electric battery, Sir Charles Wheatstone, inventor of the electric telegraph, and Sir Charles Lyell, whose geological theories, despite his own orthodox opinions, did more to undermine traditional belief in the Biblical version of Creation than anything emanating from the 'Godless college'. Durham University (1833), a truly Church foundation designed to pre-empt criticism and perhaps sequestration of the vast wealth of the dean and chapter, was a collegiate structure consciously imitative of Oxford, but with its own quota of teaching professors and modern subjects, including chemistry, mineralogy and engineering.[14]

Yet this proliferation of middle-class universities in the industrial and growing commercial cities in no way derogated from the primacy of Oxford and Cambridge which, indeed, came to supply most of their professors. Their dons and students, too, remained at least as numerous in 1900 as those of the rest of the English universities put together.[15] The professionalization of university teaching, therefore, required still more the reform of Oxford and Cambridge, which in fact accompanied and even to a large extent preceded the founding of the civic universities. There the movement for reform could scarcely come from the 'inert, almost moribund professoriate', since, though some professors like Arnold at Oxford and Sedgwick at Cambridge played a leading role, they were too few and too powerless to transform the old universities into Scottish or Continental professorial institutions. The tradition there, evolved through centuries of playing bear-leader to recalcitrant and often anti-intellectual gilded youth, was of the college tutor, the guide, philosopher and friend, rather than learned doctor, of the undergraduate, who looked to him for the formation of character and a gentlemanly way of life rather than learning and a dedicated career of scholarship. Under such model tutors as Benjamin Jowett at Oxford and Oscar Browning of Cambridge the tutorial tradition was elevated to the fine art of raising Christian gentlemen with a moral concern for the less fortunate classes and a determination to serve society and the Empire. It was a noble tradition which did much to put a touch of altruism and *noblesse oblige* back into the selfishness of the Victorian gospel of self-help, which indeed it was intended to: Oxbridge's determination to civilize and save the souls of barbarian aristocrat and philistine *bourgeois* alike.

The connection between industrialism and the reform of Oxford and Cambridge is tenuous enough. The bludgeonings of the Whiggish *Edinburgh Reviewers* and the Radical *Westminster Review and Quarterly Journal of Education* merely put the universities on the defensive, as did the nonconformist campaign of James Heywood, the Manchester M.P., in the 1840s. It was only when a sufficient body of young tutors inside the sacred walls took up the cry – heard faintly from outside – that anything was done. Mark Pattison said of 1850: 'A restless fever of change had spread through the Colleges – the wonder-working phrase "University Reform" had been uttered and that in the House of Commons. The sound seemed to breathe new life into us'.[16] It still took two Acts of parliament (Oxford 1854, Cambridge 1856) and two Executive Commissions to open them to non-Anglican students, to give the universities some real functions over against the colleges, and to reorganize the professoriate. And it took further Acts and Commissions, in 1871–2 and 1877, to abolish religious tests and the celibacy rule for dons and put the relations between the universities and colleges on a reasonable footing.[17] The social cost was considerable, too, in the abolition of the poverty clauses for most scholarships and awards which opened them to 'merit' of the kind acquired at public schools, thus ensuring that the next half-century saw fewer poor students at Oxford and Cambridge than at any time in their history.[18] Nevertheless, new subjects were introduced, especially science, laboratories built, and Oxford and Cambridge began to become modern universities offering almost as wide a range of courses as the Scottish and civic, though retaining their idiosyncratic tutorial methods both of teaching and paternal care. At the end of the process the old universities had, like the public schools before them, been transformed, but not into mere training schools for the new capitalist *bourgeoisie*. Rather had the sons of the *bourgeoisie* been converted to the aristocratic, classically oriented values of Oxford and Cambridge.[19] Indeed, it might be said that two of the most significant features of late Victorian England, the smooth transition from an aristocratic to a plutocratic society dominated by a wealthy business class with traditional paternalist ideas, and the not unconnected decline of the innovating entrepreneurial drive of British industry, were largely derived from the 'civilization' of the high capitalist middle class by the public schools and the old universities.

By 1900, then, both new systems had come into being, and there had been an explosion of student numbers. In England and Wales numbers had grown from 1,128 in 1800 and 5,500 as late as 1885 to 16,735 in 1899.[20] But the profession was still tiny – less than 2,000 university teachers in Great Britain, nearly half of them in Oxford and Cambridge – and the degree of professionalization was minimal. The Fellows of the Oxford Colleges were still, in spite of the leaven of married dons, Nonconformists and scientists, recognizably the gentlemen amateurs they had always been. And in Scotland and the English and Welsh provinces (including London) there was no recognized career structure: the lucky few (31.4 per cent in 1910) were professors,[21] all the rest underpaid assistants, for the most part without tenure of prospect of promotion. And, outside Oxford and Cambridge with between 400 and 500 dons each, they were mostly scattered in tiny groups: Manchester, the largest, had only 67 academic staff, 24 of them professors,[22] and most had less than half that number. More important, although a host of new and especially vocational subjects had been established in the universities, in no profession with the exception of medicine was it essential to have a university degree, and the vast majority of business and professional men were non-graduates.

How did university teaching (and its recent offshoots in other higher education institutions) become what I have called elsewhere the 'key profession', the profession which selects and educates, and increasingly also does the fundamental research for, the other professions?[23]

Some people, of course, would deny that it is a profession at all – at best a collection of bits of professions, assembled on the principle that those who can, do, and those who can't, teach. But professions in this very professional century come in all shapes and sizes, and few of them fit all the criteria of the classic ancient professions of the law, physic and the clergy: the specialized intellectual training, the expert technique or learned 'mystery', the fixed remuneration by fee or stipend, the sense of responsibility for the fiduciary service which the client or public must take on trust, the closed association or exclusive club which protects the public and disciplines members, and over all the legal monopoly granted by the State.[24] But then all the emerging professions and quasi-professions aspire to these criteria, and we should rather think of a rising scale of professionalism than a definitive cluster of indispensable attributes.[25] On this scale university teaching is not so advanced as the law and medicine, or any of the registered professions such as architects, mining engineers or mid-wives, but it is considerably more advanced than the civil service, the bank clerks, the management professions (with the exception of accountants) and (until the teaching certificate finally does become compulsory), the school-teaching profession.

The academic profession is now in practice developing a specialized training, however inappropriate to half of the job (the Ph.D.); an expert technique, however ill-acquired (teaching by lecture and tutorial and research in libraries and archives or laboratories); a fixed remuneration in the form of national salary scales binding on the individual institutions; a fiduciary service which the clients (the student for teaching and the public for research) are increasingly disposed to question, but in the end still have to take on trust; a closed but not quite comprehensive association, the Association of University Teachers, which accepts only staff on academic and related salary scales and has a monopoly of negotiating rights at both national and local levels; and, if not a legal monopoly of the occupation, at least a form of tenure for all those who have completed three or four years' service which is the envy of most other professions.

How did the profession of university teaching acquire these wide functions, responsibilities and rights? How did it become the key profession of the twentieth century?

First there has been the vast expansion in the size of the profession and the demand for its services. From less than 2,000 members on the eve of the First World War and less than 5,000 on the eve of the Second, it grew to about 15,000 at the time of the Robbins Report (1963) and to about 30,000 today.[26] This enormous growth reflects two connected features of modern industrial society: the growing popular demand for higher education, or at least for the paper qualifications which are increasingly the passport to high status and income (even though the race for them could, but has not yet, become self-defeating), and the growing demand from business and the professions for trained personnel who, increasingly it seems, can no longer be trained by business and the professions themselves. One has only to glance at the list of subjects now commonly taught in universities which were unknown or rare before the war – from sociology or the Hayter area studies to computer science and business studies – to realize how much of the world's work is now taught and researched into there. Indeed, *pace* the claims of the polytechnics, there is no subject or vocation with a substantial intellectual content which is not taught and studied in some British university.

Secondly, they now reach and influence a much larger fraction of society than ever before. It is not merely they teach much larger numbers of students – about 240,000 today as against about 50,000 before the war and a peak of about 85,000 after it (1949-50) – and will teach still more, even by Mrs. Thatcher's reduced estimate, by 1981 (375,000); or that the percentage of the age group going to university has risen from under 1 per cent in 1900, under 2 per cent between the wars and only 4 per cent at the Robbins Report to 8 per cent today, and will rise to 11 per cent by 1981.[27] Nor is it that the real under-graduate population is much larger than that, and must include all those taking degrees in polytechnics, technical colleges and colleges of education, and the Open University – the figures are hard to come by, but they would probably raise the percentage of the age group now to 15 per cent or more and by 1981 to something approaching 22 per cent[28] – or that the vast majority of the staffs of the non-university colleges are themselves products of the university sector. It is the much more significant fact that there is now scarcely a profession or white-collar occupation whose upper echelons are not staffed by graduates, with the partial exception of the trade unions and the entertainment industry. Even the police and the armed forces are advertising for their quota, and paying recruits while they go to college or university. Leaving aside the economic and social spin-off in improved living standards, health and environment from university research, and the cultural spin-off from the books, articles, television and radio programmes by university dons, 'pretty well every person in the country', to quote Halsey and Trow, 'is moulded, directly or indirectly by university training'.

Thirdly, universities individually are now much larger and more complex institutions than they were. Up to the time of the Robbins Report the majority of universities and university colleges had less than 2,000 students, and the largest outside Oxford and Cambridge (about 9,000 each) had about 6,000. The new universities with their plans for a 'minimum viable size' of 3,000 students were then thought to be overweeningly ambitious. Now the giants of yesterday have become the norms of today, the largest universities are 12,000 or 13,000 and still growing, and even modest new and expanding universities and expanding universities think nothing of plans for 10,000. In terms of staff this means that most universities ten years ago had less than 250 academic staff, and only a handful had over 500. Today, staffs of 500-plus are commonplace, and ones of 1,000-plus becoming familiar. With this increase in size, a profound change has taken place in the atmosphere and organization of universities. Old, informal means of communication have broken down and have had to be replaced by increasingly formal, institutionalized ones: hierarchies of committees, a veritable blizzard of duplicated paper, a whole new bureaucracy of administrators with career patterns and professional problems of their own, formal journals or house magazines to maintain contact between the central administration and the outlying staff, and so on. And the introduction of much wider representation for junior staff and students has increased the formality, the number of committees and the frequency of meetings. Leaving aside the growing pains of staff discontent and student unrest which have come with increased size, university administration for both administrators and academics has become big business, operating large management functions and controlling expenditure ranging from £3–£20 million a year. At the same time single departments have become as large in staff and student numbers and in budgetary scale as whole faculties used to be, and senior academics have increasingly been forced to become managers and administrators rather than merely teachers, with consequent changes, by no means all for the better, in their relations with their junior colleagues and students. We have now reached the point where universities are seriously discussing sending professors and other heads of department on management courses.

Along with this, fourthly, the built-in tendency in all expanding human institutions towards hierarchy has shown itself. At the beginning of the century, as we have seen, nearly a third of all university teachers were professors. Between the wars, the proportion shrank to about one-fifth. Since the war it has declined still further, to about one in nine or ten.[29] But even this does not gauge the extent of the trend: there is a higher top emerging in the shape of 'super-professors', heads of department, deans of school and the like. (In the polytechnics and technical colleges, always more hierarchical in tendency, the trend has gone much further, and they are top-heavy with non-teaching heads of departments, schools and divisions, permanent deans, deputy directors and so on.) There is now a strong, anti-authoritarian counter-current, demanding departmental democracy, rotating chairmanships, and the reduction of hierarchy generally, but whether it will effectively overcome the powerful drive, common to all professions, towards domination by the professionally most successful and prestigious, may well be doubted. Indeed, a purely democratic profession is a contradiction in terms: professions only exist because some men know more or are more skilled than others, and if it were not so the profession would have nothing to offer the public. Democracy in all non-academic matters and consultation in all academic ones are the order of the day, but a university in which the students and junior staff were already as knowledgeable as their seniors would have nothing to teach them, and might just as well shut up shop.

Fifthly, as one might expect, the demand for longer training and more paper qualifications which is such a feature of modern society has naturally affected the chief providers of qualifications, and university teachers are better qualified in terms of higher degrees than they were. It is now extremely rare for a young lecturer to be appointed without either a Ph.D. or the prospect of one, and certainly without five or six years of higher education (that is one reason why there are so few women in the profession, since they have been reluctant to spend two or three of their most marriageable years doing research). Whether they are better qualified in the true sense of being intellectually superior is another question: with the expansion the proportion of firsts amongst new entrants (if that means anything) has gone down from three-quarters before 1945 and two-thirds between 1945 and 1959, to less than half in 1960–8.[30]

Finally, the increasing professionalism of the university teacher has expressed itself, as in other rising professions, in the demand for a professional organization with real influence over the terms, conditions and standards of the profession's life and work. The Association of University Teachers grew out of an association of lecturers caught by the inflation and lagging real incomes of the First World War. It was founded in 1919 when the lecturers and professors were forced into an alliance to protect their superannuation. For fifty years it remained a professional pressure group, with some influence on the universities mainly through their relations with the Vice-Chancellors' Committee and their pressure on the State through the University Grants Committee and the Treasury, but with no real power.[31] Suddenly, in the last few years its position has been transformed. In the space of a couple of years, between 1970 and 1972, it became a registered trade union, it negotiated real negotiating powers over salaries and related matters with the University Authorities Panel and the Department of Education and Science, and it came to be recognized as 'sole bargaining agent' in every university except Oxford and Cambridge (where the difficulty is to discover with whom to negotiate). It is still of course an uneasy coalition of professors and non-professors, whose interests, for example over narrower or wider salary differentials between the lecturers' grade and the professorial average, are often in conflict, and from time to time one or the other group threatens to secede and set up on its own or join a rival union. But on the whole the vast majority recognize that there is more strength in unity than in fragmentation, and the forces of cohesion are greater than those of dissolution. Its greatest achievement has not been in the field of salaries or superannuation, or even in the pressure towards an expanded and integrated higher education system, but in the establishment of tenure, in a shorter qualifying period and on better terms than any other university system or almost any other profession.

There are even signs that it is beginning to pull together the two separate traditions of the academic profession. For fifty years the fellows of Oxford and Cambridge, with their medieval corporate privileges and guild masters' equality, felt little need for the protection and support of the A.U.T. But recently, with the cold winds of change blowing from the State through the corridors of the DES and the U.G.C., they have begun to see the value of professional solidarity and have begun to join the Association in larger numbers. At the same time, the gentlemanly dons, especially in the natural and social sciences, have begun to become much more professional, more like their colleagues in other universities, and indeed, with more interchange, much the same people. Conversely, the introduction over the last twenty years of the tutorial system, both in the form of teaching in small groups and in shape of paternal care (one of the paradoxes of this age of aggressively adult students) in the other universities, has made the Oxbridge don indistinguishable from the university teacher elsewhere. Of course, given the in-built snobbery of English society and still more of the English education system, the sense of effortless superiority – effortless? superiority? – will die hard.

Meanwhile, the most important decision facing the profession and the A.U.T. will be to determine whether to make a takeover bid for all the academics teaching to degree level in the non-university colleges, or whether to maintain the principle that the unique characteristic of the university teacher is the combination of teaching and research at the frontiers of knowledge. Whatever it decides, there can be no doubt that university teaching is now nothing like the tiny, isolated and dispersed, and almost irrelevant occupation it was at the beginning of this century. It has become not merely *a* profession, but *the* profession towards which all the rest must look for the supply of new recruits and of new ideas, on which the future of our society depends.

## Notes

1 H. Rashdall, *Universities of Europe in the Middle Ages,* new ed., F.M. Powicke and A.B. Emden, (eds.) 3 Vols, Oxford: Clarendon Press, 1936, *passim.*
2 Quoted in A. Mansbridge, *The Older Universities of Oxford and Cambridge,* London: Longmans, 1923, p.50.
3 K. Charlton, *Education in Renaissance England,* London: Routledge & Kegan Paul, 1965, *passim.*
4 *ibid.* p.136.
5 W. Harrison, *Description of England,* 1577; L. Withington (ed.), 1876, pp.252–3.
6 E. Gibbon, *Autobiography,* Oxford, 1907 ed., pp.36, 40.
7 Mrs E. Egerton, to John Egerton, 25 March 1729, Egerton, MSS, Tatton Park.
8 A. Smith, *The Wealth of Nations,* 1776; E.B. Bax (ed.), 1905, I, pp.138, 140.
9 'Vindiciae Gallicae', *Blackwood's Edinburgh Magazine,* XIII (1823), p.94.
10 G. Millerson, *The Qualifying Associations,* London, Routledge & Kegan Paul, 1964, esp. chronological list, pp.246–54.
11 S. Smiles, *Lives of the Engineers,* 1866 ed., IV, pp.105–6; *Dictionary of National Biography,* IX, pp.221 f.
12 Cf. R.L. Meek, 'The Scottish contribution to Marxist sociology', in J. Saville (ed.), *Democracy and the Labour Movement,* London: Lawrence & Wishart, 1954.
13 Cf. W.H.G. Armytage, *Civic Universities,* London: Benn, 1955, pp.173–6, 224–5.
14 *Op. cit.*
15 A.H. Halsey and M. Trow, *The British Academics,* London: Faber, 1971, pp.145, 151–3.
16 Quoted in Mansbridge, *op. cit.* p.156.
17 Cf. A.I. Tillyard, *A History of University Reform,* Cambridge, 1913, Chs VI–IX; S. Rothblatt, *The Revolution of the Dons: Cambridge and Society in Victorian England,* London: Faber, 1968, Part II; B. Simon, *Studies in the History of Education, 1780–1880,* London: Lawrence & Wishart, 1960, pp.84–94; 281–99.
18 Mansbridge, *op. cit.* pp.108–9; H. Jenkins and D. Caradog Jones, 'Social class of Cambridge University alumni of 18th and 19th centuries', *British Journal of Sociology,* 1950, I, pp.93f.
19 Cf. Rothblatt, *op. cit.* Epilogue.
20 Mansbridge, op. cit. p. XXII; Armytage, op. cit., p.223; A.N. Little, 'Some myths of university expansion', *Sociological Studies in British University Education,* Sociological Review Monograph No. 7, 1963, p.196.

21 Halsey and Trow, *op. cit.*, p.153.
22 H.B. Charlton, *Portrait of a University*, Manchester University Press, 1951, p.183.
23 H. Perkin, *Key Profession: the History of the Association of University Teachers*, London, Routledge & Kegan Paul, 1969.
24 Cf. A.M. Carr-Saunders and P.A. Wilson, *The Professions*, Oxford: Clarendon Press, 1933, pp.284–7.
25 Cf. W.E. Moore, *The Professions: Roles and Rules*, New York: Russell Sage Foundation, 1970, esp. Ch. 1.
26 University Grants Committee figure for the main grades in 1971–2 is 28,840; with research and other full-time ancillary academic staff it would be in excess of 32,000.
27 Cf. *Education: a Framework for Expansion*, p.35, London: HMSO, 1972, Cmnd. 5174; *Higher Education: Report of Robbins Committee*, p.16, London: HMSO, 1963, Cmnd. 2154.
28 The White Paper figures for all students in higher education rise from 15 per cent of the age group in 1971 to 22 per cent in 1981, but what proportion of these will be on degree courses is still unclear – *Education: a Framework for Expansion*, p.35.
29 Halsey and Trow, *op. cit.* pp.151–3.
30 Cf. Perkin, *op. cit.* Table 6, p.260.
31 *Ibid. passim.*

# 9
# WHO RUNS BRITAIN? ELITES IN BRITISH SOCIETY SINCE 1880*

THE question 'Who runs Britain?' is an endlessly fascinating one for the British. It may be of some interest to students of power and society in other advanced industrial countries too, since the answers, and still more the methods of finding the answers, may throw light on the distribution of power elsewhere, and how and why it changes over time, especially under the impact of those two most powerful forces of change, economic development and political pressure from below. The two great revolutions of the modern world, the industrial revolution and the rise of democracy, were bound to have a profound effect upon both the *amount* of power exercised by the controllers of wealth, political force and ideas in society and upon *who* those controllers were and how they exercised their power.

Industrialism and its aftermath in the bureaucratic organization of mass production and centralized services have enormously increased the wealth of society and its capacity both for doing good (improving the quantity and quality of life for the many) and for doing evil (restricting human freedom and self-development and increasing war destruction). The rise of democracy has, paradoxically, enormously increased both liberty and tyranny: both the freedom for some to choose their rulers and determine the policies they will be allowed to pursue, and the obligation for others to vote for single-party regimes of right or left which then impose a dictatorship upon society in the name of the masses (that tyranny of the majority which Aristotle called 'ochlocracy', the pathological form of democracy). Because of the vast concentrations of political and economic power in modern society, it is of some importance therefore to know who holds it and how they have changed over time.

But it is much easier to ask the question than to answer it. There are a large number of problems to be solved before an answer can be attempted: conceptual problems (what is power, and what does it mean to exercise it), institutional problems (where does it reside, and through what organizations is it exercised), sociological problems (who exercises it, how are they selected, and whether and how they are interconnected) and ideological problems (what determines the

---

* Presented at Professor Wolfram Fischer's seminar at the Free University of Berlin, 12 May 1978, at the invitation of Hartmut Kaelble.

issues to be decided, the content of the decisions, and the terms in which they will be discussed). There are even those who deny that there is a question at all. They *know* the answer already: power is the capacity to exploit the working class (the mass of the people), it is held by the ruling class who are by definition the owners of the means of production, and there is no point in arguing about how they exercise it, since they control all the institutions of the State; and all the so-called élites of society are but 'fractions of the capitalist class' (see Nicos Poulantzas, 'The Problem of the Capitalist State', *New Left Review*, 1969, and *Political Power and Social Class*, 1973). This has been dismissed, however, by other Marxists, as a kind of 'structural superdeterminism, which makes impossible a truly realistic consideration of the dialectical relationship between the State and the system' (Ralph Miliband, in his 'Reply', *New Left Review*, 1970) — in other words, it is necessary even for Marxists to consider how and through whom the capitalist ruling class turns its economic power into political control over the State.

On the other side it tends to be argued that power is so dispersed in Western democratic societies that a ruling class no longer exists, but has been replaced by a pluralist system of countervailing élites. Raymond Aron in France, Lipset and Bendix in America; David Lockwood and John Goldthorpe in England, Ralf Dahrendorf in Germany, argue that, whereas in totalitarian states there is a 'unified élite' (Aron) which concentrates all power, political, economic, military and ideological, within its grasp, in the pluralist Western democracies there is a dispersion of power between divergent élites who may overlap or interact but who nevertheless prevent any one élite from permanently dominating the rest. In particular, the separation of ownership and management in modern large-scale industry and the general rise of bureaucracy supposedly fragment the ruling class and set up dichotomous and competing groups within it. One group of young British sociologists (K. Roberts, F.G. Cook, S.C. Clark and Elizabeth Semeonoff of Liverpool University) see the same *Fragmentary Class Structure* (1977) affecting the whole of society, and eroding the old class-consciousness and class-based institutions of both the middle and the working classes.

Marxist and other believers in the unified ruling class take their stand on the continued existence of capitalist institutions, the manifest survival of economic exploitation of the many by the few, and the persistence of gross inequalities of wealth and income in the Western democracies (though they studiously ignore State capitalism and the same exploitation and inequalities in the Soviet system). But as Dahrendorf has shown, the existence of class and class conflict does not depend on the unequal distribution of material rewards, or their non-existence on the spread of welfare measures or the much disputed *embourgeoisement* of the working class. It depends above all on the unequal distribution of *power* – strictly of legitimate power, i.e. authority – both in the state as a whole and in its subordinate 'imperatively co-ordinated associations' (*Herrschaftsverbanden*), including the economic enterprise or factory. Dahrendorf attempts to 'square the circle' of reconciling Marxism with pluralist interpretations by seeing traditional, owner-managing, capitalist property in the means of production (as distinct from 'post-capitalist' separation of ownership and control) as only one form of unequal authority by the few over the many which inevitably issues in group or class conflict. We need not go all the way with Dahrendorf in his belief that industrial conflict is becoming increasingly isolated from the expanding area of 'real life' outside the work situation – on the contrary, a man's occupation still colours his whole way of life and attitude to others inside and outside the 'imperatively organized association' in which he works – in order to agree with him that it is the objective distribution of power or authority which determines the social structure and how people see themselves in relation to it. If power (following Weber) is the 'probability that one actor in a social relationship will be in a position to carry out his own will despite resistance' and authority the 'probability that a command with a given specific content will be obeyed by a given group of persons', then it is clear that the élites, i.e. those who occupy what Wright Mills has called 'the strategic command posts of society' and exercise power and authority over others, are the real rulers of society.

Whether they are a unified ruling class in Meisel's sense of possessing 'the three C's' – consciousness, cohesion, conspiracy – is, *pace* Poulantzas, Althusser and co., an empirical question to be decided by examining in each society from what classes they are recruited, how they are educated and socialized for their élite roles, to what extent they are interrelated or otherwise connected as between the different élites (e.g. by intermarriage, overlapping appointments, membership of the same clubs and societies, or sharing of a common ideology or way of life), and how they exercise their power and come to their momentous decisions.

The difficulty is not merely that there is far more theorizing about élites than hard factual research: everyone knows that societies are run by the few, but how few, which few, how selected, how cohesive, how powerful, how permanent, how and when replaced? The further and greater difficulty is that such few empirical studies as exist are both too narrow and too wide: two narrow, because they rarely cover more than one or two élites, and in sufficient depth or on a sufficiently comparative basis; and too wide, because they usually imagine that it is enough to show that élites are recruited from a large minority of the population, the middle class, the non-manual workers or the privately educated, which is so obvious as to be trivial. Élites are by definition a minority of the minority, the *crème de la crème*, and the important thing to discover about them is precisely how narrow is the social sector from which they are drawn and to which they belong, and to what extent their circles of recruitment and activity have expanded or contracted over time. That is why many research projects which distinguish only between such broad social bands as the non-manual versus the manual workers, the privately-educated versus the State-educated, or university graduate versus non-graduates can tell us almost nothing about élites that we did not already know.

What we need are finer conceptual tools to discriminate between the important gradations of power, wealth and status *within* the minority at the top end of society. In societies which are by definition unequal, and increasingly unequal towards the top end, the important movements are not between the bottom and the top but within the higher reaches, just where most élite studies obscure the differences. That is why in my computer study of c.4,500 élite positions in British society since 1880 I determined to discriminate as minutely as the sources would allow, especially at the top end of society.

(1) As far as social class or status of origin was concerned, instead of the usual distinction between two or three classes (e.g., the most important study of the British political élite, by W.L. Guttsman, merely distinguishes between the aristocracy, the middle class and the working class), I chose a ten-point scale: I broke down the upper class (about 3 per cent of the population) into large landowners, big business men and higher professional men; the middle class (about 18 per cent) into farmers (most farmers in Britain are not peasants but small capitalists), smaller business men, and lower professional men; and the working class into the non-manual supervisory and white-collar (office) workers (about 18 per cent), and the manual skilled workers (33 per cent), semi-skilled (17 per cent) and unskilled (11 per cent). (These are very approximate percentages since the change over time: e.g. the manual working class has declined from about 80 per cent in 1880 to about 60 per cent in 1970). Even this scale

is not very satisfactory, since big and small business for example can mean many things, but the sources often give only a one-word description of the father's occupation. That is why it was so important to find some indication if possible of the family's wealth, as we shall see.

(2) In education, too, it is usual to distinguish between what the British confusingly call public schools (meaning private, usually boarding, and fee-charging) and State education, though many studies do distinguish between the major and minor public schools and also the direct grant (State-subsidized private day) schools (e.g. an eclectic comparison by an American, David Boyd, of the educational background of eight modern British élite groups takes the 26 best-known public schools, other public, direct grant, State grammar, other State schools, and foreign/other education). I decided to list all the most commonly named public schools (59 of them), other public schools belonging to the prestigious Headmasters' Conference, other independent schools, direct grant schools, military schools and four types of state school – altogether no less than 70 categories, which can be analysed in various ways by the computer. For the purpose of my own analysis I decided to reduce them to seven categories: Eton and Harrow separately (the two schools most favoured by the very rich and successful in Britain), nine other major public schools, other private, direct grant, State schools, and other education (private tutors or abroad).

(3) Similarly with higher education, it is usual to distinguish between university graduates and non-graduates, and sometimes between Oxford and Cambridge and other graduates; but I decided to distinguish between 12 categories: Oxford, Cambridge, London, Scottish, Irish and other UK universities, military colleges, the Inns of Court (for barristers and judges) other professional institutions, non-university colleges, foreign higher education, and no higher education. These two categorizations of secondary and higher education enabled me to see important shifts within the educational background of the élites.

(4) Finally, the most important thing one needs to know about the élites in a capitalist or 'post-capitalist' society, is whether people can buy positions of power and influence, i.e. whether the rich are a self-perpetuating class who can replace themselves with their own children. This is a difficult question to answer, since there are no reliable sources for individual incomes, and the only publicly available source is the probate valuations of taxable property left at death. The value of this source, which is often used (e.g. by the

Inland Revenue and by the recent Royal Commission on the Distribution of Income and Wealth) for estimating economic inequality, is hotly disputed since, it is claimed, the rich have many ways of disguising or redistributing their wealth so as to escape taxation. (That is why, for example, death duties have recently been replaced by the Capital Transfer Tax, which taxes wealth whenever it is transferred, and not only at death.) But the objections to this source, though highly technical, are not nearly so great as has been imagined: the rich do not so willingly give up *all* their wealth and power to their children, and enough remains to indicate a wealthy parentage. Moreover, the taxation is so light at the lower levels (down to nothing at all below £10,000) that the increasing number of élite individuals' fathers who, as we shall see, left very little, had no reason to hide what little they had. The use of the source is amply justified by the results: the fact that it shows that some élites – large landowners, millionaires, certain company chairmen such as bankers, brewers and shipowners – continued to be recruited from rich men's sons is an indication that the change in other élites towards an influx of poorer men's sons is genuine and not just a statistical effect of increasing tax evasion.

However finely one discriminates, of course, a computer study of this kind cannot answer all the questions one would like. It cannot, for example, determine whether you have chosen the right élite individuals, the ones who really make the important decisions in society. It is fairly safe to take Cabinet ministers, top civil servants (the permanent secretaries of government departments), and perhaps senior judges. But what about the chairmen of the 200 largest companies? They must be important representatives of British capitalism, because these companies in 1963 owned about two-thirds of the assets of the 2,000 or so public companies quoted on the Stock Exchange, but are they the *right* representatives? According to Pahl and Winkler, who studied the actual process of decision-making in nineteen companies, the important decisions in British companies may not be made by the nominal head of the company, who may only be a figurehead or a nominee of some other company – a holding company, a merchant bank or an American multi-national – and the real decisions may be made by others, by the professional managers who actually run the company and control the flow of information, or by the parent company which controls the finance. But Pahl and Winkler confuse power and influence (cf. Madame de Pompadour and Louis XV, Lady Falkender and Harold Wilson). The chairman is usually the highest paid official of the company, he is nominally responsible for its success, and he has usually got to the top either by making or inheriting money or by extraordinary success as a profit-earning manager. He is at least typical of the men who run the capitalist system.

In the same way, the chairmen and deputy chairmen of the nationalized industries are typical of the men who run the *public* sector of British business. They may be chosen because of their success in other élites, in the government (like Lord Robens of the National Coal Board, or Richard Marsh of British Rail) or in private industry (like Lord Melchett of British Steel, or Lord Cobbold of the Bank of England) or they may have risen from the managerial ranks (like Sir Monty Finniston of British Steel), but they are as responsible for their enterprises as the chairmen of private sector companies. What cannot be decided by this kind of study, however, is whether they see themselves as the successors to private capitalism or as its servants and supporters.

There is a similar difficulty over the trade union leaders (of the TUC and the eight largest unions whose members comprise nearly half the unionists in the country): they are to a man drawn from the workers whom they represent, but are they their servants or their masters, and do they make the decisions – to oppose or co-operate with the capitalist system or to support or oppose government incomes policy – or do they merely reflect the wishes of their members? And if the latter, which of their members, the militant few or the apathetic many? At all events, there is no doubt in the public mind that the major trade union leaders are important: Jack Jones, late General Secretary of the largest union, the Transport and General Workers, was voted in a public opinion poll the most powerful man in the country, more influential than the Prime Minister, and his name is better known than that of any capitalist. Whether that *makes* trade union leaders more powerful than great capitalists is rather doubtful, but there is no doubt that they are at the head of their own élite, which is sometimes called the Fifth Estate of the realm.

The press, and by extension the other media, radio and television, used to be called the Fourth Estate (after the Crown, Lords and Commons), since it was thought to control public opinion and so the content and outcome of political decisions. There are still a few Marxists who believe that it is through the manipulation of the media that the ruling class translates its wealth into political control, but if this were so we should always have Conservative governments. Very few observers now believe that newspaper editors (and proprietors, who are not dealt with separately here), still less the governors of the BBC and members of the Independent Television (now Broadcasting) Authority, have any major influence on public affairs, though some individual journalists and broadcasters may; the latter cannot be picked up in a study of this kind; any more than the successful pop stars and sports personalities who undoubtedly influence the ambitions and life style of the young. These may have influence but it is in matters so trivial (hair styles and clothes and, more seriously, drug-taking) as not to constitute power in the accepted sense.

Many of the professions, the doctors, lawyers, engineers, accountants, architects, university and school teachers may be important in their own spheres, but it would be difficult to claim that the presidents of the leading professional institutions, vice-chancellors of universities or heads of the great public schools were amongst those who ran Britain. They are included because they are representative of great functional interests and leading beneficiaries in prestige and status, if not indeed in income, of the social system.

Finally, there are three groups whose success is measured either in great wealth or high status: the great landowners who once were the élite of élites and undoubtedly dominated most of the institutions of government down to the early years of this century; the millionaires, whose continued determination to die rich proves the value of the probate returns; and the newly created peers, who can be considered the publicly recognized champions of most of the other élites.

For reasons of time and expense the military and religious élites (generals, admirals, RAF air officers and bishops) were omitted from this study, but enough is known about them from other studies to make comparison possible in all aspects save wealth. These alone excepted, we can be fairly certain that our 4,500 incumbents of élite positions (3,300 individuals if we allow for double counting, chiefly between peers and the rest) contain most of the people who have any claim to share in the answer to the question 'Who runs Britain?'

What changes have taken place between 1880 and 1970 in the kind of people who have occupied the top positions in British society? At first sight, and in the terms offered by most traditional élite studies, very little. Apart from the Labour movement (a majority of leading trade unionists and a large minority of Labour cabinet ministers) very few children of the manual working class (who have constituted from 80 per cent – 60 per cent of the population) very few of the State-educated (who represent 93 per cent of all school children) and a larger but still small percentage of non-graduates (who have made up 99 per cent – 93 per cent of all school-leavers in this century) have reached the top of our great functional hierarchies.

Even in these terms, however, there has been some widening of the area of recruitment. In the nineteenth century no member of the Cabinet was the son of a working man, and even down to the First World War there was only one, John Burns, the token trade unionist in the last Liberal government. By the 1960s over a third of the Labour cabinet came from working–class families, and it was even possible to find the odd Conservative minister, Ernest Marples, son of an engine fitter though himself a self–made business man, from that class. Again, down to the First World War State-educated cabinet ministers were almost unknown, but now they are comparatively thick on the ground: nearly two-thirds of the Labour governments, including James Callaghan, Harold Wilson, Roy Jenkins, Denis Healey, Barbara Castle, Shirley Williams and other leading figures; and even some of the leading Conservatives, including Edward Heath, Margaret Thatcher and Anthony Barber. Graduates, on the other hand, have been holding their own in Conservative cabinets, and even increasing their share of Labour ones, but this is partly (as we shall see) a measure of the increasing importance of higher education as an instrument of social mobility.

Similarly, there has been a noticeable expansion of the small minority of children of the working class, (including the non-manual or white-collar working class) who became top civil servants, great company chairmen and even millionaires, from one or two in each case before 1900 to about one in six in the most recent cohort – men like Lord Armstrong, last Head of the Civil Service, whose father was an 'officer' in the Salvation Army (the equivalent of a very poor dissenting church worker), Lord Kearton, late Chairman of Courtaulds and now Chairman of the government's Industrial Development Corporation, whose father was a bricklayer, and William Morris, Lord Nuffield, the pioneer of mass-produced motor cars in Britain, who began life as a bicycle mechanic and left £3¼ million in 1963. There was a still greater expansion of the State-educated amongst the top civil servants, from none before 1900 to 25 per cent (33 per cent with direct grant), less amongst the company chairmen and millionaires, where the self-made men of the Victorian and Edwardian age, like Lord Leverhulme of Unilever or Lord Armstrong, the armaments king, have not yet been wholly replaced by the bright scholarship boys climbing the managerial ladder. In the public sector, by contrast, the heads of the nationalized industries have had substantial minorities of working-class sons (21 per cent) and of the State-educated (35 per cent), mainly because of their partial recruitment from other élites, including the Labour movement, and from rising managers within the industries.

Surprisingly perhaps, very few working–class children appear in the professional élites: very few senior judges (and none from the manual classes), only one president of the two great medical colleges, only a handful of presidential accountants, architects, civil and mechanical engineers, solicitors, great public school headmasters, or Oxbridge vice-chancellors – though other vice-chancellors show a steadily increasing percentage, to a third in the last cohort. This is perhaps because of the role of education in the recruitment of the professions, where the State-educated (mainly from the lower middle class) have made a modest but increasing appearance even amongst the judges and especially amongst the other vice-chancellors. But it must be remembered that the professional élites here dealt with are, apart from the judges, largely symbolic figures, and it is well known that the professions, notably teaching, university teaching, engineering and the like, are avenues for the upwardly mobile from the working class, though they may lack the traditional background and confidence to stand for elective office in their professional institutions.

(If we turn for comparison to the mainly educational surveys of the two main élites not dealt with here, high-ranking military officers and bishops of the Church of England we find, for example from Otley's study of Army generals since 1870 that very few working-men's sons ever reached the rank of lieutenant-general or above, but that there has been an increase since the war in the small minority of generals coming from State schools (to 11 per cent in 1959); and from various studies of bishops since the war that none are *known* to have come from the working class but that a small and slightly increasing minority (11–13 per cent) come from non-public schools.)

Thus, even in traditional terms there has been in most élites a modest increase in the rate of upward mobility from the working class and the State-educated, in line with the vertical mobility discovered by Hartmut Kaelble in Germany, S.M. Miller in the United States, and Lipset and Bendix in other industrial societies. But it is when we come to the finer measurements of mobility within the upper reaches of society that we discover the more profound changes which have been going on in Britain in the recruitment of the élites. For example, while the great landowners who used to be the master élite in British society and predominated in the House of Commons until 1885, in the Cabinet until 1905 and in the House of Lords until well after the First World War, remained much richer than all other élites except the millionaires (with whom they overlapped to the extent of 13 per cent or more), they lost their hold on the political élites through which they used to control society. Landowners' sons have shrunk from 60 per cent to only 15 per cent of Conservative cabinet ministers (and only the odd maverick among Labour ministers), from 31 per cent to only 4 per cent of newly created peers, and from 28 per cent to only 2 per cent of top civil servants. From most other élites, great company chairmen, heads of nationalized industries, judges and other professional men, they have almost disappeared.

Surprisingly, the sons of bigger business men have not taken their place. Contrary to popular opinion large capitalists and their sons have never been a majority in Conservative governments, nor for that matter in the Liberal, still less in Labour governments; in the top civil service they have increased, but only from 5 per cent to 15 per cent; and amongst newly-created peers they have shrunk from 28 per cent to 20 per cent. They have even shrunk (63 per cent – 44 per cent) amongst great company chairmen – a reflection of the rise of the professional manager – and (57 per cent – 49 per cent) amongst millionaires – a measure of the persistence of landed wealth on the one side and of the self-made business man on the other.

Privileged education is even more revealing. It remains true, as we have seen, that the privately educated still dominate most élites (the Labour movement alone excepted). But non-State education covers a wide range, from Eton and Harrow and the other great schools down to private schools of low standards and prestige, while alongside them all were (until they lost their government subsidies in 1977) the meritocratic direct grant schools which were little different in recruitment from the best State grammar schools and educationally better than most if not all private schools. The changing pattern of élite recruitment *within* the privately educated is significant. The dozen or so major public schools still have far more than their share of most élites, but they are undoubtedly losing ground to the lesser independent and State schools. In the Conservative cabinet, the great bastion of Eton and Harrow, their share has declined from two-thirds to one third, and that of the major public schools from 77 per cent – 58 per cent. In the top civil service old Etonians have declined from 41 per cent – 6 per cent, major public schoolboys from 72 per cent – 29 per cent. Amongst great company chairmen on the other hand it has persisted at 43 – 45 per cent, partly because in Britain even self-made business men send their sons to the 'best' (i.e. most expensive) schools. For the same reason it has even increased amongst judges (38 per cent – 48 per cent) and several other professions (medical presidents, civil engineers, solicitors) but slightly declined amongst the professions as a whole (32 per cent – 29 per cent). But in contrast to the old ruling class headed by the great landowners – 90 per cent of whom were educated at the great public schools, over 70 per cent at Eton alone – who were a unified élite educated in the same institutions, the new élites are drawn from a much wider range of schools.

At first sight, higher education seems to argue against this widening of the élites. In nearly all the élites there are increasing numbers of graduates, and indeed increasing numbers of Oxbridge graduates: Cabinet ministers of both major parties, top civil servants, newly-created peers, great company chairmen, senior judges and most other professions, and so on. But this is mostly an effect of the expansion of higher education in this century, from 1 per cent – 7 per cent of the population, and of the channelling of social mobility increasingly through the universities. If a working-class child or a State-educated middle-class one is to climb the ladder to élite status, the first rung is normally via the university, and until very recently it was, paradoxically, easier for really bright children to get scholarships to Oxford or Cambridge than to go to any other university. Thus both the rich, who are more expected now to prove their merit via a degree, and the poor who can normally lay claim to high status only via education, are forced through the channel of the university and, given the inborn snobbery of the English (not the Scots), preferably through Oxbridge.

But it is when we come to examine the mainspring of inequality in society, the unequal distribution of wealth, that we can measure most accurately the changing pattern of recruitment of the élites from within the higher reaches of society. Leaving aside those élites which are defined by their wealth, mostly inherited, the great landowners and the millionaires, there has been a universal decline in the average wealth of the families from which élite individuals are drawn, as measured by what their fathers left at death. This is true for most of them even in current terms, without allowing for the sevenfold inflation between 1880 (or 1900) and 1970. Allowing for inflation it is true of them all. It is best measured by the median of fathers' estates at 1913 prices, i.e. the maximum amount in real terms left by half the fathers. For Conservative cabinet ministers it has gone down from £80,000 in 1880–99 to £7,300 in the 1960s, for Labour ministers from £3,600 (in the 1920s) to £300; for top civil servants from £15,000 to £1,300; for newly-created peers from £39,300 to £2,300; for senior judges from £17,400 to £7,600; for most professional men from £5,300 to £2,200. Even for company chairmen it has gone down from over £108,000 to under £9,000, while the heads of nationalized industries have mostly been the sons of poor men who left less than £1,100 and £1,400 at 1913 prices.

What these figures mean is that all the élites are increasingly recruited from the middle ranges of society, from families which possess little capital but have enough income to send their children to the lesser private boarding schools or the more expensive or competitive day schools, and on to university. The more fragmentary social structure is reflected by a more fragmentary system of élites at the top, recruited from a much wider, though still restricted, sector of society.

Yet the question must still be asked: is there an inner circle of élite individuals who, however widely they are recruited, still control the power centres of British society? There is certainly one group of great company chairmen who appear to be a more unified and cohesive group than the rest, and have overwhelmingly come from rich upper-class families, have gone to the major public schools, especially Eton, and on to Oxford or Cambridge. These are the bankers, brewers and shipowners, to whom one might add the great landowners, with precisely the same background. Twenty-one years ago the alleged leakage of profitable information from the Bank of England was investigated by the Bank Rate Tribunal (1957), which led two sociologists at Manchester, Tom Lupton and Shirley Wilson, to trace the family connections between the people involved: Bank of England directors, other bankers, directors of eight big insurance companies, some senior civil servants, and some of the politicians, including the Prime Minister, Harold Macmillan. They found an extraordinary chain of kinship connections linking the bankers with the politicians and members of the landed aristocracy. Only the civil servants were not (for the most part) linked to the chain.

Again, a study by Michael Barratt Brown in 1968 of the concentration of British industry showed that a total of 378 'controllers' in 1958, chiefly bankers, held 881 directorships on 215 great companies, including all the major banks (29), the top 36 insurance companies, the top 120 industrial companies and 30 top overseas companies. Many of these controllers come from rich families, had been to Eton or one of the major public schools and on to Oxford or Cambridge.

Some on the other hand were certainly not from rich families, they went to State or direct grant schools and may or may not have been to university, but it could be argued that, being expert managers and 'profit doctors', they were more capitalist than the capitalists born. If there is still a capitalist ruling class, it could be argued, it resides in the bankers and other 'City men' who appear to control the 200 or so largest companies. Yet the question remains, can they, in an open and expanding society like ours, control the other élites, especially the government politicians, the civil servants and the trade union leaders? That question cannot be answered by a statistical study of this kind. It would take a piece of investigative journalism like Carl Barnstein and Bob Woodwood's *All the Presidents' Men* to put the jigsaw together – and in the end, no doubt, you would still not know for certain 'who runs Britain'. Your answer, I suggest, will depend in the final analysis on your political ideology.

# Appendix

### 1. CHILDREN OF THE UPPER CLASS
*(About 3% of occupied population)*

|  | Percentage | | | | |
|---|---|---|---|---|---|
|  | 1880–99 | 1900–19 | 1920–39 | 1940–59 | 1960–70 |
| Conservative Cabinet | 88.5 | 73.1 | 76.3 | 71.0 | 63.4 |
| Liberal Cabinet | 62.4 | 60.5 | 33.4 | — | — |
| Labour Cabinet | — | — | 28.0 | 28.4 | 28.6 |
| New Peers | 85.0 | 71.3 | 61.8 | 62.4 | 51.1 |
| Top Civil Servants | 70.2 | 48.0 | 44.7 | 36.8 | 39.2 |
| Large Landowners | 98.1 | 98.0 | 99.0 | 98.3 | 98.8 |
| Big Company Chairmen | 75.0 | 77.5 | 73.2 | 69.3 | 68.5 |
| Trade Union Leaders | — | — | — | — | — |
| Senior Judges | 50.0 | 54.2 | 46.0 | 61.4 | 75.0 |
| Oxbridge V.-C.s | 38.8 | 29.4 | 22.2 | 36.8 | 18.1 |
| Other V.-C.s | 54.6 | 51.7 | 31.3 | 20.6 | 22.6 |
| Nat's Inds. Heads | — | — | — | 32.6 | 44.9 |
| Newspaper Editors | 32.4 | 28.6 | 33.3 | 34.4 | 39.3 |
| Millionaires | 70.6 | 75.4 | 70.1 | 79.1 | 67.6 |

2. CHILDREN OF THE WORKING CLASS (INCLUDING NON-MANUAL)

(*Over 75% of occupied population*)

| | Percentage | | | | |
|---|---|---|---|---|---|
| | *1880–99* | *1900–19* | *1920–39* | *1940–59* | *1960–70* |
| Conservative Cabinet | — | 1.9 | — | 1.3 | — |
| Liberal Cabinet | — | 2.3 | 6.7 | — | — |
| Labour Cabinet | — | — | 24.0 | 35.3 | 31.4 |
| New Peers | 0.8 | 2.1 | 6.5 | 14.7 | 17.2 |
| Top Civil Servants | 1.8 | 4.0 | 10.7 | 11.2 | 19.0 |
| Large Landowners | — | — | — | — | — |
| Big Company Chairmen | 6.3 | 7.3 | 6.1 | 6.9 | 9.9 |
| Trade Union Leaders | 100.0 | 94.7 | 76.0 | 83.8 | 74.9 |
| Senior Judges | 4.8 | 6.3 | 6.0 | — | 4.2 |
| Oxbridge V.-C.s | 16.6 | — | 16.7 | 5.3 | 18.2 |
| Other V.-C.s | — | 6.9 | 6.3 | 15.4 | 32.1 |
| Nat's Inds. Heads | — | — | — | 25.5 | 16.3 |
| Newspaper Editors | 8.8 | 16.3 | 18.8 | 18.8 | 19.6 |
| Millionaires | 2.9 | 2.6 | 7.0 | 5.8 | 16.2 |

3. EDUCATED AT (ELEVEN) MAJOR PUBLIC SCHOOLS

(*About 0.25% of 14-year-olds in 1967*)

| | Percentage | | | | |
|---|---|---|---|---|---|
| | *1880–99* | *1900–19* | *1920–39* | *1940–59* | *1960–70* |
| Conservative Cabinet | 77.5 | 67.4 | 64.4 | 51.5 | 57.5 |
| Liberal Cabinet | 44.4 | 34.9 | 13.4 | — | — |
| Labour Cabinet | — | — | 10.8 | 22.8 | 24.0 |
| New Peers | 69.3 | 42.9 | 43.1 | 36.9 | 27.1 |
| Top Civil Servants | 71.1 | 47.2 | 40.6 | 31.1 | 25.3 |
| Large Landowners | 94.5 | 91.4 | 95.3 | 90.1 | 89.2 |
| Big Company Chairmen | 45.5 | 42.6 | 42.1 | 38.0 | 45.3 |
| Trade Union Leaders | — | — | — | — | — |
| Senior Judges | 38.2 | 26.7 | 34.0 | 39.3 | 48.0 |
| Oxbridge V.-C.s | 35.3 | 22.2 | 16.8 | 28.0 | 15.4 |
| Other V.-C.s | 20.0 | 25.0 | 21.0 | 5.4 | 14.0 |
| Nat's Inds. Heads | — | — | — | 23.7 | 21.7 |
| Newspaper Editors | 50.0 | 34.1 | 28.6 | 32.1 | 30.7 |
| Millionaires | 43.5 | 43.3 | 48.8 | 50.7 | 48.9 |

#### 4. EDUCATED AT STATE SCHOOLS
*(92.8% of 14-year-olds in 1967)*

*Percentage*

|  | 1880–99 | 1900–19 | 1920–39 | 1940–59 | 1960–70 |
|---|---|---|---|---|---|
| Conservative Cabinet | 3.2 | 6.1 | 7.1 | 11.5 | 15.0 |
| Liberal Cabinet | 7.4 | 14.0 | 33.3 | — | — |
| Labour Cabinet | — | — | 57.1 | 57.1 | 63.0 |
| New Peers | 9.1 | 10.1 | 12.8 | 25.9 | 36.9 |
| Top Civil Servants | — | 12.9 | 15.8 | 14.7 | 25.2 |
| Large Landowners | — | — | — | — | — |
| Big Company Chairmen | 9.1 | 11.1 | 9.1 | 14.8 | 14.7 |
| Trade Union Leaders | 100.0 | 100.0 | 96.3 | 100.0 | 100.0 |
| Senior Judges | 20.6 | 15.5 | 10.0 | 8.9 | 10.4 |
| Oxbridge V.-C.s | 17.6 | 22.2 | 27.7 | 16.7 | 15.4 |
| Other V.-C.s | 10.0 | 8.3 | 23.7 | 40.5 | 48.0 |
| Nat's Inds. Heads | — | — | — | 39.5 | 30.3 |
| Newspaper Editors | 23.4 | 20.4 | 26.9 | 23.2 | 25.0 |
| Millionaires | 34.4 | 15.8 | 12.8 | 10.4 | 19.6 |

#### 5. MEDIAN FATHER'S ESTATE AT 1913 PRICES (£000s)
*(including land where appropriate)*

|  | 1880–99 | 1900–19 | 1920–39 | 1940–59 | 1960–70 |
|---|---|---|---|---|---|
| Conservative Cabinet | 80.4 | 52.4 | 58.6 | 31.4 | 7.3 |
| Liberal Cabinet | 18.9 | 25.5 | 7.3 | — | — |
| Labour Cabinet | — | — | 3.6 | 0.8 | 0.3 |
| New Peers | 39.3 | 30.0 | 18.2 | 6.3 | 2.3 |
| Top Civil Servants | 14.8 | 11.7 | 3.9 | 1.7 | 1.3 |
| Large Landowners | 102.4 | 129.6 | 189.1 | 206.8 | 94.4 |
| Big Company Chairmen | 108.1 | 72.8 | 49.5 | 30.9 | 8.8 |
| Trade Union Leaders | — | — | 0.1 | — | — |
| Senior Judges | 17.4 | 12.4 | 7.8 | 12.9 | 7.6 |
| Oxbridge V.-C.s | 5.3 | 10.3 | 2.3 | 6.4 | 0.7 |
| Other V.-C.s | 0.4 | 8.7 | 2.6 | 1.3 | 0.9 |
| Nat's Inds. Heads | — | — | — | 1.1 | 1.4 |
| Newspaper Editors | 9.8 | 4.9 | 4.9 | 1.4 | 1.7 |
| Millionaires | 59.4 | 109.4 | 201.6 | 232.8 | 93.7 |

6. MEDIAN OWN ESTATE AT 1913 PRICES WHERE DECEASED (£000s)

(*including land where appropriate*)

| | 1880–99 | 1900–19 | 1920–39 | 1940–59 | 1960–70 |
|---|---|---|---|---|---|
| Conservative Cabinet | 136.8 | 59.5 | 44.0 | 18.7 | * |
| Liberal Cabinet | 108.1 | 53.7 | 6.2 | — | * |
| Labour Cabinet | — | — | 5.3 | 4.4 | * |
| New Peers | 119.1 | 69.4 | 56.0 | 10.4 | 6.1 |
| Top Civil Servants | 19.7 | 8.4 | 5.2 | 4.1 | * |
| Large Landowners | 282.3 | 311.3 | 274.7 | 102.7 | 22.2 |
| Big Company Chairmen | 572.3 | 118.3 | 79.8 | 36.1 | 14.8 |
| Trade Union Leaders | — | 1.1 | 0.7 | 0.5 | * |
| Senior Judges | 79.9 | 48.3 | 25.9 | 12.8 | 6.1 |
| Oxbridge V.-C.s | 10.7 | 10.7 | 8.0 | 6.9 | * |
| Other V.-C.s | 17.4 | 8.8 | 7.0 | 4.5 | * |
| Nat's Inds. Heads | — | — | — | 4.6 | * |
| Newspaper Editors | 15.5 | 5.1 | 5.0 | 3.8 | * |
| Millionaires | 1563.3 | 1265.3 | 856.2 | 516.5 | 306.4 |

\* *Note* Less than 10 deceased.

## Select Bibliography

T.B. Bottomore, *Elites and Society*, Harmondsworth: Penguin, 1966.

M. Barratt Brown, 'The Controllers of British Industry', in J. Urry and J. Wakeford (eds.), *Power in Britain*, London: Heinemann, 1973.

D. Boyd, *Elites and their Education*, Windsor, Berks: National Foundation for Educational Research, 1973.

R. Dahrendorf, *Conflicts after Class*, University of Essex, 1967.

W.L. Guttsman, *The British Political Elite*, London: McGibbon and Kee, 1963.

T. Lupton and S. Wilson, 'The Social Connections of Top Decision Makers', in Urry and Wakeford, *op. cit.* (reprinted from *The Manchester School*, vol. 27, 1959).

C. Wright Mills, *The Power Elite*, London and New York: Oxford University Press, 1959.

C.B. Otley, 'Public Schools and the Army,' *New Society*, 17 November 1966, and 'Militarism and the Social Affiliations of the British Army Elite', in J. Van Doorn (ed.), *Armed Forces and Society*, Paris: Mouton, 1968.

R.E. Pahl and J.T. Winkler, 'The Economic Elite: Theory and Practice', in P. Stanworth and A. Giddens, *op. cit.* below.

K. Roberts *et al.*, *The Fragmentary Class Structure*, London: Heinemann, 1977.

P. Stanworth and A. Giddens (eds.), *Elites and Power in British Society*, Cambridge: University Press, 1974.

# 10

# 'THE CONDESCENSION OF POSTERITY': MIDDLE-CLASS INTELLECTUALS AND THE HISTORY OF THE WORKING CLASS*

IN a deservedly much-quoted phrase, Edward Thompson set out in *The Making of the English Working Class* 'to rescue the poor stockinger, the "obsolete" hand-loom weaver, the "utopian" artisan, and even the deluded follower of Joanna Southcott, from the enormous condescension of posterity.'[1] It is no criticism of that great, rugged, sprawling, big-hearted book to say that what the English working class most needs to be rescued from is the enormous condescension of middle-class intellectuals. Ever since Marx and Engels, if not indeed James Mill and Andrew Ure, English working people have not, at least until very recently, been allowed to have their own history but have had it imposed upon them from above by self-appointed champions and apologists from the 'higher' classes. Thompson himself is something of an exception, more an old-fashioned independent country gentleman than a middle-class intellectual, living in a country house in Worcestershire and exhibiting in his concern for the long dead poor the traditional paternalism which he descries in the eighteenth-century squire.[2]

The middle-class intellectuals who engage in 'labour history', as they significantly call it, are of course mostly left-wing and predominantly Marxist, a coat admittedly of many colours. Perhaps it is an unfair sample but it is a curious fact that most of the Marxist historians of the working class I happen to know are tolerably-wealthy, often public-school boys born in the purple of the *bourgeoisie*. All the more credit to them, no doubt, for escaping from the Marxist shackles of class determinism and for sympathizing with the class from which, in their own terms, their unearned incomes are extracted. I myself am not so altruistic: born in a slum with a cold tap in the yard (we were lucky!), educated at a primary school which overlooked a slaughter-house – the source of much free entertainment – and raised in crowded streets of terraced houses between 'pot-banks' and slag-heaps until I won a lucky scholarship to a

---

* First published in an earlier version in *Social Science History*, Ohio: Kent State University, 1979, with the subtitle, 'The recent historiography of the English working class'.

university, I am too 'proletentious' – too proud of my working-class origins – to join the middle-class intellectual 'phoney proletariat'. Nor am I prepared to join with their capitalist opponents: I am proud, too of having been sued for libel for three years – unsuccessfully, I am happy to add – by the right-wing Institute of Economic Affairs, an organization funded by over 150 of the largest capitalist corporations. This is an accolade won by few of the left-wing social historians whose right to express their views on the working-class standard of living I was on that occasion defending.

The sociology of the well-heeled intellectuals of the old and new 'new left' would make a fascinating study, if they would allow someone to pursue it – they believe in studying the social conditioning of everyone but themselves. It would be presumptuous to anticipate the results but, judging solely from their own writings, it would lead one into what Eric Hobsbawm has called 'the ideology of the salariat', the psychology of marginal men caught between the upper and the nether millstones of the *bourgeoisie* and the proletariat, with great abilities but insufficient capital – 'intellectual proletarians' in Bernard Shaw's self-revealing phrase who would make themselves 'the gravediggers of capitalism', the *déclassé* children of the *bourgeoisie* with Oedipean ambitions to destroy their father and enjoy his place and power.

Whatever their rationale, the trademark of at least one kind of middle-class intellectual 'labour historian' is his condescension towards the working class which he seeks to control and manipulate. Sometimes it is unconscious and endearing, as Richard Hoggart noticed in the middle-class Marxist twenty years ago:

He pities the betrayed and debased worker, whose faults he sees as almost entirely the result of the grinding system which controls him. He admires the remnants of the noble savage, and has a nostalgia for those 'best of all' kinds of art, rural folk-art or genuinely popular urban art. . . . He pities the Jude-the-Obscure aspect of working people. Usually he succeeds in part-pitying and part-patronizing working people beyond any semblance of reality.[3]

And Hoggart aptly quotes Chekhov: 'There is peasant blood in my veins, and you cannot astonish me with peasant virtues'.

In some recent 'theoretical' Marxists it is conscious and bordering on contempt. Louis Althusser, with continental clarity and candour, puts this newer Marxist view well:

Without the efforts of intellectual workers there could be no *theoretical* tradition (in history or philosophy) in the workers' movement of the nineteenth or early twentieth centuries. . . . This is so for those reasons that Lenin, following Kautsky, impressed upon us: on the one hand, the 'spontaneous' ideology of the workers, if left to itself, could only produce utopian socialism, trade-unionism, anarchism and anarcho-syndicalism; on the other hand, Marxist socialism, presupposing as it does the massive intellectual labour of the establishment and development of a science and a philosophy without precedent, could only be the work of men with a thorough historical, scientific and philosophical formation, intellectuals of high quality.[4]

(Note, in passing, Althusser's distinction between Marxist 'science' and the 'ideology' of every other brand of thinker: as an eighteenth-century bishop put it, 'Orthodoxy is *my* doxy; heterodoxy is *your* doxy.') There are a great many manual workers who would gratefully exchange this pleasant kind of 'labour', paid for out of their surplus value, for the real labour of the fields and factories.

Now, it is true that Marx envisaged a role during the revolution for 'a portion of the *bourgeois* ideologists who have raised themselves to the level of comprehending theoretically the historical movement as a whole',[5] but neither he nor Lenin saw them as having the right to dictate to or replace the proletariat in the exercise of power (whatever happened in Soviet practice). Only since Marcuse and the Frankfurt school has truth come to be monopolized by an intellectual minority who claim the divine right to think for and control in the name of 'correct theory' the proletarian majority.[6] Unfortunately for themselves, the minorities making this claim are multiple and constantly changing and, fortunately for the rest of us, can never agree amongst themselves. In the West they are politically inept and feeble, but they have nevertheless had and are still having a pernicious effect on the study of working-class history.

Let me not be misunderstood: I am *not* saying that it is impossible for middle-class intellectuals, even Marxist ones, to write objective working-class history, and there are plenty of fine examples – Thompson, Eric Hobsbawm, Stedman Jones, Geoff Crossick – to prove me wrong if I did. Historians of every class and ideology have always had to make the effort to understand people of times, societies and social origins very different from their own, and have succeeded just so far as they have done so with imagination and empathy. Those typical non-Marxist left-wing middle-class intellectuals, Tawney and the Hammonds, had the imagination and empathy to understand both the peasants and rural labourers and their aristocratic oppressors. I myself, a middle-class intellectual of working-class origins, found it a challenge to understand the old high Tories of 1830–2 who, through their repudiation of Peel and Wellington, were the key group in the self-reform of Parliament; I discovered them to be not antediluvian reactionaries but social radicals who anticipated Keynesian economies and the welfare state over a hundred years before they became generally acceptable.[7] Marx himself, who denied in a famous passage that he was a 'Marxist', was always a more objective historian than most of his followers, including Engels: compare their different approaches to the history of the working-class family, Engels' romantic and pessimistic, Marx's realistic and optimistic.[8]

What I, like Marx and indeed Thompson and Hobsbawm, object to are those 'vulgar Marxists'[9] who think that theorizing about the working class is an adequate substitute for objective study, and that where the working class refuses to fit the theory it must be made to conform. Thompson has called this 'the politics of "substitution": i.e. the "vanguard" which knows better than the class itself what its true interests (and consciousness) ought to be. If "it" does not happen to have that consciousness, then whatever it has is "false consciousness".[10] Elsewhere Thompson speaks of 'a sophisticated, but (ultimately) highly schematic Marxism which, to our surprise, seems to spring up in the footsteps of those of us in an older Marxist tradition'. (In Marx's day 'sophistication' meant 'adulteration', so he no doubt would have sympathized with Thompson.) Thompson laments: 'So the old middle ground of historiography is crumbling on both sides. I stand on a very narrow ledge, watching the tides come up.' He rejects the 'ulterior reductionism' which would reduce all human behaviour, thought and institutions (in his particular instance the eighteenth-century rule of law) to crude class determinism modified only by 'false consciousness'.[11] As I hope to show, this reductionism, ultimately of people to objects to be manipulated (which Marx himself would also have rejected), lies at the centre of at least one stream of middle-class intellectual 'labour history'.

With the kind of labour history practised by the Society for the Study of Labour History – of which I am an enthusiastic member – I have no quarrel (though I could wish it would change its name). The history of organized labour, of the institutions, trade unions, friendly societies, socialist societies and parties through which leaders of the working class have tried to ameliorate its lot and make life more bearable for the mass of their fellows, is a necessary and inescapable part of the history of the working class. But it is not the whole of it and, since the leaders and, indeed, the participants in organized labour are often a small minority, it is often only a small part of it. Moreover, as some of its leading practitioners such as Royden Harrison have pointed out, it too often descends into an antiquarian administrative history of institutions whose only connection with the working class is that it is the 'object' of their administration. Of the life of the streets and factories, between strikes and demonstrations at least, it gives only a casual and oblique glimpse. Yet as a record of the struggles of the workers for decency and dignity it needs no other justification. The kind of labour history which offends and misrepresents the working class is the kind which treats them not as individual people to be understood for their own sake and categorized, where this is necessary, into discriminate groups which they themselves would recognize and understand, but rather as a monolithic block to be set against the opposing monolithic block of the capitalist *bourgeoisie*, the nether millstone to be ground against the upper in the theoretical mill of historical inevitability.

What is wrong with such labour history is that, though it is often full of sympathy and good will, it lacks imagination and empathy, precisely because it uses the working class as an object, a thing, an instrument of its own desire for reform or revolution. This, ironically enough, is the exact paradigm of the sin for which it condemns capitalism: that it treats 'labour' (the same abstraction as in 'labour history') as a commodity, a thing, an instrument for the production of 'surplus value' of profit. To the flesh and blood worker and his wife and children there is not much to choose between being used as a means to capitalist profit and as a means to the despotism of middle-class intellectuals. If anything, the former is the easier yoke to bear, since the capitalist merely takes your surplus value and leaves you free to protest and organize against him, while the middle-class intellectual of the authoritarian variety, left or right, wants to take your mind as well and, in the extreme event of his revolutionary success, to abolish altogether your right to protest and organize. It is precisely this belief, that he knows best what is good for you, and that any sacrifice on your part to place him in power over you is justified, which accounts for the authoritarian middle-class radical's condescension towards and manipulation of the working class. It is a species of alienation from their common humanity more demoralizing than the alienation produced by wage labour as a commodity, and leads by a sequence of moral gradations, or degradations, to the treatment of the recalcitrant as obstacles to be removed from the path of revolution.

The working class for their part, *pace* Althusser and Lenin, know only too well where this will lead: to the replacement of one set of exploiters by another, but with this essential difference, that the new set will suppress all dissent and, in particular, abolish that 'trade union consciousness' which Lenin and Kautsky found so contemptible but which to the working man is his main defence against exploitation, no less necessary *after* the revolution than before. Thus reductionism – of worker to thing, to be manipulated for the benefit of his intellectual 'superiors' – leads, not accidentally by the 'aberrations' of a Stalin or a Pol Pot, but logically and inexorably to the labour camp.

This grisly declension is not confined to Marxists, whether of the new or older generations. Perhaps the best example is that model Fabian gradualist, Beatrice Webb, who began as a paternalist rent collector for Octavia Hill and John Ruskin in the East End and ended as an apologist for Stalin's purges.[12] After her famous visit to Russia in 1932 she remarked on the cattle truck-loads of 'enemies of the state' which a friend of her niece's had seen there:

Very bad stage management. Ridiculous to let you see them: the English are always so sentimental . . . you can't make omelets without breaking eggs.[13]

This attitude, that the recalcitrant lower orders should be 'put away' for their own and the greater good, was already endemic in the benevolent, paternalistic circles from which she sprang: Octavia Hill, John Ruskin, her brother-in-law Charles Booth and their friends of the Charity Organization Society. Enjoining thrift, hard labour and paternal discipline on the deserving poor, they were left with the problem of the undeserving. For these they prescribed not merely a return to the 1834 Poor Law with its workhouse test and less eligibility but the setting up of 'labour colonies' and 'schools of restraint' designed to separate the incorrigibly idle, 'the unemployables' and 'loafers' from their families, presumably to discourage them from breeding. This was the remedy proposed not by self-conscious precursors of Hitler and Stalin but, amongst other liberal thinkers, by Canon Barnett of Toynbee Hall, William Booth of the Salvation Army, and Charles Booth the pioneer social surveyor, who went so far as to recommend 'the entire removal of this very poor class [one-twelfth of the population of London] out of the daily struggle for existence.'[14]

Some of the Fabians went further and recommended, with Sidney Ball, a Social Darwinian 'process of conscious social selection by which the industrial residuum is naturally sifted and made manageable for some kind of restorative, disciplinary, or, it may be, "surgical treatment".[15] The surgery was taken literally by Bernard Shaw and H.G. Wells, who advocated 'sterilization of the failures'.[16]

Contemporary Tory radicals and Marxist revolutionaries, however benevolent, were equally prepared to force the working class to be 'free'. John Ruskin maintained that 'all forms of government are good just so far as they attain this one vital necessity of policy – *that the wise and kind, few or many, shall govern the unwise and unkind*'[17] – as defined by Ruskin. William Morris, the ideal romantic Marxist who sought a return to 'Merrie England' via 'the road to Revolution', was as ready to break eggs to make bloody omelets as Beatrice Webb:

We are prepared to face whatever drawback may accompany this new development with equanimity, being convinced that it will at any rate be a great gain to have got rid of a system which has at last become nearly all drawbacks.[18]

David Kynaston's *King Labour* 'sees the course of working-class history in the second half of the nineteenth century as a necessary tragedy and suggests that a major reason for this was the inability of William Morris as a revolutionary socialist to influence organized labour'. That the leaders of organized labour might be wiser and kinder than their totalitarian middle-class 'friends' to resist a forced return to the poverty of hand labour and the medieval hovel is not an acceptable thought to an intellectual Marxist who laments 'the continuing post-Chartist phenomenon of 'false' consciousness, involving a misapprehension of the economic factor, a working class divided within itself and a still socially aspiring élite.'[19]

Here we come upon the chief indictment of the working class by some of its middle-class historians, that because of its divisions it fails to unite around the 'true' consciousness which they prescribe for it, and so fails to do its revolutionary duty. Even Stedman Jones, an objective Marxist of Thompson's 'middle ground of historiography', who catalogued the inhuman views of the middle class on the 'demoralized' poor of *Outcast London,* still blamed the failure of 'the dream of creating a united and Marxist-based labour movement' on 'the enormous gulf – cultural and economic – that separated skilled workers from the poor'.[20] This implies the common Marxist assumption that somewhere in the working class, between the political 'rootless volatility' of the casual poor and the 'spineless moderation' of the highly skilled, there was a potentially revolutionary majority only waiting for leadership from above and support from below. Since what Francis Place long ago called 'the ignorant' cannot be blamed for their lack of consciousness, it is 'the informed'.[21] the skilled and educated labour aristocracy, who have become the chief scapegoat for the political 'failure' of the working class. H.F. Moorhouse has explored the shifts and inconsistencies of the Marxist theory of the labour aristocracy, notably its changing definitions from pre-industrial craftsmen through factory subcontractors and pacemakers to trade union and Labour Party activists, and its self-contradictory belief that the labour aristocrats were at once cut off from the rest and dominant in their culture and politics, and has found 'lurking within the theory . . . a very simplistic theory of the development of class consciousness'.[22] Their most heinous crime is that, despite their alleged aloofness from their fellow workers and supposed gullibility towards *bourgeois* ideology, they have apparently defeated with ease the revolutionary consciousness-raising efforts of the middle-class intellectuals.

This theory, originating with Engels, seized on by Lenin to explain why Marx was wrong about the inevitability of revolution in Britain, and popularised in the last twenty-odd years by Eric Hobsbawm,[23] has recently enjoyed a revival as an explanation of the transition from militancy to moderation in the middle years of the nineteenth century. John Foster has argued in an influential book that the decline of revolutionary working-class consciousness in Oldham, and by implication elsewhere, around 1850 can be explained by 'liberalization', the chief element in which was the creation and manipulation of a *new* labour aristocracy of subcontractors and pacemakers by the capitalist employers as an instrument of social control.[24] He even claims, without evidence, that the labour aristocrats spoke a different language from their fellows (who were 'protected by dialect') and did not frequent the public house.[25] Unfortunately for Foster, the ground has been cut from under his feet by David Gadian, who has demonstrated that Oldham radicalism was a case of 'class collaboration rather than class war' and was led by millowners and manufacturers like John Halliday, John Halliwell, Joshua Milne and the redoubtable factory reformer John Fielden.[26] Stedman Jones, a more objective Marxist, further points out that a subcontracting and pacemaking labour aristocracy was not new at mid-century in engineering, still less in cotton and coal-mining, though he still argues that it was the vulnerability of skilled workers to merchanization and dilution by the unskilled which accounts for their political moderation.[27] Yet if this was so, why did the same threat in the 1890s have the opposite effect, and cause the skilled workers in the great engineering dispute of 1897 to become as militant as the unskilled 'New Unionists'?

For that conjuncture, however, J. Hinton has cleverly adapted the theory to embrace the new trade union leadership 'cut off, in its bureaucratic isolation, from the mass of workers, but claiming like the labour aristocrats of old to interpret the political will of the whole class' – a remarkable feat of remote control, if true! – and to lead it into the 'corporativism of the Labour Movement in the twentieth century'.[28] The way is clear for the final transformation of the labour aristocracy, by R.Q. Gray and others, into the 'union and party activists' who have since led the Labour Pary in the unrighteous paths of constitutionalism and reform.[29]

It is amusing to see in this the twists and turns of middle-class intellectuals seeking excuses for their own failure to manipulate and control the working class. They cannot see the simple truth, that the working class, far from being unconscious of their interests, are acutely aware of what their would-be manipulators are up to. Nothing is more galling to working people than to be told what to think by supercilious intellectuals and accused of 'false conscious-ness' if they do not. This accounts for their healthy suspicion, rising at times to derision, of intellectuals both within the Labour Party and still more in the more 'theoretical' and socially superior fringe parties further left. The exiguous support for revolutionary platforms is due not to the 'false consciousness' of the workers, who are only too aware of what Lenin called 'left-wing communism, an infantile disorder'. To the down-to-earth worker *their* dictatorship of the proletariat means the dictatorship of the middle-class intellectual, whose embrace is the kiss of Judas.

Fortunately, in the last few years the working class has at last begun to tell its own history, not in the self-justifying memoirs of the 'workhouse to lord mayor' genre but in the authentic voice of those who were more interested in their class as seen from the inside than themselves rising out of it. It began, I suppose, with Richard Hog-gart's *The Uses of Literacy* which in 1957 revealed for the first time in print the real life and attitudes of the twentieth-century working class. It was a badly structured book which compared like with unlike, the backstreets and 'ginnels' (alleyways) of the working-class Leeds of Hoggart's directly observed boyhood with the 'candy-floss world' of the contemporary working class as seen through the popular press and the mass media.[30] It displayed on the one side no awareness of the long tradition of the 'gutter press' going back through the Victorian sensational Sunday papers to the street ballads and gallows sheets which are nearly as old as printing,[31] nor on the other did it directly observe the contemporary working class except through the backward glance of the 'uprooted and anxious' scholar-ship boy. The first half, nevertheless, is a masterpiece of remembered history, which recalls the rich variety of emotional and cultural life of which outsiders, convinced that material deprivation must entail every kind of dehumanizing spiritual poverty, can hardly conceive.

In 1963 appeared *North Country Bred: A Working-Class Family Chronicle,* by Stella Davies, who had left school at 13, the fourteenth child of a warehouse labourer turned commercial traveller, and had via evening classes and part-time research become a Ph.D. of Manchester University in her 50s. I wrote in my introduction:

As far as I know, this book is unique. Family histories there are in plenty, of the rich and noble, the great and famous, or at the very least the educated and articulate. Working-class history there is in plenty, too, but apart from memoirs of exceptional individuals it is almost entirely the story of the wage-earning majority as a class, the impersonal mass which left its chief record in the criminal records and other administrative statistics of government, the 'poor' who appear in the patronizing memoirs of their betters, or the faceless institutional groupings of 'organized labour'. Working-class history from the inside, the history of real people with names and faces and lives to live which left little or no trace in the records . . . is rare indeed. And a working-class family chronicle, by a trained historian who yet spent most of her life amongst the people or the descendants of the people of whom she writes. . .is in my experience without parallel.[32]

The book, characteristically, was savaged in the Sunday press by a middle-class reviewer who said that he *knew* (ignorant of the work of R.K. Webb, Richard Altick, Lawrence Stone and others) that the working class could not write until 1870 and therefore could have no history.[33]

Since then, a plethora of rediscovered working-class autobiographies has proved him wrong. In 1972 was published in full the *Autobiography of Francis Place*, probably the oldest and certainly one of the most revealing of working-class memoirs.[34] Apart from its political importance as a major source for the London Corresponding Society, it gives the lie to those romantics like Engels who imagine that pre-industrial domestic workers 'vegetated through a passably comfortable existence, leading a righteous and peaceful life in all piety and probity, and their material position was far better than that of their successors'.[35] Place by contrast says:

It is but too common for a man and his wife whose circumstances compel them to be almost constantly together in the same room to live in great discomfort. . . . Nothing conduces so much to the degradation of a man and woman in the opinion of each other, and of themselves in all respects; but especially of the woman; than her having to eat and drink and cook and wash and iron and transact all her domestic concerns in the room in which her husband works, and in which they sleep.

And he talks of the 'sickening aversion' which prolonged labour in close surroundings brought on.[36]

A whole collection of *Autobiographies of Working People from the 1820s to the 1920s* was edited by John Burnett in 1974 under the title *Useful Toil*. As Burnett says,

One of the most remarkable characteristics of much of the writing is the uncomplaining acceptance of conditions of life and work which to the modern reader seem brutal, degrading and almost unimaginable . . . Yet most of those who experienced such conditions are not, in their writings at least, consciously discontented, let alone in a state of revolt. There is a sense of patient resignation to the facts of life, the feeling that human existence is a struggle and that survival is an end in itself.[37]

That is not what some middle-class revolutionaries want to hear, no doubt, but it is a truth which they would do well not to ignore if they wish to 'politicize' the working class.

There have, of course, been many others, too numerous to catalogue, either by working people themselves or those close to them. Amongst those most quoted are Flora Thompson, *Lark Rise to Candleford*, Mabel K. Ashby, *Joseph Ashby of Tysoe* and Robert Roberts, *The Classic Slum*.[38] As Roberts, the child of a corner shop in a working-class 'village' of thirty streets shut in between two railway lines and two main roads of greater Manchester, says,

No view of the English working class in the first quarter of this century would be accurate if that class were shown merely as a great amalgam of artisan and labouring groups united by a common aim and culture. Life in reality was much more complex . . . Inside the working class as a whole there existed, I believe, a stratified form of society whose implications and consequences have hardly yet been fully explored.[39]

Exploring it systematically, however, cannot be left to the exceptional literacy of a few working people and their close friends. The best hope of recovering the lives of the unexceptional lies in the new development of oral history.[40] Many of the oral historians are admittedly middle-class intellectuals but, unlike so many of their predecessors, they possess or rapidly acquire a proper empathy and respect for their 'subjects'. It is not possible for anyone with the least sensitivity to listen to the life stories of elderly working people, however inarticulate, without coming to respect their integrity, their vast experience of real, intractable life, their resilience under the blows of 'the system', their irrepressible sense of humour in the most appalling circumstances and, above all, the perspicacity of their observation. Their preferences for practical wisdom over intellectual theorizing is catching, and the interviewer who comes away with an unbruised sense of his own superiority must be thick-skinned indeed. In the tape recordings of the oral historian the inarticulate working class has at last found its own authentic voice.

Take for example Michael Anderson's (non-Marxist) application of sociological 'exchange theory' to the Victorian Lancashire working-class family, which comes to the condescending and dehumanizing conclusion that their relationships with kin had a 'calculative orientation', offering help only in the expectation of 'an immediate instrumental return'. This has been exploded, for a later generation at least, by Elizabeth Roberts' respondents in Barrow and Lancaster, who give numberless examples of unselfish kindness which could never be returned.[41] What material reward could an elderly grandmother expect who brought up the children of a deceased or absconded daughter, or the family which rallied round a tubercular brother, or the neighbour with a large family who fed and nursed a penniless old midwife? The 'calculative', 'instrumental' attitudes are, one suspects, in the eye of the historian.

Or consider the sermons preached at the working class from Malthus and the Utilitarians to Galton and the Fabians against their pauperizing and anti-eugenic breeding, without any consideration for their right to choose between affectionate family life and material comfort or for the difficulties of contraception. In 'Married Life and Birth Control between the Wars', Diana Gittins for the first time revealed how working-class women thought about sex and came to limit their families. When they learned nothing about sex and reproduction from their mothers, at school or from the (middle-class) family doctor, how did they come to decide that two or three children instead of five or six was the 'right' family size and where did they learn the means to achieve it? Not, despite *embourgeoisment* or 'cultural diffusion' theories, from the middle class since the latter deliberately *withheld* information, but from their own age-mates, especially at work.[42] So much for Marie Stopes and her middle-class helpers. As in other kinds of mutual aid, it was 'the poor that helped the poor'.

As for the labour aristocracy, Paul Thompson found only one such family amongst 500 respondents born before 1905: 'It seems possible that the pattern of individual occupational mobility and therefore of social structure was rather more flexibile in this period than has been assumed.'[43] In other words, as anyone knows who was born in the working class, brothers, sisters and cousins could be found spanning the whole range of manual occupations and even spilling over into non-manual work in shops, offices, insurance collecting and commercial travelling. And the prosperity and status of a particular family might turn less on the occupation of the main breadwinner than on how much he drank, how well his wife managed, how many secondary earners there were, and a host of other factors. So much for the permanent privileged élite of the labour aristocracy.

Indeed, as Raphael Samuel and his colleagues of the Ruskin History Workshop (seminar, journal and series)[44] have shown – new to outsiders, long known to insiders – the most important division in the working class is not that of the statisticians between the skilled and the unskilled but between the 'respectable' and the 'roughs'. It is a diagonal line, since it embraces many skilled workers at the top and more of the unskilled at the bottom. It corresponds, or used to correspond, only approximately to another diagonal division, between the pub-going and the church or chapel-going, though it was the amount and committedness of each that mattered, not the attendance in itself, since many went to both. But to the insider, the difference between rough and respectable neighbourhoods, or between the rough and respectable ends of the same street, is more significant than the division between the middle and working classes which, given the inter-mingling of white-collar workers with the respectable manual workers often within the same families, was a much fuzzier line. The respectable working class would feel less solidarity with the roughs, hooligans and semi-criminals than the respectable middle class today with, say, the Poulsons and Kim Philbys.

Yet while many historians have glimpsed the importance of the 'respectables', in the shape of Methodist or Dissenting Chartists, trade union leaders and Labour politicians from William Lovett and Tommy Hepburn to Keir Hardie, few have tried to understand the 'roughs'. In 'Quarry Roughs' and 'Country Work Girls in nineteenth-century England' (both in *Village Life and Labour,* edited by Samuel), Raphael Samuel and Jennie Kitteringham have tried to show, from oral interviews and written reminiscences, what made the Oxfordshire quarry workers so feared by their neighbours and the police, and why English women farm labourers were so despised.[45] In both cases rough work bred rough manners, but also a rugged independence which came from (comparatively) good, if irregular, wages and from the knowledge that, being at the bottom of the heap, you had nothing to lose by cocking a snook at authority and the respectable. More to the point, the 'rough' had their own morality and hierarchy of worth, in which strength, earning power, generosity and sheer dare-devilry were respected more than law and lace curtains. To understand the 'roughs' requires imagination and empathy even in the intellectual who has risen, almost inevitably if at all, from the respectable working class.

This is not to say that oral history can 'speak for itself' any more than traditional source-based history. The oral historian has just as critical and creative a role to play, in assessing his sources, discounting bias, collating oral and written evidence and so on, and still more in the creative evocation of the past life of his subjects, often in terms and with parallels of which they themselves may be completely unaware. The tape recorder, unimaginatively used, can lead to a new antiquarianism, whether in 'ethnomethodology', the new instant empirical sociology, or in the new demotic history. The historian, whatever his source material, needs creative imagination as well as empathy, and must aim to recreate, understand and explain rather than merely chronicle and record. But that problem is not peculiar to oral history: its solution has been the test of the good historian throughout the history of historiography.

Some of the threads of this new, more realistic and less manipulative approach to working-class history are drawn together for a key period at the turn of the present century in a recent book by Standish Meacham, *A Life Apart: The English Working Class, 1890-1914*, which draws heavily on working-class memoirs and on the tape-recorded interviews of Paul Thompson and Thea Vigne. Setting out to trace 'the patterns of working-class consciousness during the years before the First World War', he recognizes that much of the evidence comes from middle-class men and women, writing not just to record the facts but to urge reform: 'Sympathy can lie perilously close to patronage, a habit of mind the most well-intentioned reformers fought but seldom completely conquered. They wanted working-class men and women to lead not only 'better' lives, but lives defined as 'better' according to the standards and assumptions of the middle class.'[46] It seems paradoxical that a *complete* outsider, an American professor at the University of Texas whose life style must be as remote from that of the Edwardian English working class as the participants in a close encounter of the third kind, should display so much more insight into their mental and moral world than some of their patronizing fellow countrymen. A similar insight into the much abused working-class radicals of mid-Victorian England is shown by another American, Trygve Tholfsen of Columbia University, who argues that, *pace* the Webbs and the later 'schematic Marxists', they were independent of and in confrontation with the hegemony of middle-class liberalism.[47] It is perhaps *because* they are so remote, and can therefore exercise the necessary imagination and empathy without fear of damaging their *amour propre*.

For in the end the unimaginative middle-class intellectual, contemporary or historian, is a Narcissus who sees only the reflection of his own mind in his superficial view of the deep pool of the working class. As Robert Roberts perceptively observes,

the upper and middle classes, self-confident to arrogance, kept two modes of address for the poor: the first was a kindly *de haut en bas* form in which each word, of usually one syllable, was clearly enunciated; the second had a loud, self-assured, hectoring note. Both seemed devised to ensure that though the hearer might be stupid, he would know enough in general to bow at once to breeding and authority . . . It was a tactic, conscious or not, that confused and 'overfaced' the simple and drove intelligent men and women in the working class to fury.[48]

When I read of some of the more arrogant kinds of middle-class 'labour history', I share their fury, not least because its writers should and can do better, as a small and increasing number of them have begun to. The contrast between these two approaches reminds me of the two voices of Wordsworth (himself a middle-class intellectual forever patronizing or hectoring the Lake District poor about their spades or leech gathering or children's graves) in C.S. Calverley's parody. I end with it in the hope that it will prove a suitable epitaph for 'labour history' of the unimaginative and dehumanizing kind:

> Two voices are there; one is of the deep . . .
> And one is of an old, half-witted sheep . . .
> And, Wordsworth, both are thine . . .

Only when this kind of 'labour history' is laid to rest and superseded by the history of working people can we rescue the English working class from 'the enormous condescension of posterity'.

## Notes

1  E.P. Thompson, *The Making of the English Working Class*, London: Gollancz, 1963, p.12.

2  He is not above tendentiously selective quotation, however. In E.P. Thompson, 'Eighteenth-Century English Society: class struggle without class?', *Social History*, III, May 1978, pp.135–6, he quotes my *Origins of Modern English Society, 1780–1880*, London: Routledge & Kegan Paul 1969, on what he presents as a condescending description of eighteenth-century social relations 'as they may be seen from above'. He does *not* quote the succeeding paragraph (42–43) on the disciplinary social control exercised by the landlord and the harsh treatment of

those who opposed his will. As it happens, my whole argument about eighteenth-century paternalism is that it was Janus-headed and had a harsh, disciplinary face for the 'insubordinate' as well as a benevolent one for the deferential, and that class protest. always latent, was brutally suppressed whenever it became overt.

3  R. Hoggart, *The Uses of Literacy*, London: Chatto & Windus, 1957, Penguin ed. 1971, p.16.

4  L. Althusser, *For Marx*, English trans. London: New Left Books, 1969, p.24; in fact Lenin did not 'follow Kautsky', whom he repeatedly denounces in *Imperialism: the Highest Stage of Capitalism*, 1917, Moscow: Foreign Languages Publishing House, 1947, the English working class, and elsewhere.

5  *The Communist Manifesto*, 1848.

6  Cf. A. MacIntyre, *Marcuse*, London: Fontana, 1970, chap. 8.

7  H. Perkin, *op cit.*, pp.237-52.

8  K. Marx, *Capital*, Dent, Everyman ed., 1942, I, 529; F. Engels, *The Condition of the Working Class in England* in *Marx and Engels on Britain*, Moscow: Foreign Languages Publishing House, 1962, p.36.

9  Cf. E.J. Hobsbawm, 'Karl Marx's Contribution to Historiography', in R. Blackburn, (ed.). *Ideology in Social Science*, London: Fontana, 1972, esp. pp.270–3.

10  Thompson, *op. cit.* p.148.

11  E.P. Thompson, *Whigs and Hunters*, London: Allen Laine 1975, pp.258–60.

12  B. Webb, *My Apprenticeship*, London: Longmans, 1926; S. and B. Webb, *Soviet Communism: a New Civilization?*, London: Longmans, 2 Vols., 1935). In later editions the question mark was dropped.

13  'Was Mrs Webb "ruthless"? A Niece's impressions', letter from Konradin Hobhouse, *Manchester Guardian*, 4 February 1958: 'Aunt Bo . . . despised the working classes with all the zest of her admirable middle-class Victorian upbringing.'

14  S. Barnett, 'A Scheme for the Unemployed', *Nineteenth Century*, XXIV 1888, pp.753–4; W. Booth, *In Darkest England, and the Way out*, London, 1890, p.93; C. Booth, *Life and Labour of the People of London*, London, 17 Vols., 1902, I. pp.154, 166–8. The penchant of many middle-class Victorians for compulsory labour, 'state slavery' or 'semi-servitude' as a solution to the threat of the 'demoralized poor' is admirably catalogued in G. Stedman Jones, *Outcast London*, Oxford: Clarendon Press, 1971, esp. chaps. 15, 16.

15  S. Ball, 'The Moral Aspects of Socialism', *Fabian Tract* No. 72, London, 1896. p.5.

16  B.B. Gilbert, *The Evolution of National Insurance in Great Britain*, London: Joseph 1966. p.92.

17  J.D. Rosenberg, *The Darkening Glass: A Portrait of Ruskin's Genius*, London and New York: Columbia University Press, 1961, p.140.

18  A.L. Morton, 'A French View of William Morris', *Marxism Today*, 1973, p.152.

19  D. Kynaston, *King Labour: the British Working Class, 1850–1914*, London: Allen & Unwin, 1976, jacket and p.64. See also a letter by Morris of 1886: If you had only suffered as I have from the apathy of the English lower classes . . .' – E.P. Thompson, *William Morris*, London: Lawrence & Wishart, 1977 edn, p.411.

20  G.S. Jones, *op. cit.*, p.349.

21  F. Place, *The Improvement of the Working People*, London, 1834, p.10.

22  H.F. Moorhouse, 'The Marxist theory of the labour aristocracy', *Social History*, III, January, 1978, p.82; see also A. Reid, 'Politics and economics in the formation of the British working class: A response to H.F. Moorhouse', *Social History*, III, October, 1978, which quotes, p.355, Perry Anderson and Tom Nairn with approval on 'the *inadequacies* of the British working class' (my italics); though Reid

himself from his own research on the Clydeside shipbuilding industry in the early twentieth century stresses the diversity, fragmentation, job competition, inter-union rivalry and consequent inherent disunity of the working class under capitalism.

23 The origin of Engels' ideas seems to be his article 'England in 1845 and in 1885' in *The Commonweal*, London, 1 March 1885, extensively quoted in his Preface to the 1892 English edition of *The Condition of the Working Class in England*: Cf. V.I. Lenin, *Imperialism, op. cit.*; E.J. Hobsbawm, 'The Labour Aristocracy in Nineteenth-century Britain', *Labouring Men*, London: Wiedenfeld & Nicolson 1964; and 'Lenin and the Aristocracy of Labour', *Marxism Today* (1970).

24 J. Foster, *Class Struggle and the Industrial Revolution*, London: Wiedenfeld & Nicolson 1974, esp. Introduction and chap. 7.

25 *Ibid.*, p.238.

26 D.S. Gadian, 'Class Consciousness in Oldham and other North-West Industrial Towns', *Historical Journal*, XXI 1978, pp.161–72.

27 G.S. Jones, 'Class Struggle and the Industrial Revolution', *New Left Review*, XC, 1975, pp.61–9.

28 J. Hinton, 'The Labour Aristocracy', *New Left Review*, XXXII, 1965, pp.72–7.

29 R.Q. Gray, *The Labour Aristocracy in Victorian Edinburgh*, Oxford: Clarendon Press, 1976; Z. Bauman, *Between Class and Elite: the Evolution of the British Labour Movement*, Manchester University Press, 1972.

30 Hoggart, *op.cit., passim.*

31 Cf. H.J. Perkin, 'The Origins of the Popular Press', *History Today*, July 1957, see above as Essay 3.

32 C. Davies, *North Country Bred: A Working-Class Family Chronicle*, London: Routledge & Kegan Paul, 1963, 1.

33 P. Toynbee in the *Observer*, 27 October 1963, and private correspondence.

34 M. Thale, (ed.), *The Autobiography of Francis Place*, University Press Cambridge, 1972.

35 Engels, *op. cit.*, p.36.

36 Thale, *op.cit.*, p.116; for his occasional 'sickening aversion' to work see D. George, *England in Transition*, Harmondsworth: Penguin, 1931, pp.60–1.

37 J. Burnett, (ed.), *Useful Toil: Autobiographies of Working People from the 1820s to the 1920s*, London: Allen Lane, 1974, p.14: see also D. Vincent, (ed.), *Testaments of Radicalism: Memoirs of Working-class Politicians, 1790-1885*, London: Europa 1977.

38 F. Thompson, *Lark Rise to Candleford*, London: Oxford University Press, 1945; M. K. Ashby, *Joseph Ashby of Tysoe*, Cambridge University Press, 1961; R. Roberts, *The Classic Slum: Salford Life in the first quarter of the century*, Manchester University Press, 1971; see also *A Ragged Schooling*, Manchester University Press, 1976

39 Roberts, *Classic Slum*, 1.

40 The earliest exponent of 'oral history' was probably Henry Mayhew, whose vivid interviews with the street folk of London are recorded in *London Labour and the London Poor*, 4 Vols., London, 1861, which began life as much fuller articles on the working class in the *Morning Chronicle*, 1849–51; see E.P. Thompson and E. Yeo, (eds), *The Unknown Mayhew*, Harmondsworth: Penguin, 1971, and P.E. Razzell and R.W. Wainwright, (eds), *The Victorian Working Class: Selections from Letters to the Morning Chronicle*, London: Cass, 1973. Modern oral history has been pioneered by, amongst others, Paul Thompson and Thea Vigne and their journal *Oral History*, 1973 onwards.

41 M. Anderson, *Family Structure in Nineteenth-century Lancashire*, Cambridge University Press 1971, pp.110, 162–4, 179; E. Roberts 'The working-class family in

Barrow and Lancaster, 1890–1930' (unpublished Ph.D. thesis, University of Lancaster, 1978).

42 D. Gittins, 'Married Life and Birth Control between the Wars', *Oral History*, III, 1975, pp.53–64.

43 P. Thompson, 'Memory and History', *S.S.R.C. Newsletter*, No. 6, 1969, p.18, and *The Edwardians: The Remaking of British Society*, London: Wiedenfeld & Nicolson, 1975, pp.125–34.

44 See their new journal, *History Workshop* and the History Workshop Series published by Routledge & Kegan Paul, London.

45 R. Samuel, (ed.), *Village Life and Labour*, London: Routledge & Kegal Paul, 1975, parts 3, 4.

46 S. Meacham, *A Life Apart: The English Working Class, 1890—1914*, Cambridge, Mass.: Harvard University Press, 1977, p.8.

47 T. Tholfsen, *Working-Class Radicalism in Mid-Victorian England*, London: Croom Helm, 1976.

48 Roberts, *The Classic Slum*, p.109.

# 11

# PUBLIC PARTICIPATION IN GOVERNMENT DECISION-MAKING:
## The Historical Experience*

PUBLIC participation in government decision-making began with the election of their kings by the Anglo-Saxons. Archbishop Aelfric at the end of the tenth century declared: 'No man can make himself king, but the people have the choice to elect whom they like.' He proceeded, however, to pinpoint the difficulty in all representative government, that the representative once elected tended to lose touch with the electors and to represent chiefly himself until the end of his term, in this case for life: 'but after he is consecrated king, he has authority over the people, and they cannot shake his yoke off their necks'.

Even when the Crown became hereditary the notion of service by the representative and of participation in the most important government decision, who is to rule, survived in the coronation oath and the symbolic acclamation of the new monarch by the people. From this, by the principle of consent to taxation and other laws affecting the vital interests of the ruled, evolved the whole system of parliamentary and representative local government. The two levels of government are connected: the House of Commons was originally not so much the assembly of the commoners as of the *communes* of the realm, the communities of the freeholders of the counties and the free burgesses of the towns. Their consent was required before the king could raise extraordinary taxation for war or other purposes or pass laws to take any man's life or property.

The system was not particularly democratic: the freeholders and burgesses down to modern times were a minority, and because of the inherent tendency towards oligarchy in most human institutions a diminishing minority. When the American subjects of George III demanded 'No taxation without representation', more than nine out of ten of his British subjects were taxed without being represented, at least in the direct sense. In the phrase of Edmund Burke and Arthur Young, they were merely 'virtually represented' by their superiors in the social hierarchy. At the time of the Great Reform Bill only 435,000 electors in England and Wales had the vote out of a population of 14 million, that is one in 32 of the population, or about

---

* Presented as the opening address at the Royal Town Planning Institute's Oversea Summer School at the University of York on 1 September 1973.

186

one in eight of the adult males. The 1832 Reform Act added only 217,000 to that number. It was not until the Third Reform Act of 1884 that a majority of adult males received the vote, and not until the Act of 1918 that every man and a majority of women were enfranchised.

In spite of this, all government is in a sense government by consent or at least by the acquiescence of the governed. The executive rulers are by definition few, the ruled many, and even passive resistance by the majority if it is united can soon make life impossible for the most tyrannical government. That is why politics are always at bottom a battle for the mind, and why fascist governments of both the right and the left put so much effort into propaganda. How then did the unenfranchised majority in Britain before the onset of modern democracy make their desires and objections known? How did the individual, enfranchised or not, manage to participate in government decision-making?

Before the invention of the modern public inquiry, which, as we shall see, grew out of the enclosure movement which has a central place in this story, there were three main, overlapping ways in which the unenfranchised mass and/or the aggrieved individual could seek to influence government: by petition, by agitation or by riot. They overlapped because an agitation or demonstration often took the form of publicizing and presenting a petition to the monarch, to Parliament or the local magistrates, [compare the demonstrations and marches in the 1830s and 1840s for the People's Charter, which was in the form of a petition to Parliament]; equally because a frustrated agitation or rejected petition could easily lead to a riot.

Nor must we think that petitions and demonstrations were legal and accepted while riots were not. It depended in both cases on what they were for and how they were carried on. Some demonstrations however peaceful in intent, like the one at 'Peterloo' in Manchester in 1819, were held to be illegal by the government simply because they were large assemblies of non-freeholders attempting to overawe the magistrates on a question, namely universal manhood suffrage, considered at that time to be none of their business. At the same time certain riots were accepted or even connived at by the government and political parties if they were for the right object. Almost every contested election in the eighteenth century was accompanied by riots, often supported by the candidates. On hearing a riot from his deathbed the Duke of Newcastle, greatest of eighteenth century electioneers, said, 'Let them be – I dearly loved a mob'. The Sacheverell Riots of 1710, the 'Wilkes and Liberty' Riots of the 1760s, and the Gordon Riots of 1780 were violent outbreaks of national consequence deliberately started for their own ends by leading politicians, while the Church-and-King Riots of the 1790s were fomented by the government agent John Reeves to terrorize the English Jacobins. Even the bread riot, the most traditional form of organized violence in pre-industrial England, was not what it seemed. It was not a chaotic outburst of bread stealing by starving workers, but a carefully organized process in support of what the rioters took to be the law, by which the bakers and millers were forced to sell bread and flour at the statutory price fixed (or, increasingly and illegally, not fixed) by the magistrates.

All three forms of participation in government decision-making can be seen at work in the movement which did most to change the face of the country and interfere with individual property rights before modern planning legislation – the enclosure movement. The enclosure of the medieval open fields and commons took place in two main waves, in the late fifteenth and sixteenth centuries against the will of the government, and in the eighteenth and nineteenth centuries with the government's blessing and support. In the earlier period the Tudor governments' opposition to the enclosure (mainly for sheep) and 'engrossing' (consolidation) of peasant holdings was primarily for military reasons: sheep pastures maintain few men for defence and increase dependence on foreign corn. They were, however, also swayed by streams of petitions from evicted or threatened peasants and by the anti-closure riots which culminated in outright rebellions in 1536 (the Pilgrimage of Grace, ostensibly a demonstration and petition against the Dissolution of the Monasteries) and in 1549 (Kett's Rebellion). Admittedly, both rebellions failed, and over the second the government of Lord Protector Somerset fell, not to the rebels but to their fiercest opponent, the overbearing, enclosing landlord, the Duke of Northumberland. All Tudor and early Stuart governments were however, sufficiently swayed by public opinion and by occasional riots, such as those of 1607, to maintain the anti-enclosure policy.

The second and larger wave of enclosures in the eighteenth and early nineteenth centuries, when over 5,000 separate Acts were passed enclosing about 7 million acres of common field and waste, took place in a very different atmosphere, with the encouragement of all the agricultural experts, progressive landlords, Parliament and government. It used to be thought that this second wave of enclosure caused the decline of the small English landowner, the eviction and disappearance of the peasant and cottager, and their transformation into a landless labour force for the new large farms and the factories. It is now known that most of the small owners and tenants disappeared long before the main enclosures and that, far from depopulating the villages, the new agriculture on the enclosed fields required more labour than before. This was not only for hedging and ditching and the building of the new farmhouses and outbuildings out in the fields instead of in the villages: it was, more importantly, for the new rotation of crops, with four crops in four years instead of two crops and a fallow in three years, and for the increased number of animals which could be fed on the new fodder crops of clover and turnips. Not only did the labourers increase in numbers but also the farmers because many of the enclosures were financed in part by selling off portions of the common. In fact, the numbers engaged in agriculture as farmers and labourers reached their peak in absolute terms at the 1851 Census, the culmination of the process of enclosure.

Yet this did not mean that enclosure was popular or unopposed. Even Arthur Young, the most influential publicist of enclosure, admitted that 'by nineteen enclosure bills in twenty they [the poor] are injured, in some, grossly injured . . . The poor in these parishes may say, and with truth, 'Parliament may be tender of property; all I know is, I had a cow, and Act of Parliament has taken it from me'. Anti-enclosure riots, while by no means frequent, were not unknown: at Otmoor in Oxfordshire in 1814 and again in 1829 the local commoners tore down their landlords' fences, and on the second occasion the Militia and Yeomanry were called out against them. Even when 44 of them were arrested and hauled off in waggons to Oxford jail, a great crowd attacked the Yeomanry and rescued the prisoners. When they were eventually caught and tried, such was the state of public opinion that they were found guilty only of unlawful assembly, and given light sentences, the longest one of four months' imprisonment.

Enclosure is important to the history of public participation in government decision-making because the legislative process began by being tender only to property owners, providing opportunities to be heard and to object only to those who could prove a legal interest in the land to be enclosed, and ended by admitting a general public interest or, more strictly, a local community interest in the preservation of the remaining commons. In this way it closely parallels modern planning legislation, which began by allowing the right of objection by affected property owners and ended by providing, in the 1968 Town and Country Planning Act, for the active consultation of the local community in the making of the structure plan by the planning authority.

Most enclosures between 1700 and 1845 were carried out under private Acts of Parliament, some 5,400 of them, as we have seen already. This was a small fraction of the total number of private Acts for all purposes – from individual divorces to the policing, lighting and drainage of whole towns or the construction of a road, canal or railway – which in turn were usually twice as numerous as the public Acts (e.g. between 1800 and 1884 9,556 public Acts and 18,497 private Acts were passed, of which about 2,300 were private enclosure Acts). Enclosures were therefore subject to the same processes of consultation and rights of objection as other private Bill legislation, and in turn helped to develop those processes and rights.

Private Bills had their origin in petitions to the Crown for the redress of private grievances which could not be obtained otherwise than by legislation. In the case of enclosure the problem was to override the objections of a minority of the property holders or, rather, of the owners of a minority of the property and ensure to all the owners an indefeasible right in the newly distributed land. Up to the eighteenth century this had been done either by one man acquiring all the property in a manor, village or parish or by an agreement between all the owners which might or might not be registered in the court of Chancery. From about 1719 it became the practice for the leading owners in each case to petition for a private act, which would allow them to appoint commissioners and a surveyor to measure, value and reapportion the lands between the commoners according to the size of their holdings and claims in the unenclosed fields and commons.

On receiving such a petition the House of Commons, if disposed to receive it, ordered a bill to be presented and read when, at the second reading, it would be committed to a small select committee, usually consisting of local M.P.s of the area in which the place to be enclosed was situated. This would hear the petitioners together with any petitions against, and then report to the whole House. If the committee reported favourably the Bill would be passed by Commons and Lords and receive the Royal Assent. The commissioners would then be appointed, usually three of them to represent the lord of the manor, the rector or lay tithe-owner and the remaining proprietors, and give public notice in local newspapers and on the church door of their intention and their first meeting. At the meeting they would take the oath to perform their duties honestly, appoint a clerk and surveyor, and invite all those with claims and objections to bring them forward at a later meeting in one or two months' time. At later meetings claims and counterclaims would be heard, adjudged and adjusted, and after the surveyor had made his measurements and valuations, they would enroll their reallocation of the lands in an award, in the form of a parchment roll or volume, together with a map of all the holdings. One copy of the award was placed in the parish chest for local inspection and a second deposited with the Keeper of the Rolls of the county (or occasionally enrolled in one of the royal courts). They also assessed the payments to be made by each allottee towards the cost of the act, the commissioners', surveyor's and clerk's fees, the fencing of the rector's allotment and any land set aside for the poor, recreation, etc.

One can see that there were opportunities for public participation and objection at both stages of this procedure, at the parliamentary stage when counter-petitions would be heard by the select committee on the Bill and at the executive stage when the commissioners heard claims and counter-claims. These opportunities were institutionalized by the General Enclosure Act of 1801, which laid down model clauses to be enacted in all subsequent enclosure Acts, including a provision for appeals against the award to the local Justices of the Peace. The right to counter-petition Parliament was expensive and rarely used, as for example in the case of Otmoor in 1814, a large moor commonable by seven villages, which was at first petitioned against by the Duke of Marlborough and Lord Abingdon, eventually two of the largest beneficiaries. But the hearings by the commissioners were a very real safe-guard, and it is now generally believed that, especially after 1801, all those with a genuine legal claim or grievance received a reasonably fair hearing. Indeed, not only the claims of the legal commoners, that is the proprietors of strips in the open fields with appurtenant rights of mowing or grazing the adjoining meadows, commons and wastes, were recognized, but often those of the landless cottagers and squatters if they could show longstanding use on suffrance of the commons by their animals, usually for twenty years past. For both the small proprietor and the landless commoner the commissioners' procedure constituted a form of public inquiry very similar to the modern public inquiry by a planning inspector for the Department of the Environment.

The General Enclosure Act of 1845 took matters a stage further by adopting and popularizing the then uncommon Provisional Order procedure which extended the opportunity for local inquiry. This Act ended the need for a separate Bill for each enclosure, by setting up a central body of Enclosure Commissioners who could investigate applications and sanction enclosure orders by laying them before Parliament for approval. Under it the central Commissioners sent down an Assistant Commissioner to 'hold a meeting or meetings to hear objections' to the published scheme; they would then make a Provisional Order, after which they 'may cause meetings to be holden by an Assistant Commissioner for the Purpose of taking Consents and Dissents', and vary the Order laid before Parliament according to his report. Under this procedure in the next 25 years 946 enclosures covering 618,000 acres were sanctioned. The Provisional Order procedure came to be adopted for a great many other purposes, especially those affecting land use and compulsory purchase, such as the public health legislation from 1848 onwards, local government acts from 1858, the Elementary Education Act of 1870, and so on, under all of which the procedure required a public inquiry by 'a man from the ministry'. For example, under the Public Health Act of 1875, the Local Government Board was empowered

to cause to be made such inquiries as are directed by this Act, and such inquiries as they see fit in relation to any matters concerning the public health in any place, or any matter with respect to which their sanction approval or consent is required by this Act.

They could not make a Provisional Order unless public notice had been given in two successive weeks in the local press, and if objections were received a local inquiry became mandatory. And finally, a public inquiry became necessary before the Local Government Board could grant a compulsory purchase order to a local authority.

All these provisions for objections and inquiries under enclosure and other legislation, were both negative and individual: that is, they provided opportunities for individuals with a direct proprietory or pecuniary interest to oppose compulsory redistribution or purchase of their property or rights. Gradually, however, it became evident that many others besides the actual adjacent proprietors and commoners might have an interest in a piece of common land, so that it might be a valuable aesthetic and recreational asset in which the whole community had a legitimate interest. The General Enclosure Act of 1836 which (ineffectively) prohibited the enclosure of commons within ten miles of London and varying distances of other large towns, had recognized this interest. It was brought home to an aroused public opinion in the 1860s when a number of London landlords, eager for profits from building land, began a concerted attack on the remaining London commons, notably Wimbledon, Epsom, Hampstead Heath, Clapham, Plumstead, Tooting, Graveney and, most famous of all, Epping Forest, in the defence of which the City of London spent £240,000. A great outcry was raised, the Commons Preservation Society was set up in 1865 under the chairmanship of Lord Eversley, and procured the Metropolitan Commons Act of 1866 which prevented the enclosure of any common within the Metropolitan Police District and provided for the regulation of each London common by an elected body of ratepayers. Here was an example of legislation passed against the wishes of the government by the force of public opinion. An extension of this campaign, led by Henry Fawcett, the blind professor of political economy and M.P., saved the provincial commons and led to the Commons Act of 1876, which made the enclosure of most commons other than open fields virtually impossible, and provided for their regulation as public open spaces. Since then only a few thousand acres, mostly of open field, have been enclosed, and the vast majority of orders under that and the 1899 Commons Act have been for regulation only.

The preservation of the remaining commons was a great triumph for public participation over the vested interests of private property and its supporters in Parliament and government. But in most other fields, especially those affecting land purchase for housing, roads, railways, docks, reservoirs and physical development generally, public participation continued to mean primarily the right of individual proprietors to object either to the compulsory purchase of their property or, as planning legislation developed from 1909 onwards, to their prevention by authority from developing their property as they wished. In all these cases the Provisional Order procedure and the local inquiry by a Ministry inspector have become the standard means of dealing with complaints and grievances. Indeed, of the 7,500 public inquiries held every year in the late 1960s, over 6,000 were concerned with planning appeals and over 1,000 with housing, and most of the rest with highways and public health (sewerage and water) schemes. Apart from inquiries into accidents, all the rest originating in other government departments amounted to fewer than 250. Occasionally a question of great public importance like the siting of the third London airport elicits a public inquiry of a different sort, usually a Royal Commission, which listens to a much wider gamut of public opinion. But for the most part, public participation has been individual and negative.

It is true that in the later stages of the Second World War, with the enthusiasm for post-war reconstruction many cities like Manchester and Coventry began to produce plans for redevelopment which they proudly exhibited to the public. However, in so far as they and the 1947 Town and Country Planning Act thought of a more positive involvement of the public in planning their own community, it was naturally through their elected representatives on the local planning authority. Only very recently has the effectiveness of such represent-ation come to be questioned, stultified as it is by the inevitable gap between elected and electors (and some would say the corrupt self-interest of some of the former), by the party-political selection of candidates and the overriding of local issues by national political prejudices, as well as by the complex technicalities of modern plan-ning procedure which defeat many of the elected representatives themselves. The doubts led the 1968 Planning Act to make some rather woolly provisions for public participation in the planning process, and to the Skeffington Committee to tell the government what they meant.

The Committee reported in favour of more and better public participation, with real consultation on the choices available before the structure plan had become too cut and dried to be more than marginally changed. Will it work in practice? I have my doubts, for reasons which two examples will illustrate. The *Structure Plan Public Participation Report of Survey Summary Document* (note the excruciating title in which it is impossible to say at first sight which are the nouns and which the adjectives) for my home town is written in a highly abstract planners' jargon designed to discourage rather than encourage public discussions by the average citizen. I quote a typical sentence from the Objectives, printed there in capitals so as to make it 'clearer'.

Thus there is a clear choice to be made, a direct choice to resolve conflict and an indirect choice to establish relative priorities between a range of complementary policies, all of which cannot be fully achieved within the plan period because of resource limitations.

Since no concrete example of either choice is given, I suppose this means that there are two kinds of choice, between conflicting alter-natives about which we may disagree and between other desirable aims which we may all want but, because we cannot afford them all at once, we will have to list in order of preference. I wonder whether the ordinary citizen will even understand that that is what it means, let alone be able to express an opinion in terms which the planners will understand or take notice of?

The second example comes from the area in which I live now. The Development Corporation of the proposed Central Lancashire New Town wants to consult sections of the public not usually considered in the process of participation, such as early teenagers and the disabled. This is an excellent idea. However, when the Regional Studies Panel of Lancaster University (which includes representatives of many colleges and local authorities in north Lancashire) suggested an interdisciplinary study which would monitor the development of the new town, a member of the Board, himself an academic, retorted that public participation did not mean critical study by interfering academics. If participation means consultation only of the less articulate who cannot speak planners' jargon and the exclusion of the expert and well-informed, what difference, one wonders, will it make to the plan, already cut and dried, one suspects, in the planners' minds? Shall we be back in the tenth century with Archbishop Aelfric 'but after he is consecrated planner, he has authority over the people, and they cannot shake his yoke off their necks'?

## Select Bibliography

R.E. Wraith and G.B. Lamb, *Public Inquiries as an Instrument of Government,* London: Allen & Unwin, 1971.

G.W. Keeton, *Trial by Tribunal: a Study of the Development and the Functioning of the Tribunal of Inquiry,* London: Museum Press, 1960.

H.D. Clokie, and J.W. Robinson, *Royal Commissions of Inquiry,* Stanford University Press, 1937.

F.A. Clifford, *History of Private Bill Legislation,* 2 Vols. Butterworths, 1885; London: Cass reprint 1968.

W.E. Tate, *The English Village Community and the Enclosure Movements,* London: Gollancz, 1967.

L.D. Stamp, and W.G. Hoskins, *The Common Lands of England and Wales,* London: Collins, 1963.

W. Ashworth, *The Genesis of Modern British Town Planning,* London: Routledge & Kegan Paul, 1954.

A.M. Skeffington, (chairman) *People and Planning: Report of the Committee on Public Participation in Planning,* London: HMSO, 1969.

N. Dennis, *Public Participation and Planners' Blight,* London: Faber, 1972.

M. Broady, *Planning for People,* London: National Council of Social Service, 1968.

# 12

# THE HISTORY OF SOCIAL FORECASTING*

FORECASTING, the attempt to foresee the direction and shape of the future, is inherent in the nature of man. Man is most satisfactorily defined as a tool-making animal. Tool-making implies two concepts of the future, of what the world would be like tomorrow without the tool and how the action of the tool may change it. Some tools – a spear to hunt animals, a foot-plough to prepare a tilth, fire to cook food or bake pots, through to the science-based technologies of industrialism – act upon the physical environment, though also indirectly upon society. Others – chieftainship, priesthood, money, codes of law, morals and exchange, through to the 'policy sciences' of modern society – act directly upon the social environment, on man himself in his social relationships.

Not all the social sciences are practical or policy-making in the immediate sense of making forecasts for the purpose of manipulating the social environment. As with the natural sciences, some are more concerned with *gnosis* than with *praxis*, with knowledge and understanding than with policy and practice. But all must have some concept of the future, if only to take account of the likely environment in which they will have to operate, and since all *praxis* is informed by *gnosis* they all must expect their insights to be used by others to illuminate expectations or inspire policy.

If history is a social science, it would seem to be the least oriented towards the future, the most concerned with *gnosis* and the least with *praxis*. Yet all forecasting is based on knowledge of the past, or of the 'specious present' which is really the immediate past, whether by logical extrapolation of observed trends or by intuitive imagination from experience. As Duclos said in 1745, when as we shall see historians were at last becoming oriented towards the future, 'The past should enlighten us about the future: knowledge of history is no more than anticipated experience.'[1] The function of the historian, however, is not just to provide raw material for extrapolation or object lessons to emulate or avoid, but to show how men, generation after generation, have coped with their ignorance of the future and yet have played the major part in bringing it about.

---

* Presented at one of a series of seminars at the Social Science Research Council and published in C. Freeman, M. Jahoda and I. Miles, *Progress and Problems in Social Forecasting*, London: HMSO, 1976.

In relation specifically to social forecasting, the historian can perhaps help the discussion in three ways: by showing, first, how and when forecasting possible future states of society came to be a common human activity and why it has recently become an obsession; secondly, how as a corrective or antidote to this imaginative, holistic type of forecasting the emerging social sciences introduced logical, disaggregated social forecasting based mainly on extrapolation (broadly conceived) rather than intuition; and, finally, why in the last few years disaggregated or fractionated social forecasting has ceased to appeal and been challenged by a renewed demand for holistic forecasting, though on a new, more scientific basis. We can call the first the origins of macro-forecasting; the second the rise of micro-forecasting; and the third the revival of macro-forecasting in futures research.[2] Clearly, it would not be possible to fulfil this dialectical programme – thesis, antithesis, synthesis – in so brief a paper. All that will be offered is a framework for a history of social forecasting with a few of the frames lightly sketched in.

## The Origins of Macro-forecasting

The remote origins of forecasting go back to Stonehenge and earlier megalithic computers for calculating the movement of the sun and, in an agrarian society, the return of the seasons. Whether they were also used for predicting political events and social change is not known, but the first historical astronomers, the Babylonian priesthood, were also astrologers and indiscriminately predicted sidereal and human events. Many peoples down to and including the Greeks and Romans used terrestrial phenomena for prediction – dreams, oracles, the flight of birds, the behaviour or the entrails of sacrificial animals. But all these were ahistorical and irrational. Forecasting as a rational activity connecting the future logically with the past depends upon an appropriate philosophy of history.

The first people in the West to have such a philosophy were the Greeks of the fourth century B.C. But it was not very propitious for the purpose of forecasting. Plato and his followers saw history as cyclical, an endless decline from a series of golden ages endlessly restored by charismatic law-givers like Pericles. Unfortunately, since the owl of Minerva only flew at dusk, the sky whenever they stopped to reflect was darkening and the golden age was in retreat. The early Christians fixed the cycle, as it were: they pushed the golden age back to the Garden of Eden and its restoration forward to the Second Coming, when Christ would return in majesty to judge the living and the dead and begin the reign of universal peace. For the Middle Ages and Reformation Europe the Second Coming was always just around the corner. But this too was not propitious for forecasting: either the future was very short and likely to get worse before it got better; or, if the Second Coming was a long time coming, the interim forecast was 'no change' – this world would continue a vale of tears, and improvement could be hoped for only in the next, the heavenly city of St. Augustine.

Social forecasting as we know it, as a logical construction of the future on the foundations of the past, could not begin until men had some notion of history as process, as a development neither cyclical between golden ages nor isthmian between eternities but evolutionary in the sense of unfolding along a one-way continuum of time. To achieve such a philosophy, men had to escape from the tyranny of both the medieval and the ancient philosophies. The stages by which they did this, during the Renaissance and the Enlightenment, are well enough known: first, they brought the classical world to second birth, raising it to a golden age to which it had only aspired, in order to shrug off the tyranny of the 'dark ages' in between; and then, in the obscure late seventeenth-century 'battle of the books' they convinced themselves of the superiority of the 'moderns' over the 'ancients'. It would be tempting to think that the second change resulted from the growing technological superiority of early modern Europe, and this was partly so; but in general it would be to invert the historical order. Although in some respects, such as ocean shipping and navigation, fire-arms, iron making and agriculture, superior to the Greeks and Romans, in others, such as building and civil engineering, the pre-industrial Europeans of the early Enlightenment were decidedly inferior. It was their *conviction* of superiority which paved the way for industrialism and undoubted technological superiority, not the other way round. Finally, it was the philosophers of the later Enlightenment who, having convinced themselves that the present was superior to the best of the past, took the plunge into the unknown by postulating that the future would always be better than the present.[3]

'The heavenly city of the 18th-century philosophers', as Carl Becker has shown, was the future itself. As Diderot expressed it, 'Posterity is for the philosopher what the other world is for the religious man.'[4] Posterity was a just but inexorable god who would come to judge the living and especially the dead. Robespierre, the violent child of the *philosophes*, invoked it to justify the revolution within the revolution:

O posterity, sweet and tender hope of humanity . . ., it is for thee that we brave all the blows of tyranny; it is thy happiness which is the painful price of our struggles . . . Make haste, O posterity, to bring to pass the hour of equality, of justice, of happiness! [5]

The idea of progress was a cause to die for: Condorcet and Mme. Roland were amongst its rejoicing martyrs.[6]

Born in intellectual and political revolution, the idea of progress was a revolutionary philosophy. It invited men not merely to contemplate a better future but to play a part in bringing it about. It thus bridged the gap between *gnosis* and *praxis*, between forecasting and planning, between foreseeing the future and enacting it. It inspired the American and French Revolutions and all the subsequent *bourgeois*-democratic political revolutionaries and reformers who have helped (political) *liberté, fraternité* and *égalité* to triumph in modern Western society. It also inspired Marx and all the social revolutionaries who rebelled against the inequities of *bourgeois*-democracy and sought to establish (social) *liberté, fraternité* and *égalité* in both West and East. It still inspires revolutionaries, such as Charles Reich, the Rousseau of 'the revolution of the new generation' (Marcuse is its Voltaire). In *The Greening of America* (1970) he forecast a new American society, a 'Consciousness III community', in which the 'Corporate State' of the industrial-military complex would wither away and the 'happy people' of the new generation would float on a cloud of love and soft drugs, sustained by 'an amazing variety of goods' – produced, no doubt, by other people. (Like the lilies of the field, who toil not neither do they spin, it seems to be the Reichian 'happy people' who, regrettably, have withered away, and so soon.)

Since Reich's heavenly city was to be won through a 'revolution by consciousness', he could equally stand for the evolutionary tradition of social forecasting stemming from Enlightenment, which descends via the Utopian socialists. Robert Owen, as much a child of the Enlightenment as Marx, also believed in 'a revolution by consciousness', wrought by education: by reason alone men would come to accept 'the new moral world' of voluntary co-operation in place of the old immoral world of compulsory competition. The same rationalist idea of progress achieved by non-violent effort informed the Fabians, those apostles of gradualist amelioration: common sense and the need for efficiency would dictate the drift towards the future of municipal socialism and nationalization, serviced by a meritocracy in the image of Sidney Webb. Their most comprehensive and far-reaching social forecast was Bernard Shaw's

*Back to Methuselah*, in which men haul themselves up by Lamarckian evolution (kindly and non-violent, not like that nasty, brutish, Darwinian natural selection) towards the pure, self-effacing intellect of the long-lived 'ancients'.

The Fabian father of science fiction began in the same optimistic tradition. Even though H.G. Wells forecast the tank, aerial warfare and the atomic bomb, he remained for most of his life an ameliorist who expected that science and technology would be more a blessing than a curse to humanity. Even *The Shape of Things to Come* as late as 1933 ends the most destructive of wars with hope. Only at the end, with *The Fate of Homo Sapiens* (1939) and *Mind at the End of its Tether* (1945), does he abandon the idea of progress. But science fiction has never abandoned it altogether. Despite the dire threats from space invaders, mutant diseases, tyrannical plants, black clouds and colliding comets, mankind always wins through, or at least survives in hope. The optimistic humane values and the upward direction of change inherited from the Enlightenment still pervade *Buck Rogers in the 25th Century* and *Star Trek*.

Outside fiction, only the occasional serious planner now takes the optimistic view of the future begun by the Enlightenment: Constaninos Doxiadis, founder of 'Ekistics' (the science of human settlement) and the Delos Conference, cheerfully envisages a world population in the twenty-first century of 35 (American) billion, most of it concentrated in Ecumenopolis, a world city covering 40 million sq. k. (15.4 million sq. mi.), most of the inhabitable coastal plains and river valleys of the earth. In this he has been followed by the Hudson Institute, at least as far as an earth with 15–20 billion people, in which the main human problem will be the dispersal of waste heat from the abundant energy consumed, by means of enormous pipes to the edge of the continental shelves, where it will stimulate the growth of fish – Dr Pangloss could not do better.[7]

Yet there is another tradition stemming from the Enlightenment, the anti-idea of progress, or idea not so much of regress as of *'plus c'est la même chose'*. It is reactionary in both senses, dialectically and historically. Its progenitor was Malthus who, it is well known, wrote his first *Essay on Population* as an antidote to the cosmic optimism of his father, an executor of Rousseau, and of his father's idols, Condorcet and Godwin. Malthus used micro-forecasting against their macro-forecasts, extrapolation of specific trends in one sector of society to undermine their generalized vision of the whole. If the tendency of human population could be shown by past observation to increase by a geometrical ratio while the supply of food increased only by an arithmetical one, then their 'speculations on the perfectability of man and society' were a chimera, and 'the poverty and misery which prevail among the lower classes of society are absolutely irremediable'.[8] Despite his later concession of 'preventive checks' other than 'vice or misery', Malthusian overpopulation has been an ingredient in pessimistic social forecasting down to the current doomsday lobby.

Not too much was heard after the early nineteenth century of Malthusian pessimism, however, since industrialism and economic growth seemed to have postponed the population crisis indefinitely – see, for example, the 1871 Census Report on the vindication of 'the great courage' of working men in marrying and multiplying, and of the Government and territorial proprietors in insuring them against death by starvation by means of the Poor Law. In the later nineteenth century pessimistic forecasts like Sir George Chesney's *The Battle of Dorking* or Bulwer Lytton's *The Coming Race* (both 1871) preferred to emphasise the perils of war or the boredom of peace and prosperity. Even in the first half of the twentieth century the admonitory forecast, under the influence of declining post-industrial birthrates, played down the Malthusian threat and played up the horrors of war, the tyranny of the machine, philistine materialism, or the threat of totalitarianism: Wells's *The Shape of Things to Come* (1933), Chaplin's film *Modern Times* (1936), Huxley's *Brave New World* (1932) and *Ape and Essence* (1949), and Orwell's *1984* (1949). Only in the last two decades has the Malthusian threat reappeared in all its pessimism, in such works as Harrison Brown's *The Challenge of Man's Future* (1954), William and Paul Paddock's *Famine – 1975!* (1968), Paul Ehrlich's *The Population Bomb* (1968), and the 'publication explosion' of the ecology lobby.

But this brings us to the questions, why has social forecasting become since the Second World War an obsession with a large part of the human race, and why has it, with some exceptions like Doxiadis or the Hudson Institute, turned sour and rejected the idea of progress? The reasons are obvious, if somewhat paradoxical. Men have never been so affluent, have never had such long expectation of life, have never collectively had so much control over the physical environment and the means of life. And yet they have never been so afraid of the future. The threat is from men themselves, from that very power over the physical environment and the means of life which can destroy as well as create, and from the lack of self-control which may so easily release the forces of destruction. All power is power for good or evil; godlike power is power to create heaven or hell on earth. Since the Second World War first one national government, now five, tomorrow perhaps a dozen or a score, have the nuclear capacity to destroy the human race.[10]

Even if we retain enough self-restraint to avoid the nuclear holocaust, our very success in having life more abundantly threatens to become self-defeating. We are trapped in the success of our own forecasts, in the pursuit of progress (now called economic growth), in the upthrust of the exponential curves – of population, urbanization, pollution, the use of fossil fuels and minerals, of the exhaustion of the planet. Exponential curves cannot soar upwards for long without going through the roof: unless some of them unexpectedly flatten out the crisis cannot be long delayed. We are on a collision course with ourselves which threatens our destruction, or at least a savage reversal of the upward direction of change which will drastically reduce the human race. As Dr. Johnson said, 'When a man knows he is to be hanged in a fortnight, it concentrates his mind wonderfully.'

But will it concentrate his mind *effectively*, so as to defeat the prediction? That depends on the kind and quality of his thinking, and the steps he is prepared and able to take to avoid the inevitable.

## The Rise of Micro-forecasting

The techniques of traditional macro-forecasting were intuitive and holistic, because its function was an aggregate one, to predict whole future societies, a heaven on earth for revolutionaries or reformers to aim at or an admonitory or satirical hell for contemporaries to avoid. The techniques of micro-forecasting, by contrast, are logical and analytical, because its function is disaggregative, to tease out the separate strands of social development and estimate their individual speed and direction. In short, they are the techniques of the individual social sciences: induction from observed data to predictive hypotheses. As with all induction, intuition cannot be left out altogether: it is required for the 'inductive leap' between observation and hypothesis. Imagination is also required to design tests for the hypotheses, particularly difficult where experiments cannot be repeated and must wait for the future to validate them, and to estimate whether trends will become self-reinforcing and exponential or self-satisfying and abortive. But the chief technique is extrapolation from the known to unknown, from the past to the future.

The roots of micro-forecasting are therefore to be found in the emerging social sciences of the eighteenth and nineteenth centuries and their sceptical reaction against the naïve generalization of 'common sense' which informed most macro-forecasts.

Micro-forecasting as much as macro-forecasting was a product of the Enlightenment. We have already seen how Malthus used it to defeat the naïve optimism of his father and Condorcet and Godwin. Even earlier the pioneer actuaries of the eighteenth century, Esmond Halley, Richard Price and William Morgan, constructed tables of mortality for insurance purposes to defeat the naïve expectation that one man's life was as good a risk as another's.[11] The 'Scottish historical school of philosophy' – Adam Ferguson, Francis Hutcheson, Dugald Stewart, Adam Smith, John Millar and the rest – who pioneered the empirical social sciences and the economic interpretation of history used it to demonstrate the growing wealth and social complexity of nations and defeat the naïve notion of history as a concatenation of great men and great events. Their successors in one branch, the classical economists, turned anti-historical and were only concerned with the forecasting of hypothetical markets rather than the real economy as a whole, and their successors in the other, the empirical sociologists of the Statistical Societies from 1833 onwards, were more interested in data collection than forecasting. But both profoundly influenced policy, the first chiefly in the triumph of *laissez-faire*, the second chiefly in its modification in relation to public health, slum housing, illiteracy and poverty.[12] Their reformers' method was a kind of negative forecasting, to predict how costly and morally intolerable certain economic and social problems would become if they were not dealt with. But it was not social forecasting in the modern sense, only the empirical foundations for it.

The First World War with its enormous increase in state intervention and control, and therefore in the possibility of planning, gave a boost to micro-forecasting. The Committee Reports on Commercial and Industrial Policy after the war and on the prospects of individual industries were the first serious attempts at government economic planning.[13] But the economic state of Britain between the wars was so contrary to expectations that most politicians and economists ran for shelter to the old orthodoxies. While in Soviet Russia the five-year plans were under way and in America the New Deal was feeling its way towards manipulative budgetary planning, in Britain where Keynes was laying the theoretical foundations of economic planning in the *General Theory* (1936) only the exiguous distressed areas legislation displayed any government awareness of it.

The Second World War was the turning point of micro-forecasting. It provided dazzling displays, albeit for destructive purposes (the thousand-bomber raids, the anti-submarine campaign in the Atlantic, island-hopping in the Pacific, the invasion of Normandy, and the Manhattan Project), of man's technological and organizational mastery. It provided the tools and the techniques: the computer, operational research, model-building, games theory, the systems approach. And it clarified the tripartite division of the world, first into the 'haves' and the 'have-nots', the countries with and without the technological and organization know-how, secondly into the 'haves' of East and West competing with each other for economic growth and for leadership and exploitation of the Third World. Means and motivation combined to make the immediate post-war period the great age of optimistic micro-forecasting.

As the wizards of the modern world, who had only to wave the wand of capital to set the self-sustaining cornucopia flowing, the growth economists had a field day. For Kindleberger, Moore and Hoselitz, Arthur Lewis, Rostow, and the rest the panacea for the disease of under-development (poverty) was to raise the rate of capital investment from under 5 to over 10 or 12 per cent of GNP. (To be fair, most of them admitted the need for certain social and political preconditions, but these were thought to be as much within government control as the rate of capital investment.) Since those happy days of the 1950s economic optimism has evaporated. Large injections of capital have failed to move many Third World economies, and until the recent rise in the price of oil, food and raw materials at least, the gap between the 'haves' and the 'have-nots' has increased rather than diminished. Even amongst the developed countries, Keynesian techniques have failed to cure the ailing economies, and the differences between the highly successful, such as Japan and Germany, and the less successful, such as Britain and Italy, cannot be put down to differences in economic forecasting and planning. Resort has been made to elaborate econometric models, such as the American National Planning Association's PARM model of the US economy and the Cambridge Growth Model of the UK economy. But, with all due respect to their great intelligence and sophistication, their operators would be the first to admit that they could neither forecast nor cure our present discontents. Sir Alec Cairncross's concluding reflection on the Ditchley Park Conference of 1970 on Britain's economic sluggishness was that it 'was long on analysis and short on policy'.[14] The roots of economic growth or stagnation have been found to lie outside the realm of pure economics, in social attitudes, social structure, industrial relations, even in the self-validating expectation that growth will or will not take place and rewards will or will not be forthcoming.

The economists of the still-expanding economies, of course, continued smugly optimistic, until the current energy crisis. In the United States the great pundits of the 1960s, Walter Heller, Paul Samuelson, Milton Friedman and the late Harry Johnson, talked as if the problems were only those of analysing or controlling growth, or not controlling it, according to political predilection: 'Everyone seemed to be agreed that there would be no more dramatic upheavals in our economic life'. Their British counterpart, *The Economist,* in 1969 said of the American economy:

The great achievements of the 1960s are . . . that the country has been set on course . . . to semi-automatic economic expansion . . . American economic policy is now much more nearly idiot-proof.[15]

It was, unfortunately, not Arab-proof. By an accident of international pressure politics the oil-producing countries discovered that the kind of oligopolistic dealing which the advanced countries had operated for so long against them could be used to turn the tables, and permanently change the terms of trade between the primary producers and the manufacturing countries. What the outcome of this will be it would take a very shrewd forecaster to predict. It might be a much fairer world, in which the primary producers, not only of oil but of food and raw materials, could by a sort of international trade unionism redress the balance of the free market, as workers' trade unions have done within national economies, and enable the Third World to obtain, without the frenetic sacrifices of industrializing themselves, a much larger share of the profits of industry. It might equally be a still unfairer world, in which the cost of fuel to the non-oil producing countries of the Third World so reduced their disposable incomes that economic growth for them was postponed indefinitely, while the industrial West either suffered consequent depression – and, unexpectedly, a generation of deflation – or concentrated its industrial output on making Arab oil-sheikhs still richer.

The oil crisis is perhaps the best example of the nemesis of micro-forecasting. The assumption in one domain, economics, that cheap energy could be taken as a datum for optimistic forecasting was rudely upset by an unforeseen development in another, international politics, when 'a group of politically motivated men' decided to change the rules of the game and therefore the whole framework within which forecasting takes place. The failure cannot wholly be laid at the economists' door: they were only playing their own game according to their own lights. When another set of players switches off the lights, darkness suddenly reigns.

Nor have the other social sciences, playing their own particular games by their own individual lights, been much more successful. Demography is important because the population explosion can nullify economic growth by spreading it over too many bodies. The demographers have become masters of extrapolation – given the birthrate! The annual revisions of the British population in A.D. 2000 on which so much model building depends, show how difficult it is to forecast the birthrate even in so static a society as Britain.[16] How much more difficult is it to forecast in the socially and economically unstable societies of the Third World!

Educational forecasting, given the birthrate, ought to be simple. And, since those in it have been born longest and can be planned for furthest ahead, higher education forecasting ought to be simplest of all. Yet the forecasting of student numbers in Britain since the War has been a comedy of errors. It is not quite true that the U.G.C. and the government failed to anticipate the impact of the 1947 birthrate 'bulge' on the universities in 1965, but it is true, as Lord Simon of Wythenshawe pointed out at the Home Universities Conference in 1955, that they completely underestimated the 'trend' to stay on at school and qualify for university entrance.[17] Similarly, the Robbins Committee (1961–3), the first official body to apply forecasting to the whole higher education system, underestimated the demand: by 1971–2 student numbers in higher education and in the universities (463,000 and 236,000) had already passed the estimates for 1973–4 (392,000 and 219,000). The forecasts for 1981 (560,000 and 350,000) were outstripped by DES *Planning Paper No. 2* in 1970 (835,000, and 460,000). The 1972 White Paper cut the main figure back to 750,000, but even this underestimated the swing of the pendulum away from higher education. By January 1974 Mrs Thatcher had cut the figure back to 700,000, and before the end of the year Mr Reg Prentice, the new Labour Secretary for Education, had cut it back still further, to 640,000 – within sight of the original Robbins estimate of 560,000. Such are the vicissitudes of educational planning based on student demand.[18] Current application numbers suggest a decelerating rate of growth in higher education, but this may be a temporary reflection of recent graduate unemployment, now ended, and the lowness of student grants. Britain is still a long way behind most other industrial countries in student numbers, though not so far in graduate production, and may be expected to try to catch up.

Manpower planning, as the Robbins statisticians pointed out, was the only alternative to student demand as a predictive instrument. But manpower planning in Britain since the War has been even more disastrous. In 1957 the Willink Committee forecast falling demand for doctors: we are still making good the consequent shortage by importing them from the Third World. In 1961 the Zuckerman Committee forecast an adequate supply or possible surplus of scientists by 1965: the consequent shortage provoked the U.G.C.'s 2:1 increase in science: arts placed in 1967–72, at the very time when student demand was swinging away from science.[19] The DES recently cut back places for teacher training from 114,000 in 1971–2 to between 60,000 and 70,000 in 1981 – and already a teacher shortage is beginning to appear on the horizon.[20]

All this is not meant to rejoice at the discomfiture of the micro-forecasters. Social forecasting is a very difficult art. This is not primarily because human beings are unpredictable: the social sciences could not exist unless they were predictable in some respects, at least in terms of statistical probability. It is because of the number of variables involved, and even more because of their interconnectedness. 'One damn thing affects another'; and there are too many 'damn things'. That is why there is a disillusionment now with micro-forecasting, and a swing back to macro-forecasting in the shape of 'futures research', where the interconnectedness of things and the plurality of possibilities are the starting point, and where all the skills of all the social sciences can be combined in one integrated, interdisciplinary whole. But the paradox of this is that in macro-forecasting the number of 'damn things' is greater still, and the models infinitely more complex.

## The Revival of Macro-forecasting: Futures Research

'Futures research' – 'futurology', 'futuristics', 'futuribles' – is a product of the 'specious present'. As an organized discipline with societies, institutes, conferences, university courses and learned journals it came to birth in the 1960s. A few eminent intellectuals like Buckminster Fuller, Bertrand de Jouvenel, C.H. Waddington and Constantinos Doxiadis had been preaching the need to study alternative futures for years, but only in the 1960s did it suddenly 'take' and burgeon into a world-wide movement. The reasons for this are obvious enough: the upsurge of the exponential curves and the knowledge that world population would double between 1960 and 2000, the failure of economic planning to make headway in closing the gap between the industrial countries and the Third World, the realization that there were limits to growth in the earth's finite reserves of fossil fuels and minerals and the stock of cultivable land, the growing awareness of the increasing pollution of air, water, soil and the whole biosphere by man-made wastes[21] – all these came together to convince many people that micro-forecasting and disaggregated social and economic planning could not cope with the magnitude and complexity of the problems facing the world. As the OECD Symposium on Long-range Forecasting and Planning at Bellagio, Italy, in 1968 said of 'the present stage of social crisis',

Many of the most serious conflicts facing mankind result from the interaction of social, economic, technological, political and psychological factors and can no longer be solved by fractional approaches from individual disciplines. The time is past when economic growth can be promoted without consideration of social consequences and when technology can be allowed to develop without consideration of the social prerequisites of change or the social consequences of such change.

There was thus a need to plan social systems as a whole, to consider alternative possible futures and the values and norms underlying them.[22]

It would be fruitless to look for one single starting point of this movement. Prophets who had been crying in the wilderness for years suddenly found a hearing, and funds for conferences, societies, institutes. Bertrand de Jouvenel started his International Futuribles Committee in Paris in 1960, since 1970 the permanent 'Maison des Futuribles'. Constantinos Doxiadis commenced his Delos Conferences of eminent futurologists and the CIBA Foundation devoted a Symposium to 'Man and his Future' in 1963. A number of interdisciplinary study groups sprang up in different countries to concentrate research on the year 2000: the American Academy of Arts and Sciences' Commission on the Year 2000 and the Dutch 'Work Group 2000' in 1965, soon followed by the Italian Committee for the Year 2000, a Czechoslovak long-range study group, the British S.S.R.C.'s Committee on the Next Thirty Years (now the Social Forecasting Committee), and the international 'Plan Europe 2000' Group meetings in London and Brussels. Societies and institutes were founded in the United States, Britain, Denmark, Sweden, West Germany, Czechoslovakia, Yugoslavia, Romania, Japan and several other countries. World conferences on futures research were held in Oslo (1967), Kyoto (1970), and Bucharest (1972). American university courses on the study of the future increased from 80 in 1970 to 350 in 1972, Olaf Helmer occupies the first chair of futures research, at the University of Southern California, and C.H. Waddington started a course at Edinburgh. Journals began to appear, like *The Futurist*, published by the World Futures Society in Washington, and *Futures*, published at Guildford, Surrey, for an international group of leading futurologists and the Institute for the Future at Middletown, Connecticut.[23]

Thus futures research is becoming a thriving new discipline. But to what end? Is it, as Amitai Etzioni asked at the Kyoto Conference, 'the nature of a non-existent subject that people talk a lot about it without doing it'?[24] Certainly, there is a lot of talk, and some of it to little purpose. But there also seems to be some serious work, such as the Delphi techniques of forecasting innovation pioneered by Olaf Helmar and Norman Dalkey at the Rand Corporation, later at the Middletown Institute, the British vogue for PPB – Planning, Programming, Budgeting – and the cross-impact analyses which attempt to trace the chain reactions of changes in one or more sectors of society through all the rest.[25] Some of the study groups have begun to publish their findings, including the American Commission's immensely influential *The Year 2000* by Herman Kahn and A.J. Wiener (1968), the British S.S.R.C.'s much slighter *Forecasting and the Social Sciences* (1968) and the Plan Europe 2000 group's *The Future is Tomorrow* (The Hague, 1973).[26]

In the last analysis, however, interdisciplinary models are still only macro-systems built up from micro-subsystems, and the whole can be worse than the sum of the parts if the parts themselves are defective. No amount of cross-correlation and cross-impact analysis can turn bad micro-forecasts into good interdisciplinary models. It is therefore up to the individual social sciences not only to improve their co-operation but to improve their techniques. Without that the history of social forecasting has an unfruitful future.

## Notes

1  C.P. Duclos, *Histoire de Louis XI,* La Haye, 1745, preface.
2  Economists and students of management would no doubt prefer to keep 'macro' and 'micro' for large scale economic and company-level business forecasting respectively, but one man's 'macro' is another man's 'micro', and since the alternatives here, 'holistic' or 'aggregate' versus 'sectoral' or 'disaggregated' are both clumsier and similarly ambiguous I shall stick to 'macro' and 'micro'.

3  J.B. Bury, *The Idea of Progress*, London: Macmillan, 1920; C. Becker, *The Heavenly City of the 18th Century Philosophers*, New Haven and London: Yale University Press, 1932.

4  D. Diderot, *Oeuvres XVIII*, Paris: Garnier Frères, 1875–7, p.101.

5  J. Vellay, *Discours et Rapports du Robespierre*, Paris, 1908, p.155.

6  Cf Becker *op cit* pp.150–4.

7  C.A. Doxiadis, *Ekistics: An Introduction to the Science of Human Settlement*, London: Hutchinson, 1968, pp.71–2, 215–17, 447; BBC 2 Television, Horizon programme 'The Future goes Boom!', 4 and 10 March 1974.

8  T.R. Malthus, *Essay on Population*, 1803, preface to 2nd edition, London: Everyman ed. 1914, pp.1–3.

9  *Census of Great Britain, 1871, IV General Report*, p.xviii.

10  B. Ward and R. Dubos, *Only One Earth: The Care and Maintenance of a Small Planet*, Harmondsworth: Penguin, 1972; A. Peccei, *The Chasm Ahead*, New York: Macmillan, 1969; E. Goldsmith and R. Allen, *Blueprint for Survival*, Harmondsworth: Penguin, 1972.

11  Cf H.E. Raynes, *Insurance*, Home University Library Series, Oxford University Press, 1960, and *Dictionary of National Biography*, *sub* Halley and Price, Oxford University Press, 1960.

12  The 'classical' economists also helped to modify *laissez-faire* in certain respects – cf. L. Robbins, *The Theory of Economic Policy in English Classical Political Economy*, London: Macmillan, 1952. The degree to which the Statistical Societies and the Society for the Promotion of Social Science (1859) influenced policy by exposing social problems can only be gauged by reading their transactions in the *Statistical Journal* and elsewhere.

13  For the titles and references of the reports, see P. and G. Ford, *Breviate of Parliamentary Papers, 1917–39*, Dublin: Irish University Press, 1969, pp.151–60.

14  A. Cairncross, (ed.) *Britain's Economic Prospects Reconsidered*, London: Allen & Unwin, 1971, p.220.

15  A. Levi, *Journey among the Economists*, London: Alcove Press, 1974; *The Economist*, 10 May 1969.

16  Cf J. Thompson, *The Growth of Population to the end of the Century*, Social Trends No 1, 1970, and the three different projections in No 4 (1973) London: HMSO, p. 73. CF also C. Leicester, *Britain 2001 AD: A Forecast of the UK Economy at the turn of the Century*, London: HMSO, 1972.

17  Cf H.J. Perkin, *Innovation in Higher Education: New Universities in the United Kingdom* OECD, 1969, pp.62–4.

18  Robbins Report on *Higher Education* (Cmnd. 2154, 1963), p. 284; *DES Planning Paper No 2: Student Numbers in Higher Education*, London: HMSO, 1970, p. 37; *Education: a Framework for Expansion* (Cmnd. 5174, 1972), pp.34–7.

19  *Committee to Consider the Future Numbers of Medical Practitioners and the Appropriate Intake of Medical Students*, London: HMSO, 1957, *The Long-term Demand for Scientific Manpower*, London HMSO, 1961, cf. the review of the past failures of manpower planning and the need for a Manpower Council in the *Report from the Commons Expenditure Committee on Further and Higher Education*, London: HMSO, 1972, pp. x–xiii. See also B. Ahamad and M. Blaug, *The Practice of Manpower Forecasting*, Amsterdam: Elsevier, 1973.

20  'Further drops in graduates wanting to train as teachers' (15 March 74) *Times Higher Education Supplement*.

21  Cf. Ward and Dubos, *op. cit.*; also D.H. Meadows, D.C. Meadows, J. Randers and W.W. Behrens. *The Limits to Growth*, New York: Universe Books, 1972, and the

two issues of *Futures* devoted to it, February and April 1973, reprinted in H.F.D. Cole, C. Freeman, M. Jahoda and K.C.R. Pavitt (eds) *Thinking about the Future*. London: Chatto and Windus, 1973.

22 'The Bellagio Declaration on Planning', quoted in *Futures*, I, 1968–9, pp.182–4.

23 The most comprehensive source for all developments in this field is *Futures*, vols I–V, 1968–73, Guildford, Surrey: IPC, and the Institute for the Future: Middletown, Connecticut.

24 Quoted in *Futures* II, 1960 p.188.

25 Cf. numerous articles in *Futures*, I–V, 1968–73, passim.

26 Cf. also R. Brech, *Britain 1984: A forecast prepared for Unilever* London: Darton, Longman and Todd, 1963; D. Calleo, *Britain's Future*, London: Hodder and Stoughton, 1969; H.F.D. Cole *et al* (op. cit), O. Helmer, *On the Future state of the Union*, Institute for the Future, Report R.27. Middletown, Connecticut, 1972; H. Kahn and B. Bruce-Biggs, *Things to Come: Thinking about the Seventies and Eighties*, New York: Macmillan, 1972; J. McHale, *The Future of the Future*, New York: Brazilles, 1969; J. McHale, The Changing Pattern of Futures Research in the USA, *Futures* V, 1973, pp. 257–71; M. Maruyama, *et al*. *Human Futuristics*, Hawaii: University Press, 1972; Plan Europe 2000 *Fears and Hopes for European Urbanization*, The Hague: Nijhoff, 1972; F. Polak, *The Image of the Future*, London: Jossey-Bass, 1973, now obtainable through Elsevier: Amsterdam; A. Toffler, *The Futurists*, New York: Random, 1972; B.R. Jones, 'Social Forecasting in Lucas', *Social Trends 1979*, London: HMSO, 1978.

(These are only a few examples of the immense literature on futures research being published currently.)

# 13
## SOCIAL HISTORY IN BRITAIN*

A quarter of a century ago I published an article called 'What is Social History?' (See Essay 1). It was very much a young man's first faltering attempt at the outset of his career to define the subject which he was the first university teacher in Britain to be paid specifically to teach. By today's standards it was a bad article, too modest, apologetic, deferential and namedropping. Instead of taking my elders and betters by the throat in the modern manner and demanding to know why they did not write the kind of history I intended to write – and so much better, of course – I gently pointed out how many of them, from Namier and Neale to Trevor-Roper and Asa Briggs, were covertly or overtly engaged in the social approach to history. Still, it was a good question, and at that time much in need of an answer. Social history, I said, was the Cinderella of English historical studies. There were no chairs and no university departments, no learned journals, and few if any textbooks.

It would be easy at this point to draw a classic 'before and after' contrast and intone 'how different from us!' There are now several chairs of social history in Britain: by cheating – naming my own chair – I managed to occupy the first of them, in Lancaster in 1967, and since then Michael Flinn in Edinburgh, John Burnett at Brunel, Joyce Youings at Exeter, Rodney Hilton at Birmingham (in medieval social history), Norman McCord at Newcastle, and Royden Harrison at Warwick Universities have joined the eponymous few, while, more significantly, almost every chair of economic history on changing occupants has added 'and social' to its title. There are still no unhyphenated undergraduate departments – though many in economic and social history – but there are two postgraduate centres for the study of social history, at the new universities of Warwick and Lancaster, and the Social Science Research Council's research unit for the History of Population and Social Structure at Cambridge. Since 1968 one-year postgraduate degree courses have been established at Aberystwyth, Essex, Lancaster, Manchester, Swansea and Warwick with S.S.R.C. approval and support, and since 1974 even an undergraduate degree course at Lancaster. There are several old-established series of social history volumes, notably Heinemann's Kingswood Social History Series

* First published in the Jounal of Social History, X, Winter 1977.

founded about 1956 by H.L. Beales and O.R. McGregor, and Rout-ledge and Kegan Paul's Studies in Social History edited since 1961 by myself, latterly with the assistance of my colleague Eric Evans. Two learned journals have been founded in 1976, *Social History* edited by Janet Blackman and Keith Nield at Hull University and *History Workshop*, edited by S. Alexander and others which grew out of Raphael Samuel's ten-year old history workshops mainly on oral history of the working classes at Ruskin College, Oxford. There are in addition the specialized and somewhat older *Bulletin of the Society for the Study of Labour History*, founded in 1960 and now edited by Royden Harrison and J.L. Halstead, the *Urban History Yearbook* founded by the late H.J. Dyos, and *Oral History*, founded in 1971 and edited by Paul Thompson of Essex University, and of course the always socially oriented *Past and Present* founded as long ago as 1952. The final assurance that the subject had arrived was the launching at a conference at Lancaster University in January 1976 of the Social History Society of the United Kingdom, with Asa (now Lord) Briggs as President.

Social history in Britain has undoubtedly come a long way since 1953, and it would be hypocritical not to rejoice in its current popularity. But it still has much farther to go before it catches up with the Americans or the French. Britain is still in social history an underdeveloped country and we need much more capital investment and intensification of skills before we achieve technological maturity and maximum output. The best British work, as one might expect of a country steeped in history and with a high tradition of individual craftsmanship, vies with the best anywhere, but it is on a small scale and is produced by a relatively few virtuosos. It is still mainly a cottage industry worked by isolated individuals with here and there a workshop operated by a small team. Factories and mass production are still in the future. The bigger, older and more prestigious univer-sities, which could more easily afford to develop the subject, have neglected it most, and for the most part it has been left to the newer, smaller and less well-known to develop it with their more limited resources and influence.

The exception which tests the rule is the Cambridge Group for the study of Population and Social Structure. This was not, however, an institutional creature of Cambridge University but the brainchild of three individual members of staff who received little or no help from the University. In the early 1960s Peter Laslett, an historian of pre-industrial political and social ideas, Anthony Wrigley, a geog-rapher, and Roger Schofield, an historian with an interest in quantitative techniques, became interested in applying the methods of the French *Annales* school of historical demography, pioneered by Louis Chevalier and Le Roy Ladurie, to English pre-industrial society. They formed the Cambridge Group as an informal research unit to co-ordinate the activities of hundreds of amateur researchers up and down the country, recruited to pillage the parish registers and complete the forms which the Group designed for feeding into the computer. Out of this work emerged three stimulating books, Laslett's *The World We Have Lost,* (1965), which focused attention on pre-industrial English society and its unexpectedly modern family social structure, *An Introduction to English Historical Demography* (1966) and *Nineteenth-Century Society: Essays in the Use of Quantitative Methods for the Study of Social Data* (1972), two symposia edited by E.A. Wrigley which described and applied their new techniques. They also founded a small journal, *Local Population Studies,* to publicize their methodology. Laslett claims that the Group's work in research and seminars goes beyond the *Annales* school in systematic application of technique and rigorous appraisal of social structure; although it must be admitted that the technique *has* to be more refined to extract sense from the less informative English records and the social structure depends on a few lucky finds such as the fortuitous seventeenth-century incumbents' 'censuses' of the villages of Colyton in Devon and Clayworth in Nottinghamshire.

As the work grew it attracted project grants from the Social Science Research Council, awarded on the individual applications of the three protagonists. Finally, in 1973 the S.S.R.C. was persuaded, unprecedently for an independently founded research programme, to grant them the status of a research unit. This guaranteed them permanent financial support, independent of Cambridge University, now running at £62,000 a year. It is in effect an indictment of that great and wealthy University, perhaps inevitable in view of its unwieldy structure and resistance to innovation, that it could not find so small a sum for one of its most famous recent enterprises.

This is not to say that the Cambridge Group has been an unqualified success. Its pioneering techniques of family reconstitution from parish registers and census returns and of computer 'microsimulation' of population change have been universally acclaimed, but the 'pay-off' in reinterpretation of pre-industrial social life has so far been disappointingly meagre. Some of the best work, no doubt stimulated by them, has been produced elsewhere, for example by Michael Anderson of the University of Edinburgh on *Family Structure in Nineteenth-Century Lancashire* (1971) and W.A.

Armstrong of the University of Kent on *Stability and Change in an English Country Town: York, 1801-51* (1974). The Group still hopes to throw light on the demographic and social origins of industrialism and has recently expanded its interests into nineteenth-century quantitative history and history of education and it attracts scholarly visitors from all over the world, but its failure to expand its foothold in Cambridge itself beyond the three original pioneers confirms the limited commitment of the older universities to social history.

The new universities founded in the wave of enthusiasm for educational innovation of the 1960s were by definition more open to new ideas and subjects, and several of them attracted younger historians of a social bent. The leading pioneer both of social history and of the 'new map of learning' pursued by the new universities was Asa Briggs, who became Professor of History, Dean of Social Studies and eventually second Vice-Chancellor of the first of them, the University of Sussex opened in 1961. (He is now Provost of Worcester College, Oxford.) There he continued, with his characteristic energy and spontaneity, to publish social histories of great breadth and penetration, from *Victorian Cities* (1963) to *The History of Broadcasting in the United Kingdom,* (1961–70; three volumes). Yet the new map of learning of which he was the chief cartographer was, paradoxically, not one on which social history found an institutional position. The 'school' approach to higher education, with broad groupings of interdisciplinary scholars in social studies, European studies, English and American studies, and so on, left the social and indeed other historians spread-eagled between several schools with no recognized centre or focus of activity.

This dispersion was taken to extremes at the new University of Essex, where history as such was not taught at all until 1975, except as an adjunct to social studies in the person of a single reader in social history. That Paul Thompson was able to build a reputation on so narrow a base and to found the journal and Society of *Oral History,* says much for his talent and ingenuity.

Oral history, indeed, has become one of the growth areas of social history. There are at least seventy research projects currently being pursued. They include Paul Thompson's own work on social life at the beginning of the century, published in his book *The Edwardians* (1975), and his ex-research assistant, Thea Vigne's work on Edwardian childhood, Theo Barker's and Michael Winstanley's project at the new University of Kent on local social conditions and attitudes in the same period, an M.A. project by Pam Taylor at the Birmingham University Centre for Contemporary Cultural Studies (the creation of Richard Hoggart and more literary than historical) on working women 1916-40, the recording of personalities involved in the labour movement in connection with John Saville and Joyce Bellamy's *Dictionary of Labour Biography* at Hull University, Elizabeth Roberts' study of working-class life in Lancaster and Barrow, 1890–1930, at Lancaster University, a Manchester Polytechnic study of the motor industry and other aspects of industrial life at Coventry, work on various aspects of Manchester life at the Oral History Unit, Manchester Polytechnic, Norman McCord's interviews with Independent Labour Party workers at Newcastle University, Brian Harrison's with former suffragettes at Oxford, Raphael Samuel's study of Headington Quarry workers for the History Workshop at Ruskin College, Oxford (published in *Village Life and Labour,* 1975), and two projects on the social history of coal mining, in South Wales and Yorkshire, at the University College of Swansea and the University of York. It is significant, however, that more oral social history projects are being pursued outside the universities and polytechnics at museums, galleries, centres and societies of local history and folklore, than inside.

The first university-supported institutional development in social history was the postgraduate Centre for Social History at the new University of Warwick. This was established in 1968 by that great historian of the English working class, Edward Thompson. It concentrated, naturally, on labour history and has been aided since 1973 by the invaluable Modern Records Centre in the University Library which collects primary historical sources with particular reference to labour relations. During Thompson's directorship its research followed his expanding interest in pre-industrial social protest, so brilliantly anatomized in his article on 'The Moral Economy of the English Crowd in the Eighteenth Century' *(Past and Present,* 1971). The product was two seminal books on pre-industrial crime and social protest. Thompson's own *Whigs and Hunters* (1975) sets out to explain the Black Act of 1725 which added no less than fifty new capital offences to the statute book out of the two hundred or more created by that bloody-minded century. It does so in terms of the war between the Whig aristocrats who dominated government and had acquired, and often purloined, the forest rights of the Crown, and the forest dwellers whose farms suffered the depredations of the deer and of the hunters themselves, and whose sole redress was to black their faces and revenge themselves by night on their oppressors' game, property and sometimes persons. The great merit of the book is that, while it could so easily have become a reductionist

Marxist diatribe against class oppression and the sins of property, it looks beyond to the unique feature of the contemporary English landed aristocracy , that it chose to defend itself and its property not by arbitrary power but by the rule of law, which in turn became the foundation of expanding freedoms for the rest of society. The rule of law was not ideological humbug but 'a legacy as substantial as any handed down from the struggles of the seventeenth century to the eighteenth'.

The second book, *Albion's Fatal Tree* (1975), (the gallows which ineffectively terrorized the smugglers, poachers, wreckers of ships, food-rioters and machine-breakers as well as the common murderers, highwaymen and pick-pockets of eighteenth century England), is a collection of essays by the industrious apprentices – apart from one splendid essay on anonymous letters as a source of 'under-history' by the master himself – which shows that smuggling, deer-stealing, stripping wrecks and the like were customary occupations protected by the collective defiance and testamentary silence of the people which in many cases officialdom and property-owners acquiesced in and condoned. Both books are a refreshing change from the traditional sort of labour history which so often strays from the reality of social life into the boring bureaucracy of trade unions and proletarian parties.

Since Thompson's departure for full-time research and writing, the Warwick Centre, under the direction of Royden Harrison, expanded its interests in the direction of general social history. With seven members, it has added to its M.A. course in Comparative British and American Labour History another on Comparative Social History which aims to acquaint students with the practice of the discipline in the United States and Western Europe, with an emphasis on working-class consciousness, the impact of war on society, and immigration and prejudice, themes with a special attraction for the politically oriented young.

A rather different postgraduate Centre for Social History has just been launched at the University of Lancaster. It is not strictly a new departure, since it merely brings together and gives a label to a group of historians and a range of activities which have been in existence for several years. There are in fact no less than twenty social historians attached to the Centre, though their first loyalty is to their undergraduate departments of History, Economics, Educational Research, German, Religious Studies, and Russian and Soviet Studies. This is much the largest group of social historians under one institutional umbrella in Britain. Its M.A. course in Modern Social

History provides teaching and research training in the study of industrialism and society at the regional, national and international levels. One productive feature of the course is the research carried out by the students for seminar papers and dissertations, which each year is centred on a theme chosen by the students themselves, such as local urban élites in a given period, industrial colonies, or holiday resorts. Some of this work has issued in publications based at least in part on students' dissertations, such as J.D. Marshall's 'Kendal in the Late Seventeenth and Eighteenth Centuries' *(Transactions of the Cumberland and Westmoreland Antiquarian and Archaeological Society,* 1975) or H.J. Perkin's 'The Social Tone of Victorian Seaside Resorts' (Essay 5, above).

The Centre also offers research supervision in a wide range of social history from the most local to that of Africa, Austria, France, Germany, Russia, Spain the United States, medieval Britain and Europe, and Byzantium, as well as the history of religion, education, working-class movements, leisure and holidays, and the cinema. It also has a strong interest in the history of culture and ideas and the relation between science and society. S.S.R.C. research projects have been completed on the computer analysis of the social origins and economic worth of élites in British Society since 1880, on the working-class standard of living and the quality of life in Barrow and Lancaster, 1890–1930 (mentioned under oral history above), and on vagrancy in Tudor and Stuart England. The director also edits and publishes the *Newsletter* for the new Social History Society of the United Kingdom, of which he is Chairman. Recent books by Lancaster historians include *The Contentious Tithe: the Tithe Problem and English Agriculture, 1750–1850* by Eric Evans (1976), *Lancashire* (City and County Histories, 1974) by John Marshall and his *The Lake District at Work, Past and Present* (with M. Davies-Shiel, 1971), *The General Strike* by Gordon Phillips (1976), *The Age of the Automobile* by Harold Perkin (1976), *Carlism and Crisis in Spain, 1931–39* (1975) by Martin Blinkhorn, and *Visions of Yesterday* (1973), a study of the cinema of empire by Jeffrey Richards; and articles include 'Vagrants and the Social Order in Elizabethan England' *(Past and Present, 1974)* by A.L. Beier, 'Gregory King and the Social Structure of Pre-industrial England' *(Tansactions of the Royal Historical Society, 1976)* by Geoffrey Holmes, 'Reason and Emotion in Working-Class Religion, 1794–1824' (in D. Baker, ed. *Heresy, Schism and Religiou. Protest,* 1972) by Stewart Mews, *The Blackpool Landlady* (Manchester: University Press, 1978) by John Walton, 'The German Labou Movement, 1848–1919' *(European Studies Review, 1976)* by Dic

Geary, and on 'African Labour in the Chartered Company Period' (*Rhodesian History,* 1970) by John MacKenzie.

In addition to these eponymous institutions there are other universities with institutional commitments to certain aspects of social history. Among these Alan Everitt's postgraduate Department of Local History at the University of Leicester is the oldest and most successful. Founded by those doyens of English local history, W.G. Hoskins and the late H.P.R. Finberg, it set out to concern itself with social entities rather than areas and to portray in each case-study 'the origins, growth, decline and fall of a local community,' in other words that very history of society, albeit on the local scale, which a comprehensive social history ought to be. The occasional papers of the Leicester school have set a new professional standard in local social history which has left the antiquarian tradition of the old school far behind.

At the same university the Department of Economic History has, through the much-missed Jim Dyos, become the focus of urban history in Britain. The Urban History Society, which he founded as an offshoot of the Economic History Society in 1964, has fostered a similar tradition of community development studies as applied to towns and cities. Its approach was exemplified by a collection of essays, *The Study of Urban History* (1968), edited by Dyos, and culminated in the massive two-volume symposium on *The Victorian City: Images and Realities* (1972), edited by Dyos and Michael Wolff. Its annual conferences provide a meeting place for the many social historians interested in urban aspects of their subject and its *Yearbook* a comprehensive record of their activities.

Labour history is also widely diffused, and besides Warwick there are at least five university departments which have carved out a special niche in it. Pride of place must go to Birkbeck College, University of London, the only part-time university institution for mature students, which grew out of the first of the Mechanics' Institutes, where Eric Hobsbawm, of *Labouring Men* (1964) and so many other pioneering books, heads the History Department. Ruskin College, Oxford, a similar though pre-university institution for working men, has naturally developed a special interest in working-class history, and the history workshops organized by Raphael Samuel in the last dozen years have spawned both the journal of that name (1976) and a series of books beginning with *Village Life and Labour* (1975), already mentioned. At Hull University John Saville has pioneered with S.S.R.C. support the multi-volume *Dictionary of Labour Biography*, and Janet Blackman and

Keith Nield of his Department of Economic and Social History have founded the new journal, *Social History,* whose first two numbers are heavily weighted towards working-class history. At the University of Newcastle Norman McCord and D.J. Rowe have pursued an effective if lonely quest for the coal miners, dockers and seamen of the industrial North East, while at the University College of Swansea David Egan and David Smith have mounted an S.S.R.C. team project to recover the coalmining life of the green valleys of South Wales.

A few other universities have taken the interdisciplinary approach with a large social historical element. Manchester has an M.A. course on Late Victorian and Edwardian Britain: Economy and Society, 1870–1914, organized by Michael Rose, Secretary of the Social History Society, which includes social and economic history, literature and social and political thought. Keele has an M.A. in Victorian Studies, embracing literature, social and intellectual history. Birmingham has one in English Society and Culture in the Middle Ages run by the Departments of English and of Medieval History. London has an intercollegiate M.A. in European Area Studies which includes such themes as religious change and society in early modern Europe and European working-class movements.

In addition to these institutional developments there are large numbers of social historians, eminent or aspiring, working in ones and twos in almost every British university and a number of polytechnics. Amongst the leaders are Christopher Hill, former Master of Balliol College, Oxford, author of eleven books on the seventeenth century, mainly from the point of view of the underdog; Henry Pelling in Cambridge, author of *Popular Politics and Society in Late Victorian Britain* (1968), a refreshing non-Marxist collection of essays on labour history; Gareth Stedman Jones, also of Cambridge, Marxist historian of *Outcast London* (1971); Keith Thomas of Oxford, author of a prizewinning anthropological account of *Religion and the decline of magic: studies in popular beliefs in sixteenth and seventeenth century England* (1971); Brian Harrison, also of Oxford, of *Drink and the Victorians* (1971) and pioneer of the history of moral as distinct from social reform (see his penetrating essay in *Pressure from Without in Early Victorian England,* edited by Patricia Hollis, 1974); John Harrison of Sussex University, the authority on *Robert Owen and the Owenites* (1969); Valerie Pearl, Professor of London history at University College London, who founded the *London History Journal;* Christopher Smout of Edinburgh on *A History of the Scottish People, 1530-1830* (1969); Olwen Hufton of Reading, author of the prizewinning book on *The Poor of Eighteenth-Century France, 1750–1789* (1974); John Burnett of Brunel University, London, pioneer of the history of diet; and John Foster of Strathclyde University, Glasgow, a somewhat idiosyncratic Marxist historian of *The Class Struggle and the Industrial Revolution* (1974). They are not alone: the new Social History Society has more than 500 professional social historians amongst its members, and is still growing. In the national lists of *Theses in Progress and Theses Completed* published annually by the London University Institute of Historical Research, those on aspects of social history far outnumber any other category. The publisher's catalogues bear witness to the popularity of social histories in every shape and variety.

And yet as an organized discipline social history is, if not a Cinderella, still something of an orphan. With only three permanent stables in which, officially at least, to lay its head, though with many a temporary dosshouse up and down the country, with only one unhyphenated undergraduate degree and half a dozen postgraduate courses, it can hardly claim to be more than a struggling infant with an uncertain future. From some points of view, perhaps, it has been too successful. There is now scarcely a political, economic or intellectual historian who would not claim to place his specialism firmly in a social context: 'We are all social historians now'. Everything happens in society; *ergo,* everything is a social happening.

Yet there are still immense ranges of human experience which fail to get a fair share of attention in traditional political, economic and intellectual history. Women are the bigger and arguably the better half of the adult human race, but despite the recent burgeoning of women's studies their academic as distinct from polemical history is still neglected in Britain. (One literally new woman sociologist – the product of a sex-change operation – recently put forward a syllabus for a new course on 'her-story', a retort to male chauvinistic 'his-story'!) Apart from Ivy Pinchbeck's and Margaret Hewitt's seminal works on *Women Workers in the Industrial Revolution* (1926) and *Wives and Mothers in Victorian Industry* (1958), there has been little specific work by British historians (as distinct from Americans, such as Patricia Branca's *Silent Sisterhood: Middle-Class Women in the Victorian Home,* 1975) on women's roles in industry or social life. Their inescapable involvement in the reproduction of the species has found expression in a number of studies of the decline of fertility which accompanied late industrialism, the best of which are by J.A. Banks, *Prosperity and Parenthood in Late Victorian England* (1954), and J.A. and Olive Banks, *Feminism and Family Planning in Victorian England*

(1964), and a number of hagiographies have sung the heroines of feminist reform, such as Josephine Kamm's unfortunately named *Rapiers and Battleaxes* (1966) and Constance Rover's *Love, Morals and the Feminists* (1970). We need an updating of O.R. McGregor's seminal bibliography of two decades ago, 'The Social Position of Women in England, 1850–1914' (*British Journal of Sociology,* 1955), preferably extended as far as possible on either side. (A small step towards it is Jeffrey Weeks' 'Note on Sources: The Women's Movement', *Bulletin for the Study of Labour History,* 1974). The only recent general work on women's economic role over the last three centuries is a paper by Eric Richards, a Briton at Flinders University, Australia, on 'Women in the British Economy since 1700' (*History,* 1974), which argues by analogy with more recently developing countries that female participation rates during industrialization followed a U-shaped curve, i.e. declined and then expanded again. Unfortunately, the theory is marred by a failure to define economic participation uniformly in societies so differently organized as pre-industrial and industrial England, in that in the first all wives and daughters of domestic tradesmen are assumed to be industrially occupied while in the second women at home are assumed to be unproductive. The verdict at best must be 'not proven'. Much more remains to be done on the social history of women.

More still remains to be done on that other large segment of the human race, from a quarter to half according to period, children of both sexes. The same pair of pioneering ladies, Pinchbeck and Hewitt, have recently produced a two-volume history of *Children in English Society* (1969 and 1973), but it is much more a history of government policy towards orphans and other deprived children than a social history of children in general. History of education there is in plenty, and some of it has begun to escape from the old prison of administrative and legislative antiquarianism and into genuine social history of education, notably the work of Brian Simon (*Studies in the History of Education, 1780–1870,* 1960 and *Education and the Labour Movement, 1870–1920,* 1965), of Kenneth Charlton, (*Education in Renaissance England,* 1965), of John Hurt (*Education in Evolution,* 1971), of Lawrence Stone ('Literacy and Education in England, 1640–1900', *Past and Present,* 1969), of Richard Johnson ('Educational Policy and Social Control in Early Victorian England', *Past and Present,* 1970) and Michael Sanderson ('Literacy and Social Mobility in the Industrial Revolution in England', *Past and Present,* 1972). But a new interest is becoming discernible in the social history of childhood itself rather than the manipulation of children by educators. It was stimulated by the French historian Philippe Ariès's brilliantly evocative and entertaining *Centuries of Childhood* (1960, translated 1962) and to a less extent in Britain by Peter Coveney's *The Image of Childhood* (1967, first published under the excruciating title *Poor Monkey*, Lady Macbeth's ironic endearment for her baby, in 1957), a study of children in literature, and has produced at least one useful symposium, *The History of Childhood* (1974), edited by Lloyd de Mause. A characteristically illuminating new interpretation is offered by J.H. Plumb in 'The New World of Children in Eighteenth-Century England' (*Past and Present*, 1975). Looking at the new educational philosophies, the new school syllabuses, the new books, the new toys and toyshops, the new clothes, the new 'consumerism' of childhood generally, he discerns a new attitude on the part of upper and middle-class parents: 'Children, in a sense, had become luxury objects upon which their mother and fathers were willing to spend larger and larger sums of money, not only for their education, but also for their entertainment and amusement. In a sense they had become superior pets . . .,' but pets out of whom sexual vices like masturbation, earlier taken for granted or even encouraged, had to be cruelly beaten. 'Childhood had become more radiant, but there were dark and lowering clouds.' A full-scale social history of English childhood of this quality and insight, and not only for one century, is a high priority.

In his preamble Plumb mentions other gaps in the history of eighteenth-century England, which yawn equally in most other periods: 'there is no good history of sex, none of prostitution; not even a good history of attitudes to women. Death has been ignored, and so has food. Animals, except as a part of husbandry or the meat market, have no history'. It is not that one cannot find books on these subjects, but they are often written not by social historians with a feel for the living quality of past societies, but by specialists who murder to dissect, and cut away organs in which they are interested without any awareness of their vital relation to the whole society. Historians of sex are the worst offenders. Generally drawn from other disciplines, notably literary criticism, psychiatry or medicine, their tubular professional vision both distorts the significance of their own partial sources and shuts out the wider perspectives of ordinary life. Ronald Pearsall in *The Worm in the Bud: the World of Victorian Sexuality* (1969) is continually surprised and titillated by the historically unsurprising dichotomy between Victorian moral pretensions and sexual appetites. Dr. Alex Comfort in *The Anxiety Makers* (1967) seems to believe that his handful of Victorian doctors who wrote obsessively on the perils of masturbation, excessive intercourse and venereal disease were actually read by those for whom they were intended. A slight acquaintance with 'Walter's' *My Secret Life* (1966) or any of the contemporary pornographic magazines such as *The Pearl* (1879-80) would have cured their historical naïvety. For a sane, and hilarious, antidote to the portentous pomposity of most writings on Victorian sexuality there is still nothing to compare with Cyril Pearl's *The Girl with the Swansdown Seat* (1955). And the best general perspective on the history of sex and morals appears, surprisingly, in a now very old history of costume, James Laver's *Taste and Fashion from the French Revolution until Today* (1937) which advanced the engaging hypothesis that permissive times of loose morals and clothing, such as the French Revolution or the 1920s (and the 1970s?) saw a decline in prostitution, while uptight times of censorious morals and tight lacing such as the mid-Victorian produced record numbers of prostitutes. We need a quantitative social historian to test that theory.

Leaving aside the social history of death (done for France by Ariès), food (which has received some attention in the Industrial Revolution standard of living controversy, and from John Burnett in *Plenty and Want*, 1966), and animals (which need a study to connect the early Victorian suppression of cruelty with the late twentieth-century wildlife conservation movement), one of the more obvious gaps is the history of leisure. Leisure occupies an ever increasing percentage of our waking lives, and has begun to attract the attention of geographers like H.B. Rodgers (*The Pilot National Recreational Surveys* published by the British Travel Association and the University of Keele, 1967 and 1969) and J. Allen Patmore (*Land and Leisure,* 1970), planners like K.K. Sillitoe (*Planning for Leisure,* published by the Government Social Survey, 1969) or Sir George Young (*Tourism: Blessing or Blight?* 1973), and sociologists like Michael Smith. Stanley Parker and Cyril Smith (*Leisure and Society in Britain,* 1973), but apart from J.A.R. Pimlott's excellent but dated *The Englishman's Holiday* (1947) there is still no general social history of leisure. There are a few recent works on particular aspects, such as Eric Mackerness's *Social History of English Music* (1964) and Dennis Brailsford's *Sport and Society: Elizabeth to Anne* (1969), but the definitive work remains to be written, perhaps soon. A great many histories of seaside resorts are in preparation, by John Myerscough of Sussex University on the economic history of Brighton and Blackpool. John Walton of Lancaster University on the social history of Blackpool, and John Whyman of the University of Kent on Margate and Ramsgate, for example, and James Walvin of the University of

York has published a popular history of holidays, *Beside the Seaside* (1978. The first serious attempt to relate leisure to the problems of class and social control is Peter Bailey's *Leisure and Class in Victorian England* (1978).

The poor and underprivileged have had a considerable share of attention from the founding fathers of social history, Engels, Marx, the first Arnold Toynbee, Tawney, the Webbs, the Hammonds and the Coles down to the current and flourishing schools of labour historians. On the poor law itself recent work by John Marshall and Michael Rose (see their parallel pamphlets on *The Old Poor Law, 1795–1834*, 1968, and *The Relief of Poverty, 1831–1914*, 1972, with their excellent bibliographies), Brian Inglis (*Poverty and the Industrial Revolution*, 1971), and Mark Blaug ('The Myth of the Old Poor Law and the Making of the New', and 'The Poor Law Report Re-examined', *Journal of Economic History*, 1963 and 1964) has thrown doubt on the long-accepted certainties of that much abused topic. More interesting, perhaps, because more concerned with the poor themselves than with their bureaucratic treatment is the renewed search for the records of individual working lives, as in the autobiographies of working people collected by John Burnett in *Useful Toil* (1974), the interviews of Victorian working women recorded by *Munby, Man of Two Worlds* (by D. Hudson, 1972), and the present-day oral historians' tape recordings of elderly workers and their wives and children in Essex, Kent, Oxfordshire, Barrow and Lancaster, referred to above. The Victorian slum dwellers have enjoyed, if that is the word, a revival, with popular reprints of selections from *The Unknown Mayhew* (edited by Edward Thompson and Eileen Yeo, 1971), *Charles Booth's London* (edited by A. Fried and R. Elman, 1969) and the social explorers of 'Darkest England' (*Into Unknown England, 1866–1913*, edited by Peter Keating, 1976).

Even the darkest England of all, the England of the criminal and the lunatic, is beginning to attract its explorers J.J. Tobias's pioneering *Crime and Industrial Society in the Nineteenth Century* (1967), though statistically naïve, broke the ground, and V.A.C. Gatrell and T.B. Hadden's sophisticated study of 'Criminal Statistics and their Interpretation' in Wrigley's *Nineteenth Century Society* has shown how to till it. Much of the best work on industrialism and crime, K.K. MacNab's thesis on 'Aspects of the History of Crime in England and Wales, 1805–60' (Sussex University, Ph.D., 1965) is still unpublished, but pre-industrial social protest and crime have been amply studied by Edward Thompson and his colleagues in *Whigs and Hunters* and *Albion's Fatal Tree*, reviewed above. Much other work is in hand, some of which was presented at the Social History Society's conference, at Birmingham in January 1977, on the theme, 'Crime, Violence and Social Protest'. Lunacy is less well-served but there is an excellent book on the private madhouse in the eighteenth and nineteenth centuries, *The Trade in Lunacy* (1972), by W.L. Parry-Jones and a forthcoming one on the English lunacy reform movement by an American at Charleston College, South Carolina, Peter McCandless.

The pauper, the criminal and the lunatic then are being well-surveyed. Not so the rich and overprivileged at the other end of the social scale. On the assumption that political and economic history have dealt excessively with the politically and economically powerful, social history has often seen itself as redressing the balance by concentrating on the lower orders. Yet this is a misleading assumption. While it is true that political and economic history have been mainly written around upper-class politicians and wealthy entrepreneurs the social origins, connections, organization and even the exercise of power by those who lead and control society have been comparively neglected by both sociologists and historians. As one sociologist, Anthony Giddens, puts it – and but for the middle class it would be equally true of social historians – 'sociologists in this country have given a great deal of attention to studies of the manual working class, and to the "new" middle class, but they have paid much less heed to the upper echelons of the class structure' *(Elites and Power in British Society,* edited by P. Stanworth and A. Giddens, 1974). This neglect of élite studies is surprising, since not only are the life chances and experience of the working and middle classes controlled or at least influenced disproportionately by those who occupy what Wright Mills has called the command posts of society, but mobility in and out of the élite groups may be the key to the stability or revolutionary potential of a society. If, to paraphrase Ralf Dahrendorf *(Conflict after Class,* University of Essex, 1967), there is an inverse correlation between the rate of upward mobility and the intensity of class conflict, then the extent to which the élites are closed or open to newcomers from below may make the difference between violent social revolution and a viable class society, as I argued in *The Origins of Modern English Society, 1780–1880* (1969).

The history of élites is, however, now beginning to attract the attention of British social historians. In addition to the pioneering works of R.K. Kelsall on *Higher Civil Servants in Britain* (1955) and W.L. Guttsman on *The British Political Elite* (1963), 'Elites in Society' was the theme of the founding conference of the new Social History

Society at the University of Lancaster in January 1976, where, after an opening address by Francois Bédarida on a French view of the British 'establishment', papers were presented by J.C. Holt on 'Political Elites of Norman and Angevin England', Peter Laslett on the demography of the landed élite in pre-industrial society, Olwen Hufton on the bating of French aristocrats by poachers and rioters in eighteenth-century Languedoc, David Higgs on the decline of the nobility in nineteenth century France, Christopher Turner on the Puritan leadership of seventeenth-century Massachusetts, R.J. Morris on the urban élite of early Victorian Leeds, A.A. MacLaren on the recruitment of elders to the early Victorian Scottish Church. amd Arthur Marwick on the image of the British upper-class in 1930-50. An interim report was also presented on my S.S.R.C. project on the recruitment of élites in British society since 1880, an updated version of which, with the benefit of computer printouts, was given at the annual Conference of Anglo-American Historians at the University of London in July. My research assistant Dr. W.D. Rubinstein, an American now at the Australian National University, Canberra, has a forthcoming book on British millionaires (see his 'Men of Property: some aspects of occupation, inheritance and power among top British wealth holders' in the Stanworth and Giddens symposium). There are also studies of élites in being or in contemplation at the University of Salford (John Garrard on urban élites in nineteenth-century Salford. Blackburn, Bolton and Rochdale), the University of Exeter (G.D. Mitchell and E.W. Martin on the declining power and influence of rural élites since 1900) and the University of Durham (Duncan Bythell and M.J. Daunton on social mobility into the ranks of the industrialists in nineteenth century England). The Open University in its fourth-level History course on Sources and Historiography takes 'British Elites, 1750–1950', as one of its three themes (along with 'Popular Politics' and 'Poverty and Social Policy'). The history of élites in the next few years is likely to become one of the growth areas of social history in Britain.

What of the people in between who, in Hilaire Belloc's 'Garden Party', 'looked underdone and harrassed, and out of place and mean, and horribly embarrassed'. They are certainly underdone by social historians and embarrassed by an almost total lack of serious studies. Since Roy Lewis and Angus Maude's somewhat frivolous *The English Middle Classes* (1949) there has been no full-scale study. W.J. Reader's *Professional Men* (1966) deals mainly with the three learned professions of divinity, physic and law in the nineteenth century, and his *The Middle Classes* (1972) is an entertaining but very short illustrated essay. There are a large number of histories of particular professions, usually house histories of professional bodies, and many company histories and biographies of business men, but the unique class which more than any other made the Industrial Revolution and modern society has still to find its historian.

No doubt there are many other gaps, too numerous even to catalogue in a short paper, but which should be regarded as challenges and opportunities rather than disfigurements. The history of religion, once so sectarian and introverted, is beginning to be related to the social context out of which it grows, with books like Kenneth Inglis's *Churches and the Working Classes in Victorian England* (1963, J.D. Gay's *The Geography of Religion in England* (1971), Alan Everitt's *The Pattern of Rural Dissent: the Nineteenth Century* (1972), D.M. Thompson's *Nonconformity in the Nineteenth Century* (1972), W.R. Ward's *Religion and Society in England, 1790–1850* (1972), R.C. Richardson's *Puritanism in the North-West* (1972), Edward Royles's *Victorian Infidels* (1973), A.D. Gilbert's *Religion and Society in Industrial England: Church, Chapel and Social Change, 1740–1914* (1976) and John Bossy's *The English Catholic Community, 1570–1850* (1976). But we still need a definitive work on the relation between religion and social control and a less 'Evangelical' explanation of the rise of Victorianism— what I have called the moral revolution— than those of M.J. Quinlan, Muriel Jaegar and F.K. Brown.

There are now more adequate accounts of social problems and the development of social policy since the old Poor Law than once there were, notably Derek Fraser's *The Evolution of the Welfare State* (1973), J.R. Hay's pamphlet *The Origins of Liberal Welfare Reforms, 1906–14* (1975), Jose Harris's *Unemployment and Politics, 1886–1914* (1972), Patricia Thane's *Old Age Pensions* (1976), Enid Gauldie's *Cruel Habitations: a History of Working-Class Housing, 1780–1918* (1974) and the whole series of works on relative poverty and the distribution of income by B. Abel-Smith and P. Townsend (*The Poor and the Poorest*, 1965), J.C. Kincaid (*Poverty, Inequality and Class Structure*, 1974) and A.B. Atkinson (*The Economics of Inequality*, 1975). But we still need a convincing explanation of the paradox of increasing proverty and discontent in the midst of rising national income and living standards in twentieth-century Britain.

A great deal more attention needs to be paid to the history of social thought, a neglected field which has been left to the sociological hagiographers of 'great thinkers'. The real texture of common thought about society and their place in it by ordinary people, the changing language and concepts in which people expressed their deference or discontent, such as was revealed by Asa Briggs for the Industrial Revolution in his famous article on 'The Language of "class" in early nineteenth century England', (A. Briggs and J. Saville, eds. *Essays in Labour History 1960*), would both illuminate other periods and show where the 'great thinkers' got their key concepts from. Perhaps the oral historians, taking a lead from their near-neighbours, the sociological ethnomethodologists, could make a start on the modern end of this.

It occurs to me how overwhelming a proportion of the works mentioned above are concentrated in the period from the sixteenth century onwards. I do not think that this is entirely a reflection of my own interests and inclination. Much more work is being done in all kinds of history of the modern period than in that of the Middle Ages. There is of course Rodney Hilton's school of medieval social history at Birmingham which produced his highly successful account of the West Midlands in the reign of Edward I, *A Medieval Society*, in 1966 and now his 1973 Ford Lectures on *The English Peasantry in the Later Middle Ages* (1975), which modify in a leftward direction the earlier work by M.M. Postan, J.Z. Titow, and H.E. Hallam. There are new insights into medieval religion like Christopher Brooke's *The Monastic World, 1100–1300* (1974) and Jonathan Sumption's *Pilgrimage: an Image of Medieval Religion* (1975) to place beside those of R.W. Southern, Norman Kohn and Gordon Leff. There are a few general collections of essays and histories with a social bent like J.M. Wallace-Hadrill's *Early Medieval History* (1976) or A.A.M. Duncan's *Scotland: the Making of the Kingdom* (1975). But for the most part medieval scholarship continues to be obsessed by the chronicles of war, the struggles of the monarchy, church and baronage, and the estate-charters and terriers, perhaps owing to the tyranny of the sources through which the robust social life of the times is seen as in a glass darkly.[1]

Finally, if, as I suggested in my original paper, to justify itself social history must issue in comprehensive social histories, how many has nearly a quarter of a century produced? Not as many as we should like. It would be invidious to name any, save those which have emerged in the all too fleeting survey above, but two negatives can be stated without offence: there is still no successor to Trevelyan's *English Social History* of 1942, a one-volume, comprehensive social history of England which incorporates the new structural approach which he left out; and despite the History of British Society from 1780 onwards edited by Eric Hobsbawm there is still no multi-volume social history which applies that approach to the whole history of England. Gaps so wide and obvious as these are a challenge and an opportunity. If and when they are filled, social history in Britain may have justified itself.

## Notes

1 Since this was written, the publication of Alan MacFarlane's *The Origins of English Individualism*, Oxford: Blackwell, 1978, has opened up an exciting debate on the real attitudes of medieval English men and women towards each other and their kin and neighbours which shows them to have been different from their continental counterparts from the earliest known times of which we have knowledge.

# ACKNOWLEDGEMENTS

Acknowledgement and grateful thanks for permission to reprint are due to the following: for Essay 1, to the Librarian of the John Rylands Library, Manchester, and to my friend Norman Franklin and Routledge & Kegan Paul Ltd.; for Essay 2, to the Council of the Royal Historical Society; for Essay 3, to Peter Quennell and Alan Hodge, Editors of *History Today*; for Essay 4, to my friend Bentley B. Gilbert, Editor of the *Journal of British Studies*; for Essay 5, to my friend Gordon Forster, Editor of *Northern History*; for Essay 7, to my friend John Butt, I.F. Clarke and David & Charles (Holdings) Ltd.; for Essay 8, to Tom Cook, Brian Simon, Harold Silver and the History of Education Society and to Methuen & Co. Ltd.; for Essay 10, to James Q. Graham, Jr. and Robert P. Swierenga, Editors of *Social Science History;* for Essay 11, to the Royal Town Planning Institute; for Essay 12, to Christopher Freeman, Marie Jahoda, Ian Miles and the Social Science Research Council; and for Essay 13, to my friend Peter N. Stearns, Editor of the *Journal of Social History*. I should also like to thank Dr. W.D. Rubinstein, now of Deakin University, Victoria, Australia, for the immense labour of researching the data on the élite individuals in Essay 9 and for preparing them for the computer, and Mrs. Jean Roberts for programming the data.

# INDEX